Accounting Information Systems

Steven M. Bragg

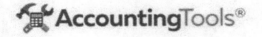

For more information about AccountingTools® products, visit our Web site at www.accountingtools.com.

ISBN-13: 978-1-64221-019-4

Printed in the United States of America

Table of Contents

Preface

The accountant needs a thorough knowledge of the main processes at work in a business. There are activities related to sales, expenditures, production, and human resources, all of which have an impact on the role of the accountant. In *Accounting Information Systems*, we cover the nuts and bolts of these activities and how the related transactions roll up into the general ledger and financial statements. In addition, the book extensively addresses the controls related not just to accounting systems, but also to the underlying computer systems on which they are built, and the ways in which someone could fraudulently penetrate these systems. In total, the book is designed to give the accountant a thorough grounding in systems, transaction processing, controls, and systems development activities.

You can find the answers to many questions about accounting information systems in the following chapters, including:

- How do subsidiary ledgers interact with the general ledger?
- How can data flow diagrams be used to document a system?
- Under what circumstances will fraud be more likely?
- What is the process for designing a system of controls?
- What preventive controls can be applied to an information system?
- What is the procedure for processing a customer order?
- What are the systems for calculating the amounts of raw materials to be purchased?
- How is a master production schedule derived?
- What presentation formats are available for the financial statements?
- What are the components of the systems development life cycle?

Accounting Information Systems is designed for anyone who wants to obtain a thorough understanding of business processes and the controls that protect them.

Centennial, Colorado
January 2019

About the Author

Steven Bragg, CPA, has been the chief financial officer or controller of four companies, as well as a consulting manager at Ernst & Young. He received a master's degree in finance from Bentley College, an MBA from Babson College, and a Bachelor's degree in Economics from the University of Maine. He has been a two-time president of the Colorado Mountain Club, and is an avid alpine skier, mountain biker, and certified master diver. Mr. Bragg resides in Centennial, Colorado. He has written the following books and courses:

7 Habits of Effective CEOs	Conflict Management
7 Habits of Effective CFOs	Constraint Management
7 Habits of Effective Controllers	Construction Accounting
Accountant Ethics [for multiple states]	Corporate Bankruptcy
Accountants' Guidebook	Corporate Cash Management
Accounting Changes and Error Corrections	Corporate Finance
Accounting Controls Guidebook	Cost Accounting (college textbook)
Accounting for Casinos and Gaming	Cost Accounting Fundamentals
Accounting for Derivatives and Hedges	Cost Management Guidebook
Accounting for Earnings per Share	Credit & Collection Guidebook
Accounting for Income Taxes	Crowdfunding
Accounting for Intangible Assets	Developing and Managing Teams
Accounting for Inventory	Effective Collections
Accounting for Investments	Effective Employee Training
Accounting for Leases	Employee Onboarding
Accounting for Managers	Enterprise Risk Management
Accounting for Mining	Entertainment Industry Accounting
Accounting for Retirement Benefits	Fair Value Accounting
Accounting for Stock-Based Compensation	Financial Analysis
Accounting for Vineyards and Wineries	Financial Forecasting and Modeling
Accounting Information Systems	Fixed Asset Accounting
Accounting Procedures Guidebook	Foreign Currency Accounting
Agricultural Accounting	Franchise Accounting
Behavioral Ethics	Fraud Examination
Bookkeeping Guidebook	Fraud Schemes
Budgeting	GAAP Guidebook
Business Combinations and Consolidations	Governmental Accounting
Business Insurance Fundamentals	Health Care Accounting
Business Ratios	Hospitality Accounting
Business Valuation	How to Audit Cash
Capital Budgeting	How to Audit Equity
CFO Guidebook	How to Audit Fixed Assets
Change Management	How to Audit for Fraud
Closing the Books	How to Audit Inventory
Coaching and Mentoring	How to Audit Liabilities

(continued)

On-Line Resources by Steven Bragg

Steven maintains the accountingtools.com web site, which contains continuing professional education courses, the Accounting Best Practices podcast, and thousands of articles on accounting subjects.

Accounting Information Systems is also available as a continuing professional education (CPE) course. You can purchase the course (and many other courses) and take an on-line exam at:

www.accountingtools.com/cpe

Chapter 1
Overview of Accounting Information Systems

Introduction

Any business that wants to collect and use information in a reasonably coordinated manner needs to have an *accounting information system* (AIS) in place. An AIS is a formal structure used by an organization to collect, store, manage, and report its financial information. This structure has the following components:

- The data being collected about an organization's business activities
- The software into which data is entered, and which then processes the data
- The information technology infrastructure within which the software is embedded
- The procedures needed to ensure that data is correctly collected and processed
- The internal controls employed to safeguard the system
- The employees who use the system

The output of an AIS has many users, including management, investors, creditors, auditors, regulators, and taxation authorities.

In this chapter, we explore the nature of data and information, the characteristics of useful accounting information, business transactions, and several related topics that are intended to lay the groundwork for a more detailed discussion of AIS in the later chapters of this book.

Data and Information

Data are stored in an AIS. Data are facts that are collected, stored, and used by an organization. There are many types of data needed by a company, as noted in the following exhibit.

Types of Data

Topic	Data Collected
Billings	Units sold, price per unit, date of sale, customers to whom units were sold
Employees	Pay rates, hours worked, social security number, age, marital status, tax deductions
Fixed assets	Units on hand, description, acquisition price, useful life, depreciation method, salvage value
Inventory	Units on hand, safety stock level, cost per unit, storage location, supplier name
Suppliers	Number of units purchased, delivery dates, quality ratings, purchase prices

Once data have been organized and processed within a context that gives it meaning and relevance, it is referred to as *information*. Information is an essential input for managers, who need it to make higher-quality decisions, as well as to reduce the level of uncertainty. Examples of information are noted in the following exhibit. A primary function of an AIS is to transform data into information.

Types of Information

Topic	Resulting Information
Billings	Days required to issue invoices, bad debts per customer, uncollected receivables
Employees	Overtime worked by employee, employee turnover rate, average pay rate increase
Fixed Assets	Maintenance costs per asset, estimated years before replacement needed, asset utilization rates
Inventory	Time period since inventory was last used, value remaining in inventory if resold now
Suppliers	Supplier quality ratings, benchmarked supplier pricing, innovation contributions by supplier

The amount of data stored by the AIS of even a moderate-sized business is immense, so the system is needed to sort through and condense it into a more usable form. For example, an AIS is routinely used to present to a collections clerk only those invoices that are more than a certain number of days overdue for payment, and only in relation to customers in the clerk's designated collection area. This can reduce the amount of actionable information presented to an employee by a factor of 100 – or more. As another example, an AIS can be used by a business desperately in need of cash to locate those specific fixed assets that have relatively low utilization levels and which are not too old, thereby highlighting the assets most likely to be sellable at a reasonable price without adversely impacting the operations of the business. Thus, an AIS can be useful in the following ways:

- *Improves decisions.* For example, an AIS can present the profit margins for each product by region, so that management can make better decisions about whether it should introduce existing products into its newest sales regions.
- *Improves scheduling.* For example, an AIS can be used to schedule when raw materials need to be ordered, so that they will arrive in time for the production of the goods into which they are incorporated.
- *Reduces uncertainty.* For example, an AIS can present the trend lines for product sales, so that managers can determine when old products should be terminated or replaced.

The uses to which information can be put are almost limitless, but a business is constrained by the costs incurred to obtain data. Some data may be unusually difficult to collect or process, so the decision to do so must be balanced against the uses to which the data can be put, as described in the following example.

EXAMPLE

Epic Rest Hotels builds and operates low-maintenance hotels that require 20% fewer maintenance staff than competing hotels. To gain more insights into the activities of the remaining maintenance staff, the CFO authorizes the hiring of an analyst, who spends nearly all of her time inputting the detailed contents of their timesheets into an electronic spreadsheet, noting the time spent on a variety of maintenance tasks.

After entering this information, summarizing it into reports, and presenting it to the management team for six months, the CFO finds that the information has not been used at all to further reduce the maintenance requirements of the company's hotels. During that time, Epic Rest incurs $40,000 in salary and fringe benefits to employ the analyst. Based on this disappointing cost-benefit analysis, the CFO concludes that the data collection should be stopped and the analyst laid off.

As the example points out, the best intentions to use new information may not actually yield actionable results. Nonetheless, one should at least make an attempt to calculate the cost to collect new data and discuss how it will be used, to see if it makes sense to invest in the collection activity.

The types of information collected should be strongly supportive of the operational strategy of a business, so that employees will know if they are making progress in the manner targeted by management. For example, the strategy of a chain of sushi restaurants is to deliver the highest-quality product by ensuring that the fish are exceedingly fresh. Accordingly, the AIS tracks the number of hours from when the fish leave the fishing boat until they are delivered to each restaurant, as well as the number of hours from when the fish arrive at the restaurant until they are sold to customers. Decisions taken based on this information include siting restaurants only within 100 miles of the ocean, maintaining minimal safety stocks of inventory, and temporarily setting lower prices to sell inventory when it is approaching the company-imposed sell-by date.

Characteristics of Useful Accounting Information

Given the preceding discussion of the relevance of information, one should certainly be aware of the characteristics of useful accounting information. If the following characteristics are not present, then one might question why data is being collected at all:

- *Prepared objectively*. The accountant should record and report on transactions from a neutral perspective, without any bias that would give the reader an incorrect impression about the financial position, results, or cash flows of a business.
- *Consistency of recordation and presentation*. A particularly important characteristic is for the accountant to record information using a consistent application of accounting standards, and to present aggregated results in the same way, for all periods presented.

- *In support of decisions.* An experienced accountant will prepare financial reports that provide the specific information needed by management to reach a decision. That is, the accountant does not just issue the same boiler-plate reports, month after month. It may also be necessary to create new reports that deal with new situations confronting a business.
- *Matches reader knowledge.* The accountant should prepare reports that are tailored to the knowledge of the reader. Thus, a short address at a shareholders meeting may call for an aggregated presentation of just a few key performance metrics, while a presentation to an institutional inves-tor may call for a considerably more detailed report.
- *Reliability and completeness of information.* The accounting system should be comprehensive enough to be able to routinely collect, record, and aggre-gate all transactions, so that users of the information are assured that they are reading about the complete results of a business. This also means that there are no "surprises" that appear as retroactive adjustments to the financial statements.
- *Timely information.* The information is presented quickly enough to give managers enough time to make decisions.

AIS and Business Processes

Every organization is engaged in certain key business processes. A *business process* is a set of connected tasks that result in the completion of a goal. These processes are not always visible to customers, but are needed to maintain the operations of the business. Examples of common business processes are:

- Acquire funding
- Acquire or construct fixed assets
- Collect payments from customers
- Design products
- Conduct marketing campaigns
- Pay employees and contractors
- Pay suppliers
- Process product returns
- Produce financial statements
- Purchase inventory and schedule its use
- Recruit, hire, and train employees
- Remit taxes to the government
- Sell goods and services

The AIS is closely linked to business processes, in order to make them more efficient. For example, an essential business process is paying employees. Someone needs to compile the hours worked by each employee, multiply these hours by the person's pay rate, deduct taxes and other items, and process payments. An AIS module assists with these activities by accumulating standard pay rate information, accepting hours worked information from a variety of sources, automatically calculating gross pay, automatically subtracting deductions to arrive at net pay, and processing payments by check or an electronic payment method.

Transactions

A *transaction* is a business event that has a monetary impact on an organization's financial statements, and which is recorded as an entry in its accounting records. Examples of transactions are:

- Paying a supplier for services rendered or goods delivered.
- Paying a seller with cash and a note in order to obtain ownership of a property formerly owned by the seller.
- Paying an employee for hours worked.
- Receiving payment from a customer in exchange for goods or services delivered.

Transactions are frequently the result of activities involving other parties, such as suppliers and customers, but they can also be the result of internal activities. For example, the movement of raw materials from the warehouse to the production floor for inclusion in a manufacturing process is a transaction, and so is recorded in the accounting records. Nonetheless, transactions are frequently the result of exchanges with outside parties, which are called *give-get exchanges*. These transactions involve the swap of one item for another, such as selling goods for cash, or buying raw materials for cash. The typical organization engages in a massive number of give-get exchanges each year, mostly involving the sale of goods and services, as well as the purchase of supplies and inventory. Given the high volumes associated with give-get exchanges, the associated processes tend to be extremely robust, with in-depth support from the AIS. The full range of give-get exchanges are usually aggregated into the following transaction cycles:

- *Expenditure cycle*. Involves all activities related to the purchase of inventory for further processing or immediate resale in exchange for current or future payments. The give-get exchange is to obtain supplies and inventory in exchange for cash. Typical activities include:
  - Requisition goods and services
  - Issue purchase orders to suppliers
  - Receive goods
  - Process the return of goods to suppliers
  - Store received items
  - Receive supplier invoices
  - Process any applicable discounts and allowances
  - Pay suppliers
  - Prepare management reports

- *Production cycle.* Involves the conversion of raw materials into finished goods. The give-get exchange is to give labor and raw materials in exchange for finished goods, which are later converted into cash. Typical activities include:
  - o Schedule production
  - o Requisition raw materials
  - o Manufacture products
  - o Store finished goods
  - o Prepare management reports

- *Sales cycle.* Involves all activities related to the sale of goods or services in exchange for current or future payments. The give-get exchange is to give goods or services in exchange for cash. Typical activities include:
  - o Receive customer orders
  - o Examine requests for customer credit
  - o Review availability of ordered goods
  - o Back order any items not in stock
  - o Pick goods from stock
  - o Ship goods to customers or provide services
  - o Issue invoices to customers
  - o Log in payments received from customers
  - o Deposit cash and checks at the bank
  - o Contact customers regarding late payments
  - o Process bad debts
  - o Process any sales returns
  - o Prepare management reports

- *Human resources cycle.* Involves all interactions with job candidates, through their hiring, training, evaluation, and eventual discharge. The give-get exchange is to obtain labor in exchange for cash. Typical activities include:
  - o Recruit, interview, and hire employees
  - o Train employees
  - o Evaluate employee performance
  - o Discharge employees
  - o Collect employee work hours information
  - o Prepare payroll
  - o Disburse payroll payments
  - o Remit payroll taxes
  - o Update payroll records
  - o Prepare management reports

- *Financing cycle.* Involves all activities required to obtain debt or equity funding from third parties, as well as the payment of dividends, principal, and/or interest to those parties. The give-get exchange is to obtain cash from funding sources and eventually pay it back or pay back a return on the invested funds. Typical activities include:
    - Forecast cash requirements
    - Issue debt/equity securities to investors
    - Borrow money
    - Pay interest to lenders
    - Pay dividends to investors
    - Retire outstanding debt
    - Prepare management reports

An additional activity within each of these transaction cycles is that the underlying AIS shares information across the organization, so that employees anywhere in the company, no matter which module they may happen to be using, can potentially access information that is consistently presented across the platform. This is not the case when a business chooses to install different systems that do not share information; in this case, it is likely that there will be inconsistencies in the information being used, depending on where people are working within a company.

EXAMPLE

Ongoing turf wars within Atlas Machining Company result in each department purchasing and operating its own software. Thus, the customer orders inputted in the order entry department and used by the production department do not necessarily align with the billing information being manually forwarded to the accounting department by the shipping staff. In addition, the credit department relies on the historical sales information stored by the accounting department to evaluate credit requests, which does not incorporate any new orders currently in the system operated by the order entry department.

Organizations may make use of the preceding transaction cycles to a lesser or greater extent, depending on the nature of their operations. For example, a manufacturing company that sells exclusively through a few distributors will have a robust production cycle, but a relatively low-volume sales cycle. Or, a services business such as a gym will have a greatly reduced expenditure cycle, since it is not providing goods to its customers.

AIS Subsystems

An AIS is comprised of many subsystems. For example, one system deals with accounts payable, while another is designed to handle accounts receivable, and a third processes payroll. Each of these subsystems is designed to have a similar look and feel, making it easier for users to seamlessly shift from one subsystem to the next. Also, each subsystem may rely on information from other subsystems in order to operate in the most efficient manner possible, so a programming change made to one subsystem could have negative consequences for the other subsystems, potentially rendering them inoperable. The interlinking nature of accounting subsystems makes it more difficult to adjust subsystems for larger organizations, since they typically have the most complex operations.

Benefits of an AIS

When an AIS has been properly configured to work with the unique business processes of an organization, it can trigger a significant jump in the firm's efficiency. These improvements are likely to arise in the following areas:

- *Continual monitoring.* The system can monitor the output coming from processes all over the organization and flag situations that appear to be incorrect, or which are approaching maximum tolerance levels. For example, data entry controls can reject transactions that are outside of established limits, such as attempting to input weekly hours worked for an employee that exceed 168 hours (which is the total number of hours in a week). Or, the system can monitor product quality and notify management when a production process is trending towards the upper or lower boundary of predetermined specification limits. The continual monitoring concept can be extended to flag any suspicious activities, such as payments being made to employees or suppliers that are well outside of the norm, or of large amounts of credit being granted to new customers.

- *Continual updates.* The system can constantly update information, so that employees will not make mistakes caused by using outdated information. For example, the inventory records are updated with the latest quantities and storage locations, so that the purchasing staff knows how much additional inventory to order, and the warehouse staff knows exactly where to go to pick units from stock.

- *Coordination with third parties.* The system can be made accessible to suppliers and customers, who can use the system to more closely integrate their operations with those of the business. For example, suppliers can directly access the system to see when the company will need to order from them again; the concept can be extended to an automated interface that issues orders into supplier systems. Similarly, customers can directly access the system to see when the company will be able to ship them previously ordered items, or to send new purchase orders directly into the company's order entry function.

- *Decision support.* The system can produce many types of reports that can assist in improving the quality of decisions made. For example, the system can generate reports that specify profit and volume levels by customer, so that management can decide whether to drop any unprofitable customers or to expand its selling efforts with unusually profitable ones.

- *Information distribution.* The system can distribute information to anyone, anywhere in the organization, which can be used to monitor conditions and improve performance. For example, the chief executive officer can access a performance dashboard to review operating and financial conditions throughout the business, and drill down into the underlying data to obtain more information, as needed. Or, project managers can access human resources files to see if anyone in the company has specific knowledge that they need to deal with a critical project issue.
- *Variance analysis.* The system can automatically compare actual results to budgeted or standard baseline amounts and report unusually large variances to management for further action. This concept is especially useful when the system is only configured to report on significant variances, so that management does not fritter away its time reviewing masses of minor variances.

Impact of an AIS on the Organization

A fully-configured AIS should be able to make information available to anyone, anywhere within an organization. Though this capability is usually constrained, so that employees only have access to what they *need* to see, the fact remains that the greater availability of data can democratize an organization, leading to pressure by employees to drive decision making down within the organization. The result can be fewer levels of management, with front-line employees taking on more responsibility.

Summary

A comprehensive AIS is needed to assist in running the operations of a business, as well as to collect, summarize, and interpret the data generated by the firm. The AIS can be integrated into operations throughout an organization, not just the accounting department, in order to maximize the benefits to be gained from it.

Being able to effectively interact with an AIS is one of the most essential parts of the accountant's job, since it is *the* tool for extracting meaning from the flood of data with which the modern organization is inundated.

Chapter 2
Transaction Processing

Introduction

How does an organization channel data about its activities into its accounting information system (AIS)? And once the data has been stored in the AIS, how does the system convert it into useful information? In this chapter, we discuss the concept of transaction processing, which is the flow of data into, through and out of an AIS. We pay particular attention to the database that underlies an AIS, which is comprised of the general ledger and any supporting subledgers.

The Data Processing Cycle

The set of operations used to transform data into useful information is called the *data processing cycle*. This cycle involves the inputting of data into the AIS, storage of the data, processing activities, and the output of information from the system. We cover each of these activities in the following sections.

Stage 1: Data Input

The beginning stage in the data processing cycle is data input. This activity is usually prompted by a business activity, such as the sale of goods to a customer. The amount of data to be collected in this stage can vary significantly, depending on what management wants to do with the resulting information. The greatest extent of the data to be input includes the initiating business activity, the people involved in the activity, and the resources impacted by it. One must decide whether it is cost-effective to input this much data, or if a subset of the maximum amount will be sufficient for the needs of the business. The following example addresses the concept.

EXAMPLE

The owner of a newly-formed importing business intends to import washing machines and sell them to distributors, where all sales will be on credit, and the sales staff will earn a commission on each sale. Since every sale will be on credit, the company must issue an invoice; to prepare an invoice, it will need to collect the following data:

- Customer name and address (to ensure that the invoice is sent to the right place for payment)
- Date of the sale (in order to calculate the days remaining before payment must be received)
- Identification of the product, the number of units sold, and the unit price (in order to calculate the total billing)
- Any applicable discounts (which are subtracted from the gross sale)
- Delivery instructions (to ensure that the washing machines are delivered to the correct location)

The only person involved in the activity at the point of sale is the salesperson, who must be identified in order to calculate a commission payment. It may also be useful to record the name of the person delivering the washing machines to the customer, in case there are questions about the delivery.

The company must also record a reduction in the inventory records caused by the reduction in the number of washing machines on hand, since this is a resource that is being impacted by the sale.

Data is typically input into an AIS from *source documents*, which are the physical basis upon which business transactions are recorded. They usually contain the following information:

- A description of the transaction
- The date of the transaction
- A specific amount of money
- An authorizing signature (in some cases)

Examples of source documents and their related business transactions that appear in the financial records are:

- *Bank statement*. This document contains a number of adjustments to a company's book balance of cash on hand that the company should reference to bring its records into alignment with those of a bank.
- *Cash register tape*. This document can be used as evidence of cash sales, which supports the recordation of a sale transaction.
- *Credit card receipt*. This document can be used as evidence for a disbursement of funds from petty cash.

- *Deposit slip.* This document is sent to the bank along with any cash deposits, so that the bank can properly identify the account in which the cash will be deposited.
- *Lockbox check images.* These images support the recordation of cash receipts from customers.
- *Packing slip.* This document describes the items shipped to a customer, and so supports the recordation of a sale transaction.
- *Purchase requisition.* This document is submitted by an employee who wants to have specific items purchased by the company.
- *Receipt.* This document is used as evidence that goods have been purchased.
- *Sales order.* This document, when coupled with a bill of lading and/or packing list, can be used to invoice a customer, which in turn generates a sale transaction.
- *Supplier invoice.* This document supports the issuance of a cash, check, or electronic payment to a supplier. A supplier invoice also supports the recordation of an expense, inventory item, or fixed asset.
- *Time card.* This document supports the issuance of a paycheck or electronic payment to an employee. If employee hours are being billed to customers, the time card also supports the creation of customer invoices.

Source documents are frequently prenumbered, so that each document is uniquely identified. Otherwise, a data entry person will have trouble determining whether a document has already been entered into the system, or if a document is missing. Some documents, such as deposit slips, are only created once a day, so the current date is used instead as the identifying number.

A different type of source document is the *turnaround document*, which is a document sent out to a third party, who is supposed to fill in the document and return it to the company. For example, the corporate secretary could issue a voting document to shareholders, where they are supposed to vote for the board of directors by filling in an oval next the names of the people on the ballot. Once this ballot is returned, it can be scanned into the system. Similarly, a seller issues an invoice to its customers with a tear-away slip at the bottom, which they are supposed to return with their payments. Upon receipt, the cash receipts clerk uses the information on the slip to identify the customer who is submitting a payment.

Where possible, it is most efficient to use an automated system to input data, such as by using bar codes or document scanning systems. Doing so minimizes the need for data entry labor, increases the speed of data entry, and reduces the data entry error rate.

An essential element of the data input stage is to improve the probability that captured data have been correctly and thoroughly entered. There are several ways to do so, including the following:

- Automate data entry, thereby eliminating the risk of keystroke errors.
- Improve the layout of source documents, making it easier to identify data on the documents.

- Improve the layout of data entry screens. For example, the presentation of fields in which data will be entered can mimic how the data appears on source documents. On-screen text can also clearly state what is to be entered into each field. There may also be pull-down menus that present all possible options to select for each field. The end result should be an uncluttered screen that simplifies how data are to be entered.

The data input stage has several controls built into it, to flag certain transactions from being entered or to ensure that they are properly authorized. For example, the entry of data for a customer order may be flagged by the system if the customer has not been paying its invoices on time, or the approval of expanded customer credit may be automatically routed to the credit manager for approval. In addition, many fields in a data entry screen may only accept certain inputs, such as the correct two-letter code for a state in a ship-to address. These monitoring controls are quite effective at keeping incorrect data from being entered into the AIS.

Stage 2: Data Storage

The second stage in the data processing cycle is data storage. Data must be stored in an organized manner that allows for its rapid retrieval. To maximize rapid retrieval, accounting information is stored in ledgers. A *ledger* is a book or database in which accounting transactions are stored or summarized. A *subsidiary ledger* is a ledger designed for the storage of specific types of accounting transactions. If a subsidiary ledger is used, the information in it is then summarized and posted to an account in the *general ledger*, which in turn is used to construct the financial statements of a company. The account in the general ledger where this summarized information is stored is called a *control account*. Most accounts in the general ledger are not control accounts; instead, transactions are recorded directly into them.

Posting refers to the aggregation of financial transactions from where they are stored in subsidiary ledgers, and transferring this information into the general ledger. Information in one of the subsidiary ledgers is aggregated at regular intervals, at which point a summary-level entry is made and posted in the general ledger. In a manual bookkeeping environment, the aggregation may occur at fixed intervals, such as once a day or once a month. For example, if the source ledger were the accounts receivables ledger, the aggregated posting entry might include a debit to the accounts receivable account, and credits to the sales account and various sales tax liability accounts. When posting this entry in the general ledger, a notation could be made in the description field, stating the date range to which the entry applies.

In a computerized bookkeeping environment, posting to the general ledger may be unnoticeable. The software simply does so at regular intervals, or asks if you want to post, and then handles the underlying general ledger posting automatically. It is possible that no posting transaction even appears in the reports generated by the system.

Posting to the general ledger does not occur for lower-volume transactions, which are already recorded in the general ledger. For example, fixed asset purchases may be so infrequent that there is no need for a subsidiary ledger to house these transactions, so they are instead recorded directly in the general ledger.

A subsidiary ledger can be set up to offload data storage for virtually any general ledger account. However, they are usually only created for areas in which there are high transaction volumes, which limits their use to a few areas. Examples of subsidiary ledgers are:

- Accounts receivable ledger
- Fixed assets ledger
- Inventory ledger
- Purchases ledger

Note: Subsidiary ledgers are used when there is a large amount of transaction information that would clutter up the general ledger. This situation typically arises in companies with significant sales volume. Thus, there may be no need for subsidiary ledgers in a small company.

As an example of the information in a subsidiary ledger, the inventory ledger may contain transactions pertaining to receipts into stock, movements of stock to the production floor, conversions into finished goods, scrap and rework reporting, and sales of goods to customers.

In order to research accounting information when a subsidiary ledger is used, drill down from the general ledger to the appropriate subsidiary ledger, where the detailed information is stored. Consequently, if there is a preference to conduct as much research as possible within the general ledger, use fewer subsidiary ledgers.

The following chart shows how the various data entry modules within an AIS are used to create transactions which are recorded in either the general ledger or various subsidiary ledgers, and which are eventually aggregated to create the financial statements.

Transaction Flow in the Accounting System

Part of the period-end closing process is to post the information in a subsidiary ledger to the general ledger. This is usually a manual step, so it is essential to verify that all subsidiary ledgers have been appropriately completed and closed before posting their summarized totals to the general ledger.

General Ledger Overview

A general ledger is the master set of accounts in which is summarized all transactions occurring within a business during a specific period of time. The general ledger contains all of the accounts currently being used in a chart of accounts, and is sorted by account number. Either individual transactions or summary-level postings from subsidiary ledgers are listed within each account number, and are sorted by transaction date. Each entry in the general ledger includes a reference number that states the source of the information. The source may be a subsidiary ledger, a journal entry, or a transaction entered directly into the general ledger.

The format of the general ledger varies somewhat, depending on the accounting software being used, but the basic set of information presented for an account within the general ledger is:

- *Transaction number*. The software assigns a unique number to each transaction, so that it can be more easily located in the accounting database if the transaction number is known.
- *Transaction date*. This is the date on which the transaction was entered into the accounting database.

- *Description.* This is a brief description that summarizes the reason for the entry.
- *Source.* Information may be forwarded to the general ledger from a variety of sources, so the report should state the source, in case there is a need to go back to the source to research the reason for the entry.
- *Debit and credit.* States the amount debited or credited to the account for a specific transaction.

The following sample of a general ledger report shows a possible format that could be used to present information for several transactions that are aggregated under a specific account number.

Sample General Ledger Presentation

Trans. No.	Trans. Date	Description	Source	Debit	Credit
Acct. 10400		**Acct: Accounts Receivable**	**Beginning balance**		**$127,500.00**
10473	3/22/xx	Customer invoice	ARL	93.99	
10474	3/23/xx	Customer invoice	ARL	47.80	
10475	3/24/xx	Credit memo	ARL		43.17
10476	3/25/xx	Customer invoice	ARL	65.25	
18903	3/26/xx	Cash receipt	CRJ		1,105.20
			Ending balance		**$126,558.67**

It is extremely easy to locate information pertinent to an accounting inquiry in the general ledger, which makes it the primary source of accounting information. For example:

- A manager reviews the balance sheet and notices that the amount of debt appears too high. The accountant looks up the debt account in the general ledger and sees that a loan was added at the end of the month.
- A manager reviews the income statement and sees that the bad debt expense for his division is very high. The accountant looks up the expense in the general ledger, drills down to the source journal entry, and sees that a new bad debt projection was the cause of the increase in bad debt expense.

As the examples show, the source of an inquiry is frequently the financial statements; when conducting an investigation, the accountant begins with the general ledger, and may drill down to source documents from there to ascertain the reason(s) for an issue.

We will now proceed to brief discussions of the accounts receivable ledger and purchase ledger, which are representative of the types of subsidiary ledgers that can be used to compile information within the accounting system.

The Accounts Receivable Ledger

The accounts receivable ledger is a subsidiary ledger in which is recorded all credit sales made by a business. It is useful for segregating into one location a record of all amounts invoiced to customers, as well as all credit memos issued to them, and all payments made against invoices by them. The ending balance of the accounts receivable ledger equals the aggregate amount of unpaid accounts receivable.

A typical transaction entered into the accounts receivable ledger will record an account receivable, followed at a later date by a payment transaction from a customer that eliminates the account receivable.

If a manual record of the accounts receivable ledger were to be maintained, it could contain substantially more information than is allowed by an accounting software package. The data fields in a manually-prepared ledger might include the following information for each transaction:

- Invoice date
- Invoice number
- Customer name
- Identifying code for item sold
- Sales tax invoiced
- Total amount billed
- Payment flag (states whether paid or not)

The primary document recorded in the accounts receivable ledger is the customer invoice. Also, if a credit is granted to a customer for such items as returned goods or items damaged in transit, a credit memo is also recorded in the ledger.

The information in the accounts receivable ledger is aggregated periodically and posted to a control account in the general ledger. This account is used to keep from cluttering up the general ledger with the massive amount of information that is typically stored in the accounts receivable ledger. Immediately after posting, the balance in the control account should match the balance in the accounts receivable ledger. Since no detailed transactions are stored in the control account, anyone wanting to research customer invoice and credit memo transactions will have to drill down from the control account to the accounts receivable ledger to find them.

Before closing the books and generating financial statements at the end of an accounting period, all entries must be completed in the accounts receivable ledger, after which the ledger is closed for that period, and totals posted from the accounts receivable ledger to the general ledger.

The Purchase Ledger

The purchase ledger is a subsidiary ledger in which is recorded all purchases made by a business. It is useful for segregating into one location a record of the amounts the company is spending with its suppliers. The purchase ledger shows which purchases have been paid for and which ones remain outstanding. A typical transaction entered into the purchase ledger will record an account payable, followed at a later date by a payment transaction that eliminates the payable. Thus, there is likely to be an outstanding account payable balance in the ledger at any time.

If a manual record of the purchase ledger were to be maintained, it could contain substantially more information than is allowed by an accounting software package. The data fields in a manually-prepared purchase ledger might include the following information for each transaction:

- Purchase date
- Supplier code (or name)
- Supplier invoice number
- Purchase order number (if used)
- Identifying code for item purchased
- Amount paid
- Sales tax paid
- Payment flag (states whether paid or not)

The primary document recorded in the purchase ledger is the supplier invoice. Also, if suppliers grant a credit back to the business for such items as returned goods or items damaged in transit, credit memos issued by suppliers would be recorded in the purchase ledger.

The information in the purchase ledger is aggregated periodically and posted to a control account in the general ledger. The purchase ledger control account is used to keep from cluttering up the general ledger with the massive amount of information that is typically stored in the purchase ledger. Immediately after posting, the balance in the control account should match the balance in the purchase ledger. Since no detailed transactions are stored in the control account, anyone wanting to research purchase transactions will have to drill down from the control account to the purchase ledger to find them.

Before closing the books and generating financial statements at the end of an accounting period, all entries must be completed in the purchase ledger, after which the ledger is closed for that period, and totals posted from the purchase ledger to the general ledger.

Coding Methods

Data must be organized in a logical manner, which calls for the use of consistently-applied coding methods. Coding methods involve the classification of data by systematically assigning numbers and/or letters to them. Here are several examples of coding methods:

- *Block codes.* Under block coding, a range of numbers is set aside for a specific set of data. For example, the 1000 to 2000 number range in the chart of accounts (described later in this chapter) may be set aside for asset accounts. Or, an office supplies distributor sets aside inventory codes A100 through A500 for use in identifying different types of storage boxes. The use of block codes makes it easier for a user to identify data based on the codes.

- *Group codes.* When group codes are used, specific digits within a number are assigned a certain meaning. The concept is most commonly applied to products, where each digit of their related product numbers is used to describe them. For example, a lawn mower is assigned the product code 8B12E. The first digit (8) states that the mower has an eight horsepower engine, while the second digit (B) describes the blue color of the housing, the third and fourth digits (12) describe the product features (self-powered), and the final digit (E) describes the language (English) in which its product manual is printed.
- *Mnemonic codes.* Mnemonic coding incorporates a pattern of letters or numbers that make it easier to remember the subject of the code. For example, a customer invoice originating from the Minnesota sales region could be numbered MN4382, thereby using the "MN" state code to identify the source of the invoice. Or, a mountain bike model could be identified with the code MTFATMED, where MT identifies the bike as a mountain bike, the FAT code states that it is a fat-tire model, and the MED code identifies the frame size as a medium.
- *Sequence codes.* Consecutive numbering is used to uniquely identify an item. For example, customer invoices, purchase orders, and inventory count tags are all prenumbered in a numerical sequence. When accounting for these items, it will be readily apparent when a document is missing, since there will be a gap in the numerical sequence.

The coding method chosen may continue to be employed within an organization for many years, so one should consider in detail how a certain method will be used, and how it may need to evolve as the company changes over time. Here are several issues to consider:

- *Potential growth.* If there is an expectation of significant growth in the business, be sure to leave enough room in the coding to accommodate that development. For example, if there is an expectation in a distribution business that the firm will eventually be distributing thousands of office products, it makes little sense to have a three-digit or four-digit product code, since there will eventually be more products than available codes. Similarly, a rapidly-growing business may need employee codes of more than three digits, since such a short code only allows for 999 employees.
- *Complexity.* The coding structure used should be as simple as possible, to aid employees in memorizing the meaning of the structure. Thus, a six-digit product code is much more usable from an employee perspective than a 17-digit code. Also, incorporating mnemonic elements into a code can make it easier to understand. An added benefit is that a less-complex and shorter code generally results in fewer data entry errors.
- *Consistency of application.* Where possible, the coding structure should be applied across the organization, with no outlier pockets of non-compliance. Allowing variations in the coding structure increases the level of complexity

in managing data. This is a particular problem in a business that engages in a large number of acquisitions, since each of its acquired businesses have different coding methods; if these disparate entities are to coordinate their activities, it may be necessary to adopt a company-wide coding methodology.

Overview of the Chart of Accounts

An excellent example of coding is the *chart of accounts*, which is a listing of all accounts used in the general ledger, usually sorted in order by account number. The accounts are typically numeric, but can also be alphabetic or alphanumeric. The account numbering system is used by the accounting software to aggregate information into an entity's financial statements.

Accounts are usually listed in order of their appearance in the financial statements, starting with the balance sheet and continuing with the income statement. Thus, the chart of accounts begins with cash, proceeds through liabilities and shareholders' equity, and then continues with accounts for revenues and then expenses. Many organizations structure their chart of accounts so that expense information is separately compiled by department; thus, the sales department, engineering department, and production department all have the same set of expense accounts. Typical accounts found in the chart of accounts include:

Assets

- *Cash*. Contains the amounts of petty cash and bank account balances. There is usually a separate account for each bank account, and a separate account for all petty cash.
- *Marketable securities*. Contains the valuations of any investments that the company has made in marketable securities. In a smaller business, excess funds may be kept in a savings account at the bank, in which case these funds appear in a cash account.
- *Accounts receivable*. Contains the balances of trade and non-trade receivables. Trade receivables are with customers, and non-trade receivables are with everyone else, such as employees. Trade receivables arise when sales are made on credit, with customers promising to pay as of a later date.
- *Allowance for doubtful accounts*. Contains a reserve against expected future losses on accounts receivable. The account has a negative balance.
- *Prepaid expenses*. Contains the unconsumed balances of any payments made, such as prepaid rent and prepaid insurance.
- *Inventory*. Contains the balances of raw materials, work-in-process, and finished goods inventory.
- *Fixed assets*. Contains the amounts paid for fixed assets, such as machinery, furniture and fixtures, and computer equipment. This account may be subdivided into a separate account for each classification of fixed asset.

- *Accumulated depreciation.* Contains the grand total accumulation of depreciation charged against fixed assets over time. The account has a negative balance.
- *Intangible assets.* Contains the purchase costs of non-tangible assets, such as purchased patents, licenses, organization costs, and copyrights.
- *Accumulated amortization.* Contains the grand total accumulation of amortization charged against intangible assets over time. This concept is quite similar to accumulated depreciation. The account has a negative balance.
- *Goodwill.* Contains any excess amount paid to the owners of an acquired business that exceeds the fair value of the assets and liabilities acquired.
- *Other assets.* Contains all other assets that do not fit into the descriptions for the preceding asset accounts.

Liabilities

- *Accounts payable.* Contains the complete set of all payables owed to suppliers, based on invoices submitted by the suppliers.
- *Accrued liabilities.* Contains estimated liabilities for which no documented supplier invoices have yet been received.
- *Taxes payable.* Contains the liabilities for all types of taxes owed, including sales and use taxes, property taxes, payroll taxes, and income taxes. There is usually a separate account to track each of these types of taxes.
- *Wages payable.* Contains the estimated amount of wages owed to employees that have not yet been paid.
- *Notes payable.* Contains the remaining balances of loans owed to lenders. There may be a separate account for each loan owed, so that payments are not confused among the different loans.

Stockholders' Equity

- *Common stock.* This account is used by corporations, which issue shares. It contains the amount of funds received by a business in exchange for the sale of its stock to investors.
- *Additional paid-in capital.* This account contains any additional amounts paid to the organization by an investor for shares in the business, which exceeds the par value of the shares.
- *Retained earnings.* Contains the accumulated amount of any earnings generated by a business.
- *Capital account.* This account is used by unincorporated entities to show the amount of funds contributed to the business by its owners.
- *Drawing account.* This account is associated with the capital account that was just referenced. It contains the amounts of funds withdrawn from the business by its owners.

Revenue

- *Revenue.* Contains the gross amount of all sales recognized during the reporting period.
- *Sales returns and allowances.* Contains the amount of any credits granted to customers for sales returns and allowances. This account balance offsets the revenue account.

Expenses

- *Cost of goods sold.* Contains the cost of all direct labor, direct materials, and factory overhead associated with the sale of goods and services.
- *Advertising expense.* Contains the recognized cost of advertising expenditures.
- *Bank fees.* Contains the fees charged by a company's bank to process transactions.
- *Depreciation expense.* Contains a depreciation charge that reflects the consumption of assets over time.
- *Payroll tax expense.* Contains the cost of all taxes associated with the payment of salaries and wages.
- *Rent expense.* Contains the cost of the rent associated with the facilities used by a business.
- *Supplies expense.* Contains the cost of all supplies consumed by a business.
- *Utilities expense.* Contains the aggregated cost of all utilities, which may include water, heat, electricity, waste disposal, and so forth.
- *Wages expense.* Contains the cost of salaries and hourly wages incurred by a business to compensate its employees.
- *Other expenses.* Contains a variety of incidental expenses that are individually too small to warrant the use of a separate account.

Several of the preceding accounts could be broken down into additional accounts in order to refine the data gathering into more selective buckets. This is especially common for the revenue and cost of goods sold accounts, since a large number of transactions flow through them. For example, the revenue account could be broken down into any of the following:

- Sales by individual sales region (such as by the northeast region and the southeast region)
- Sales by specific product or by product line (such as by sedans, SUVs, pickup trucks, and subcompacts)
- Sales by types of customer (such as retailers, distributors, and direct sales)

The sample set of accounts just noted will vary substantially by type of business. For example, the accounts used by a manufacturing business may vary substantially from those used by a cattle rancher, mining company, casino, or vineyard.

Nonetheless, the presented accounts can be considered a reasonable baseline, to which changes can be made to meet the requirements of a specific business.

There are a number of ways to structure the chart of accounts, as noted in the following sub-sections that describe three-digit and five-digit charts of accounts.

The Three-Digit Chart of Accounts

A three-digit chart of accounts allows a business to create a numerical sequence of accounts that can contain as many as 1,000 potential accounts. The three-digit format is most commonly used by small businesses that do not break out the results of any departments in their financial statements. A sample three-digit chart of accounts appears in the following example.

Sample Three-Digit Chart of Accounts

Account Number	Description
010	Cash
020	Petty cash
030	Accounts receivable
040	Allowance for doubtful accounts
050	Marketable securities
060	Raw materials inventory
070	Work-in-process inventory
080	Finished goods inventory
090	Reserve for obsolete inventory
100	Fixed assets – Computer equipment
110	Fixed assets – Computer software
120	Fixed assets – Furniture and fixtures
130	Fixed assets – Leasehold improvements
140	Fixed assets – Machinery
150	Accumulated depreciation – Computer equipment
160	Accumulated depreciation – Computer software
170	Accumulated depreciation – Furniture and fixtures
180	Accumulated depreciation – Leasehold improvements
190	Accumulated depreciation – Machinery
200	Other assets
300	Accounts payable
310	Accrued payroll liability

Account Number	Description
320	Accrued vacation liability
330	Accrued expenses liability – other
340	Unremitted sales taxes
350	Unremitted pension payments
360	Short-term notes payable
370	Other short-term liabilities
400	Long-term notes payable
500	Capital stock
510	Retained earnings
600	Revenue
700	Cost of goods sold – Materials
710	Cost of goods sold – Direct labor
720	Cost of goods sold – Manufacturing supplies
730	Cost of goods sold – Applied overhead
800	Bank charges
805	Benefits
810	Depreciation
815	Insurance
825	Office supplies
830	Salaries and wages
835	Telephones
840	Training
845	Travel and entertainment
850	Utilities
855	Other expenses
860	Interest expense

In the example, each block of related accounts begins with a different set of account numbers. Thus, current liabilities begin with "300," revenue items begin with "600," and cost of goods sold items begin with "700." This numbering scheme makes it easier for the accountant to remember where accounts are located within the chart of accounts. This type of account range format is also required by the report writing module in many accounting software packages.

Note: It is wise to include gaps in the chart of accounts numbering sequence, which leaves room for the addition of more accounts at a later date. For example, the preceding sample chart of accounts includes account 340, Unremitted Sales Taxes. The controller may eventually find that clustering the sales tax remittances for multiple states in one account leads to remittance errors, and so decides to use account 341 for New York sales tax remittances, 342 for Massachusetts remittances, and 343 for Rhode Island remittances.

The Five-Digit Chart of Accounts

A five-digit chart of accounts is used by organizations that want to track information at the departmental level. With a five-digit code, they can produce a separate income statement for each department. This format duplicates the account codes found in a three-digit chart of accounts, but then adds a two-digit code to the left, which indicates specific departments. The three-digit codes for expenses (and sometimes also revenues) are then duplicated for each department for which management wants to record information. A sample of the five-digit chart of accounts format follows, using the accounting and production departments to show how expense account codes can be duplicated.

Sample Five-Digit Chart of Accounts

Account Number	Department	Description
00-010	xxx	Cash
00-020	xxx	Petty cash
00-030	xxx	Accounts receivable
00-040	xxx	Allowance for doubtful accounts
00-050	xxx	Marketable securities
00-060	xxx	Raw materials inventory
00-070	xxx	Work-in-process inventory
00-080	xxx	Finished goods inventory
00-090	xxx	Reserve for obsolete inventory
00-100	xxx	Fixed assets – Computer equipment
00-110	xxx	Fixed assets – Computer software
00-120	xxx	Fixed assets – Furniture and fixtures
00-130	xxx	Fixed assets – Leasehold improvements
00-140	xxx	Fixed assets – Machinery
00-150	xxx	Accumulated depreciation – Computer equipment
00-160	xxx	Accumulated depreciation – Computer software
00-170	xxx	Accumulated depreciation – Furniture and fixtures
00-180	xxx	Accumulated depreciation – Leasehold improvements

Account Number	Department	Description
00-190	xxx	Accumulated depreciation – Machinery
00-200	xxx	Other assets
00-300	xxx	Accounts payable
00-310	xxx	Accrued payroll liability
00-320	xxx	Accrued vacation liability
00-330	xxx	Accrued expenses liability – other
00-340	xxx	Unremitted sales taxes
00-350	xxx	Unremitted pension payments
00-360	xxx	Short-term notes payable
00-370	xxx	Other short-term liabilities
00-400	xxx	Long-term notes payable
00-500	xxx	Capital stock
00-510	xxx	Retained earnings
00-600	xxx	Revenue
00-700	xxx	Cost of goods sold – Materials
00-710	xxx	Cost of goods sold – Direct labor
00-720	xxx	Cost of goods sold – Manufacturing supplies
00-730	xxx	Cost of goods sold – Applied overhead
10-800	Accounting	Bank charges
10-805	Accounting	Benefits
10-810	Accounting	Depreciation
10-815	Accounting	Insurance
10-825	Accounting	Office supplies
10-830	Accounting	Salaries and wages
10-835	Accounting	Telephones
10-840	Accounting	Training
10-845	Accounting	Travel and entertainment
10-850	Accounting	Utilities
10-855	Accounting	Other expenses
10-860	Accounting	Interest expense
20-800	Production	Bank charges
20-805	Production	Benefits
20-810	Production	Depreciation
20-815	Production	Insurance

Account Number	Department	Description
20-825	Production	Office supplies
20-830	Production	Salaries and wages
20-835	Production	Telephones
20-840	Production	Training
20-845	Production	Travel and entertainment
20-850	Production	Utilities
20-855	Production	Other expenses
20-860	Production	Interest expense

The preceding sample chart of accounts shows an exact duplication of accounts for each department listed. This is not necessarily the case in reality, since some departments have accounts for which they are the only probable users. For example, the accounting department in the example has an account for bank charges that the production department is unlikely to use. Thus, some accounts can be avoided by flagging them as inactive in the AIS. By doing so, they do not appear in the formal chart of accounts.

Audit Trail

A useful benefit of having a well-constructed data storage system is that it provides a detailed audit trail. An *audit trail* is the documented flow of a transaction from its point of origin to its final point of use. It is used to investigate how a source document was translated into an account entry, and from there was inserted into the financial statements. The audit trail can be used in reverse, to track backwards from a financial statement line item to the originating source document. A well-constructed AIS should have a clear audit trail for all transactions.

An audit trail is used by both external and internal auditors to trace transactions through the system, as well as by the accounting staff to track down errors and the causes of variances in the financial statements.

EXAMPLE

An auditor is examining the books of Inscription International, a maker of pens, and wants to verify Inscription's reported sales figure. She does so by tracing the sales figure back to the sales journal, which provides her with a listing of all invoices generated during the year, summing to the annual sales total. She takes a random sample of those invoices and traces their recorded sales amounts to the source documents, which are customer purchase orders and shipping documentation.

Stage 3: Data Processing

The third stage in the data processing cycle is data processing. This involves ongoing processing to keep the data in the AIS current. There are four processing activities, which are:

- *Creating records*. This is the initial entry of data into the system, such as recording the receipt of a new product at the receiving dock, the hiring of a new employee, or the issuance of a purchase order to a supplier.
- *Reading records*. This is the ongoing retrieval of existing data, such as accessing a customer's payment history to see if it deserves an increased credit line, or accessing the usage history of an inventory item when determining how much of it to reorder from a supplier.
- *Updating records*. This is the periodic updating of records with additional information, such as adding a new inventory item to the record for a warehouse location, once the inventory has been physically moved to that location.
- *Deleting records*. This is the periodic elimination of records, such as when customers are purged from the AIS when they are no longer in business.

The most effective type of data processing is *real-time processing*, where records are updated as each transaction occurs. By using real-time processing, stored information is always current, which allows management to rely on the AIS when making decisions. For example, when inventory records are being updated in real time, one can rely with great confidence on the reported amount of inventory on hand, which assists with reordering decisions. Real-time processing can be a major competitive advantage, especially when a business relies on its AIS when dealing with customers. For example, a business can quote customers a delivery date based on the on-hand inventory balances reported in its AIS.

A less-effective type of data processing is *batch processing*, where updates are made at longer intervals, such as once a day or month. This is an efficient approach, in that the system requires less processing time. However, the longer updating interval means that the impacted records are not being updated as transactions occur, and so could contain information that is no longer current. Consequently, batch processing is normally used for applications that are only accessed occasionally, such as periodic payroll processing.

Stage 4: Information Output

The final stage in the data processing cycle is information output, which is the transfer of organized information to users. The manner of presentation can be any of the following:

- *Document*. This is a piece of printed or electronic matter that provides information or evidence, or which serves as an official record. For example, an invoice is a document that is (usually) printed and mailed to a customer.

Or, a pick list is used by the warehouse staff to pick inventory items from stock. Another example is the receiving report, which itemizes the goods that were accepted at the receiving dock during a certain period of time.

- *Query*. This is a request for information from the AIS, typically to answer a question that needs an immediate answer. A query may be made through an AIS specialist who has the best knowledge of how to extract information from the system, or a user may attempt to do so directly. For example, a baby stroller manufacturing firm has just been made aware of a design flaw that may require a product recall, so the chief executive officer has a staff person generate a query to identify all product returns in the past month that relate to this specific issue. When the same query is made on a routine basis, it is more likely to be converted into a report (see next item).

- *Report*. This is a document that has been organized into a narrative, graphic, or tabular form, which is used to provide feedback about operations or to assist in making decisions. For example, a business issues financial statements to its investors to report on its financial condition. Or, it generates reports about product line profitability, which can be used to make decisions about whether to expand or terminate specific products or entire product lines. Another example is a report about the safety measures taken to deal with hazardous materials, which is issued to the relevant regulatory agency. Certain reports may be issued on a regular basis, such as a management flash report that documents key ratios, or they may be issued on a one-time basis in response to specific requests, such as a query about bad debt write-offs related to a product.

An AIS tends to generate a large number of reports, because requests for new reports are always being added, while few of the old ones are being deleted. The result is an increased level of inefficiency, as report recipients have to spend more and more time wading through reports. This issue can be mitigated by periodically examining the reports being issued to see if they are still relevant. If not, possible options are to delete them from the system, lengthen the intervals at which they are produced, combine them, or alter their formats to make them more readable.

Summary

The accountant has a massive impact on the way in which data are organized within an AIS, since the accounting department is responsible for how the general ledger and subsidiary ledgers are structured. These structural decisions can have a long-term impact on how well data are handled by the system, so it pays to explore all possible options, possibly with the help of an outside expert, before committing to a specific coding methodology and account code structure.

Chapter 3
Systems Documentation

Introduction

The documentation of a system is needed so that one can fully understand how the system works. A comprehensive set of documentation should reveal all aspects of the data processing stages that were covered in the preceding chapter. In this chapter, we cover the graphical and narrative descriptions used in a systems documentation project, with a particular focus on data flow diagrams, flowcharts, and business process diagrams.

Need for Systems Documentation

There are multiple reasons why a business needs to have adequate documentation of its systems. They are as follows:

- *Audits*. Systems documentation is commonly used for auditors, who need to understand how systems and their related controls operate. This information is needed to develop an opinion about the robustness of a company's system of internal controls. This is especially important for a publicly held company, which is required by the Sarbanes-Oxley Act of 2002 to establish an adequate system of internal controls, whose effectiveness must be evaluated by its auditors.
- *Controls*. Proper documentation can be used to highlight where controls may be lacking in a system, or where there are overlapping controls that could present opportunities for the selective reduction of controls.
- *System development or selection*. The documentation for an existing system can form the basis for the development of systems configuration documents for a proposed new system that needs to contain many of the capabilities of the old system.
- *Training*. Systems documentation can be used as the basis for training materials for system users. This is especially effective if the systems documentation is regularly updated to reflect changes in the underlying systems, and the revised documentation is then used to update training materials.

The preceding points become more urgent as a business grows in size, since its systems gradually increase in complexity and would otherwise be excessively difficult to understand.

Data Flow Diagrams

A *data flow diagram* graphically portrays the flow of information for a process, including the sources of data, where the data goes, where it is transformed and stored, and where it is delivered. The diagram uses common symbols, such as rectangles, circles and arrows, as well as short text labels, to display data inputs, outputs, storage points and the routings between endpoints. The essential symbols used in a data flow diagram are noted in the following exhibit.

Symbols Used in Data Flow Diagrams

Symbol	Name	Description
	External entity (square box)	External entities originate and use data that flow between the entity and the system being diagrammed. These data flows are the inputs and outputs of a data flow diagram. External entities are typically placed near the boundaries of a diagram, since they are external to the system being documented. They can also indicate the presence of a separate system.
	Process (circle)	Processes document activities that change or transform data flows. Because of their transformational role, processes should always have inputs and outputs on a data flow diagram. Each process may be given a short title that describes its function and labeled with a reference number that refers to additional information at the bottom of the page. Processes typically begin in the top left corner of the diagram and finish near the bottom right corner.
	Data store (rectangle or two parallel lines)	Data stores hold data for later access; they do not generate any operations. A data store may contain files or documents held only briefly, or on a longer-term basis. The flows into a data store may include operations that alter the stored data.
	Data flow (Curved or straight line)	Data flows indicate the movement of data between external entities, processes and data stores. An arrow on a data flow indicates the direction in which the data is moving. These flows are labeled with the type of data or the associated process or data store.

A generic data flow diagram appears in the following exhibit. The diagram shows data originating on the left side of the diagram from an outside source and then proceeding through three processing steps. Along the way, data flows out of the process following each processing step, with the data coming out of the second processing step being sent to storage. In the diagram, a data source represents the entity that sends data to the system, while the data destination represents the entity that receives data from the system.

Generic Data Flow Diagram

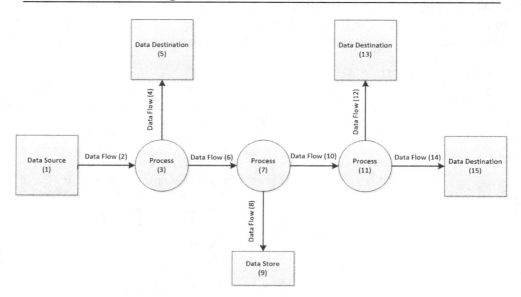

We expand upon the preceding generic data flow diagram by adding names to each of the data sources, data destinations, and processes to describe an accounts payable system. The revised version appears in the following exhibit.

Payables Data Flow Diagram

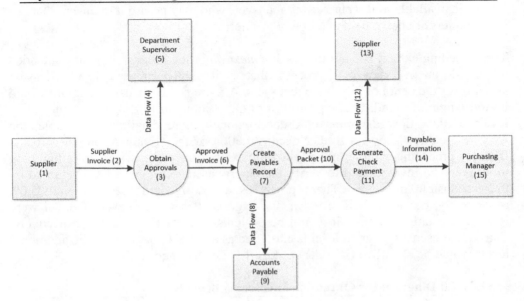

A data flow diagram may be accompanied by a narrative description. This description provides additional information about the diagram that may not otherwise be apparent. A sample narrative for the preceding payables data flow diagram is:

> When the company receives an invoice from a supplier, the payables staff logs in the invoice, retains a copy, and then sends it out to the responsible manager for approval. If the invoice has not been returned within one week, a payables staff person tracks down the responsible manager and requests that the invoice be examined immediately.
>
> Once approval is received, the invoice is entered into the accounts payable software. If the entered invoice number from that supplier is already present in the system, it will kick out the invoice as a duplicate. Once entered, the system uses the invoice payment terms to automatically schedule the related check to be included in a later check run.
>
> When checks are printed, the invoice is attached to the check and sent to an authorized check signer, who reviews the attached invoice before signing the check. The check is then separated from the invoice and mailed to the supplier, while the invoice is stapled to a copy of the check remittance advice to show proof of payment, and then filed by supplier name.

The completed payables record, including evidence of payment, is then made available to the purchasing manager, who may peruse it to ensure that suppliers are being paid in a timely manner.

The preceding exhibit is classified as a *context diagram*, because it is only intended to provide an overview of a process; that is, it only portrays a data processing system, not the detail of its component parts. A more comprehensive diagram would be too tangled to read. Consequently, it is quite common to drill down into lower levels of data flow diagrams in order to obtain more detail. For example, the following exhibit shows a further deconstruction of the Obtain Approvals process from the preceding exhibit. In the following exhibit, the processes are to initially log in all received invoices and to verify that approved invoices have been returned by the responsible managers. These processes are designated as "1.0" and "2.0", respectively, denoting their order in the diagram. If a further level of detail were required for either process, it would be designated as "1.1" or "2.1", respectively. Thus, the presented diagram level is classified as a Level 0 diagram, while additional levels would be classified (in order) as Level 1, Level 2, and so forth.

Level 0 Diagram for Obtaining Invoice Approvals

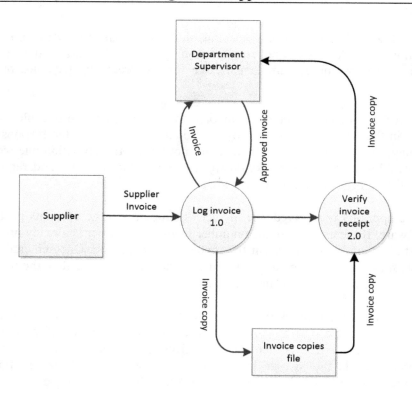

One should keep the following best practices in mind when developing data flow diagrams:

- *Investigate the system.* The development of a sufficiently clear and detailed set of data flow diagrams calls for an in-depth investigation of the system being documented. This will likely require the accountant to interview those involved in the process, observe how the various processes are conducted, and possibly have users complete a questionnaire.
- *Begin with a context diagram.* A context diagram is useful for defining the general system that will be documented. If something does not appear on the context diagram, then it will be excluded from the documentation effort.
- *Eliminate insignificant items.* Documentation of every possible aspect of a system can result in a confusing tangle of diagrams. It makes more sense to focus on those aspects of the system that are used on a repetitive basis, ignoring tasks that are only encountered on an occasional basis.
- *Define the system.* A system may spill over into adjacent systems, resulting in a massive documentation effort that never seems to end. If so, the accountant will need to designate boundaries for the documentation effort, and exclude everything outside of those boundaries.
- *Aggregate data flows.* When there are data elements that flow to the same processes, entities or data stores, show them as a single data flow.
- *Aggregate processes.* When processes are logically related and are completed at the same time, show them as a single process.
- *Identify data flows.* Assign a label to each data flow, except when data is being transmitted to a data store (in which case the data flow is obvious).
- *Use multiple layers.* Be willing to create multiple levels of diagrams, especially when using a single level would result in an excessively muddled diagram.
- *Conduct a walkthrough.* Conduct a joint walkthrough of the diagram(s) with someone else who is knowledgeable in the targeted system, to see if there are any errors or omissions that need to be corrected.

Flowcharts

A *flowchart* is a diagram that graphically describes a system. Each step in a process is represented by a box or some similar graphic, which contains text that briefly describes the step. It helps a user to visualize what is going on in a system, though the graphical nature of the presentation may not be that useful when a process is unusually complex. Flowcharts can be subdivided into the following four classifications:

- *Document flowcharts.* Portrays the flow of documents through a system, including where they are created, distributed, and disposed of.
- *Data flowcharts.* Depicts the flow of data through a system.
- *System flowcharts.* Represents the relationships between the input, processing, and outputs of a system.

- *Program flowcharts.* Portrays the sequence of coded instructions in a computer program, enabling it to perform certain operations.

Flowcharts are frequently used to clarify narrative descriptions of systems, and so can be an excellent training tool for someone who is unfamiliar with a system. They are also used to provide an overview of a system that is being analyzed for process improvements.

Given their role in clarifying processes, it can make sense to minimize the number of symbols used. The four symbols appearing in the following exhibit should be sufficient for most applications, though there are many other symbols available that can be used, portraying communication links, manual operations, electronic output, computer processing, and so forth.

Standard Flowchart Symbols

Symbol	Discussion
	Process: This is the primary symbol used in a flowchart. State each step within a process box. It is possible that a simplified flowchart will contain no other shapes.
	Decision: This is used when a decision will result in a different process flow. The decision symbol can be overused. Try to restrict its usage to no more than two per flowchart. Otherwise, the flowchart will appear overly complex. If more decision symbols are needed, consider subdividing a flowchart into multiple documents.
	Document: This symbol is particularly useful for showing where an input form is used to collect information for a process, though it can also represent a report generated *by* a process.
	Database: This symbol is used less frequently, and shows when information is extracted from or stored in a computer database. In most cases, the use of a database can be implied without cluttering up a flowchart with the symbol.

An example of a flowchart that documents the handling of cash receipts from customers appears in the following exhibit. The flowchart is clearly much simpler to understand than the following narrative of the same process, requiring only a few moments for a user to gain an understanding of the underlying process. The narrative description is:

1. **Accept and record cash.** If the business is paid by a customer in cash, record the payment in a cash register. If there is no cash register (as may

36

be the case in a low-volume sales environment), the sales clerk instead fills out a two-part sales receipt, gives a copy to the customer, and retains the other copy.

2. **Match receipts to cash.** Compare the amount of cash received to either the cash register receipt total or the total of all sales receipt copies, and investigate any differences. Complete a reconciliation form for any differences found.

3. **Aggregate and post receipt information.** Summarize the information in the cash register and post this information to the general ledger as a sale and cash receipt. If the cash register is linked to the company's accounting system and is tracking individual sales, then sales are being recorded automatically, as is the reduction of goods in the inventory records. If sales clerks are manually completing sales receipts, summarize the information in the sales receipts and record the sales and any related inventory reductions in the general ledger.

4. **Deposit cash.** Prepare a bank deposit slip, retain a copy, and enclose the original slip along with all cash in a locked container for transport to the bank. After counting the cash, the bank issues a receipt stating the amount it has received.

5. **Match to deposit slip.** Compare the copy of the deposit slip to the bank receipt, and investigate any differences. A variation is to compare the cash receipts journal to the bank receipt.

Cash Receipts Flowchart

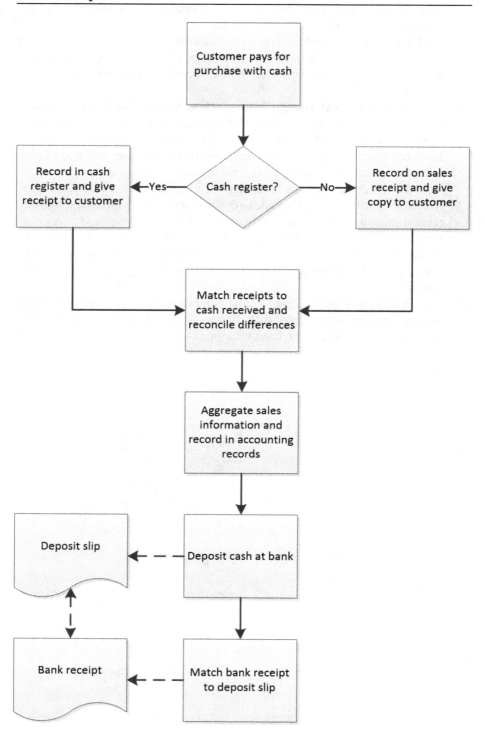

One should keep the following best practices in mind when developing flowcharts:

- *Standardize the flow.* The information in a flowchart should begin at the top or in the top left corner and proceed to the bottom or bottom right corner, thereby establishing a standard flow.
- *Minimize information.* Ideally, a flowchart should contain much less information than a narrative description of a system, so that only the highlights of the basic process steps are revealed.
- *Eliminate insignificant items.* Strip out minor steps that are rarely used. It makes more sense to focus on those aspects of the system that are used on a repetitive basis.
- *Terminate the flowchart.* If any activities or documents continue off the bottom of the flowchart, identify the name of the flowchart in which the description continues. Otherwise, the reader does not gain a complete understanding of the underlying process.
- *Conduct a walkthrough.* Conduct a joint walkthrough of the flowchart with someone else who is knowledgeable in the targeted system, to see if there are any errors or omissions that need to be corrected.

Business Process Diagrams

A business process diagram (BPD) graphically depicts the flow of business processes. The intent is to give readers a simplified, easy-to-understand overview of a process. A minimal number of symbols are used in a BPD, usually just a rectangle to describe activities, and arrows to indicate the flow of activities. The diagram reads from left to right and from top to bottom. A sample BPD for the purchase of goods appears in the following example.

When preparing a BPD, one should keep in mind the best practices noted previously for data flow diagrams and flowcharts. In addition, consider the following:

- *Simplify the format.* Since this is a high-level diagram, simplify it as much as possible by only using two columns. The first column states who is engaged in an activity, while the second column describes their activities.
- *Stay high level.* A BPD is constructed at such a high level that there is no need to delve into the details of exactly which documents are used, or which software is employed to process data. This means that a BPD is much less likely to require revision as certain aspects of a system are altered over time.

Purchasing Business Process Diagram

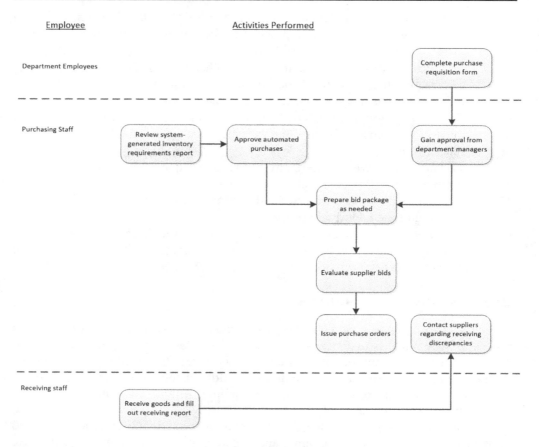

Summary

The approaches to systems documentation described in this chapter are quite useful for a variety of purposes. Systems development personnel are more likely to need data flow diagrams, while control analysts and auditors are more likely to be preoccupied with flowcharts. Business process diagrams and flowcharts can be inserted into training materials to be used by anyone wanting to gain familiarity with a process. In short, a significant amount of documentation is needed for an organization's key systems.

Chapter 4
Databases

Introduction

At the heart of an accounting information system (AIS) is a database in which data are stored. In this chapter, we discuss the nature of a database, how it is structured, how it can be queried, and several related topics.

The Nature of a Database

A *database* is an organized collection of data that is designed to make data more easily accessed, manipulated, and updated. A *database management system* (DBMS) is a sophisticated software program that defines, manipulates, retrieves, and manages the data stored in a database. The DBMS is able to manipulate the data format, field names, record structure, and file structure. It also delineates the rules to validate and manipulate the data in the database. The person who manages a DBMS is called the database administrator.

It can be useful to view the logical structure of a database, a sample of which appears in the following exhibit. The structure resembles a pyramid, where a set of fields about a specific entity roll up into a record. In the example, there may be dozens of fields that describe a supplier, including its tax identification number, primary contact, secondary contact, phone numbers, and so forth. In the second row from the bottom, there are many records describing suppliers that are stored in a supplier file. This file is designed to aggregate similar records. When these files are centrally managed, they are known as a database. Since the database can access data in any of the files of which it is comprised, users can extract a greater range of information from the system than would be the case if they could only access one file at a time.

Databases were built because businesses originally stored data on an ad hoc basis, which frequently resulted in each department or location maintaining its own files, with no centralized access to anything. A common outcome was that data needed to be loaded into more than one file, which presented both efficiency and data entry error problems. Also, there was no centralized way to update the data, making it either quite expensive to do so on a file-by-file basis, or resulting in old records that were essentially not usable, or similar records that were accurate in one file but not in another.

Logical Structure of a Database

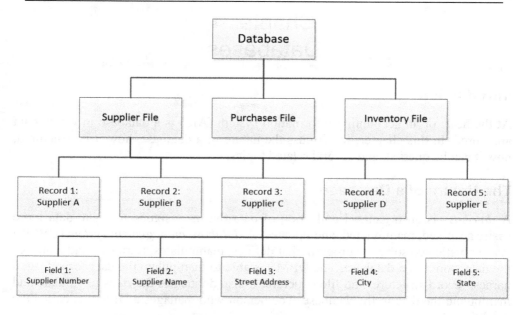

Advantages and Disadvantages of a Database

Databases are generally considered to be a substantial benefit to any organization, for the following reasons:

- *Cross-functional analysis.* Users can define relationships between different data, such as the association between product types and customer returns, in the preparation of reports for management consumption.
- *Data access.* Users can use query languages to access data, thereby making it easier to collect and interpret it.
- *Data independence.* Data are stored independently of application programs. For example, a single pool of inventory data can be used by programs that address purchasing, production management, warehousing, picking, and shipping.
- *Data security.* Access to the data is controlled in a consistent manner through a single interface, thereby improving data security.
- *Simplified application development.* Since the data are independent of application programs, it is easier to create and modify the programs.
- *Single-location data storage.* Data items are usually only stored once, thereby minimizing the risks of having redundant data and that the redundant data are inconsistent. Single-location storage also minimizes the amount of data entry, storage, and retrieval costs. Also, since data are only stored once, updates only need to be made to data elements one time.

Though the preceding advantages are substantial, they must be weighed against the following disadvantages:

- *Setup time*. Database systems can be difficult to configure, and may require an extended implementation period. This will include training time for programmers and system users.
- *Setup cost*. A comprehensive database can require a substantial expenditure for hardware and software. In addition, the conversion from a file-based system to a database can be quite expensive.
- *Ripple effect of data corruption*. Since data are only stored in one place, any corruption of the data will impact all application programs using it.

Database Terminology

There are many terms associated with databases. We note several of the more pertinent ones below, since they are useful for developing a basic understanding of databases. The terms are:

Data-Related

- *Data item*. This is a unit of data that is stored in a record, describing a particular attribute, such as the first name, middle name, or last name of an employee in an employee record.
- *Record*. This is a collection of data items, usually in a fixed sequence. For example, an employee record may include that person's name, address, pay rate, start date, date of birth, and so forth. Records are an efficient way to store and access data.
- *Record layout*. This is a document that shows the sequence of the data items stored in a file, as well as the length of each one and the type of data being stored. A sample record layout appears in the following exhibit.

Sample File Record Layout

Employee Number (numeric) Characters = 6	Employee Name (alphanumeric) Characters = 24	Employee Address (alphanumeric) Characters = 32	Employee Social Security Nbr. (numeric) Characters = 9	Employee Tax Deductions (numeric) Characters = 2	Employee Salary (numeric) Characters = 6

- *Physical view*. The manner in which data are physically stored within a database.
- *Logical view*. The representation of data in a meaningful format, telling users what is in a database.

A DBMS links the physical storage locations of data with the logical view of the data as expressed by each user. This linkage allows users to access data without knowing exactly where it is physically stored. Another advantage is that the

DBMS can change the physical location of data (usually to optimize access time) without impacting the activities of users.

Data Dictionary

- *Data dictionary.* This is a central repository of information about data, such as their meaning, usage, format, and relationships with other data. Thus, it describes the structure of a database, providing guidance on the interpretation and accepted meanings of data. It is useful for avoiding data inconsistencies across a database, and makes data easier to analyze. A data dictionary is an essential tool for the design of a database and its subsequent documentation. A sample data dictionary appears in the following table for data related to employees.

Sample Data Dictionary

Data Element	Description	Records Located In	Source	Field Length	Programs Used In	Outputs Used In	Authorized Users
Employee number	Unique employee identifier	Employee record, payroll record	Form I-9	6	Employee file update, payroll processing	Payroll register, staff summary	Unrestricted
Employee name	Complete employee name	Employee record, payroll record	Form I-9	20	Employee file update, payroll processing	Payroll register, staff summary	Unrestricted
Employee address	Street, city, state, and zip code	Employee record, payroll record	Form I-9	35	Employee file update, payroll processing	Payroll register, staff summary	Unrestricted
Social security number	Full nine-digit number	Employee record	Form I-9	9	Employee file update	Staff summary	D. Denton
Pay rate	Rate paid per hour or pay period	Employee record, payroll record	Pay rate change form	8	Employee file update, payroll processing	Payroll register, staff summary	D. Denton
Date of birth	Stated in MM/DD/YY format	Employee record	Form I-9	6	Employee file update	Staff summary	D. Denton
Cost center	Department to which expense is charged	Employee record	Department hiring form	4	Employee file update, payroll processing	Payroll register, staff summary	Unrestricted

Data Extraction

- *Report writer.* This is software that configures and prints a report based on a pre-defined description of its layout. Once a report has been created, it can be stored for future use. A report writer both simplifies and standardizes the creation of reports, which is quite useful in an accounting environment where many standardized reports are issued on an on-going basis.

- *Database query language*. This is any programming language that requests and retrieves data from a database by sending queries to it. It requires users to input a structured command that is similar to English, and so requires relatively little advance training.

A report writer and a database query language are essential tools for database users.

Schemas-Related

- *Schema*. This is a diagram that describes the tables and corresponding fields contained within a database. Boxes represent individual tables, and lines show how tables are connected. The lines may also indicate the flow of data. The three levels of schemas are:
  - o *Internal-level schema*. This defines the physical storage structure of a database. It defines how the data will be stored in a block.
  - o *Conceptual-level schema*. This describes the structure of a whole database, noting what data are to be stored in the database and the relationships among the data. Database administrators and programmers engage at this level.
  - o *External schema*. This describes the end user interaction with a database. It describes that part of the database that a specific user group is interested in, and hides the remainder of the database from that group. Each of these views is called a subschema.

Of particular importance is the ability of the external schema to hide data from certain user groups. For example, the subschema available to the payroll department would provide them with the data needed to process wage and salary payments to employees, but does not give them access to data about accounts payable or fixed assets.

The following exhibit portrays how the three-schema architecture functions.

Three-Schema Architecture

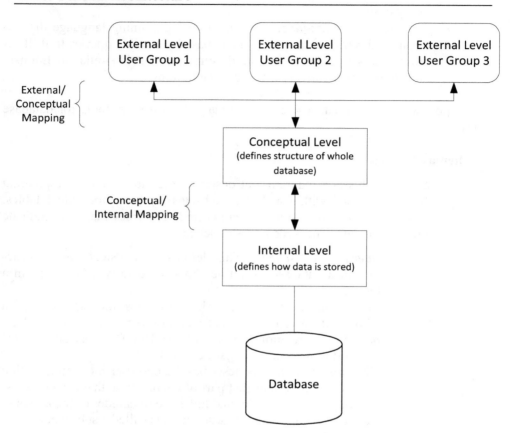

The DBMS uses the three-schema system to translate the request of a program (or a user query) for data into the specific storage locations needed to physically access the data.

Relational Databases

A relational database is a set of tables from which data can be accessed or reassembled in many ways without having to reorganize the underlying tables. Each row in a table represents instances of a type of entity, while the columns represent values attributed to that instance. A sample table that includes these concepts appears in the following exhibit.

Sample Employee Table

Employee Number	Last Name	First Name	Sex	Date of Birth	Salary	Department
EN1202	Sullivan	Linda	F	10/21/X3	82,000	IT
EN1248	Hanford	Jenny	F	11/14/X0	57,000	Materials
EN1214	Butler	Wendy	F	12/31/X2	38,500	Marketing
EN1450	McArdle	Trevor	M	06/06/X4	68,750	Accounting
EN1641	Goodrich	Carlos	M	11/03/X7	48,250	Materials

Each row within a table is assigned a unique *primary key*. It is essentially a unique address for that row. In addition, a *foreign key* is used as a field in one table that uniquely identifies a primary key in another table. The foreign key is used to link two tables together. This capability is used to produce data in response to user queries that are extracted from different tables and then stitched together for the purposes of the user. For example, the following table links the currency rate information from the CurrencyRateID table with the sales order information stored in the SalesOrderHeader table. The reason for the linkage is that currency rate information can now be included in the responses to any queries about sales orders.

Sample Link between Tables Using Keys

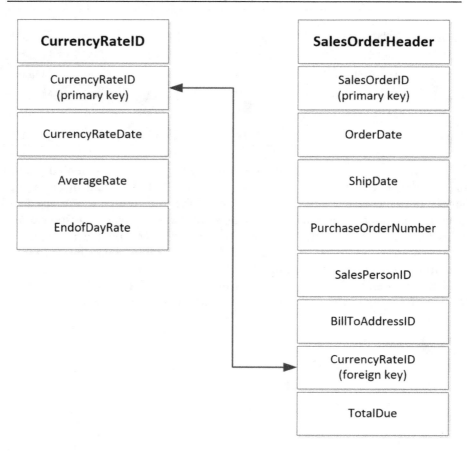

Relational databases are highly useful, for the following reasons:

- *Flexibility*. It is relatively easy for users to carry out complex queries of the data.
- *Accuracy*. Data is only stored once, thereby eliminating any data duplication.
- *Security*. Access to specific data can be limited to allow access only to predefined users.
- *Extendibility*. After a database has been created, it is relatively easy to add a new data category to it without having to modify existing applications.

Data Warehouses

The preceding database discussion was based on the assumption that it would be primarily used to support current operations, where transactions were being routinely run through it. However, there is another use for a database, which is to serve as a data archive that can be accessed as part of ongoing financial and operational analyses. This latter use mandates a different type of database, where the focus is on storing very large amounts of data, rather than supporting current transaction processing requirements. A database that supports such analyses is called a *data warehouse*; this is a large store of data that has been accumulated from a number of sources within a business, and which is used to assist in the formulation of management decisions.

The usual approach for searching through a data warehouse for relevant information is *online analytical processing* (OLAP). Someone can use OLAP to consolidate data, drill down through data, or slice and dice the data. Consolidation involves the aggregation of data, such as combining the sales data for all North American sales divisions for each of the past ten years. This information could potentially be used to generate sales forecasts. Drilling down allows a user to move from aggregated data down into the detail of the supporting data. For example, one could use drill down tools to learn more about the individual product sales that comprise the most recent annual sales figures. Slicing and dicing is useful for viewing data from varying perspectives. For example, one could view North American sales by individual salesperson, or by distribution channel, or by customer. One can use these tools to uncover many insights into a business, such as bad debt trends among certain customers, product failure rates based on where they were produced, and changes in customer order rates by state.

Despite the obvious advantages of data warehouses, many companies have not found them to be cost-effective, usually because they were not properly assembled or maintained. This is a particular problem when the data is assembled from multiple databases that contain overlapping data that may not be consistent with each other. The most useful data warehouses are those that have been thoroughly verified. Data verification is especially necessary whenever a new database is added, since there would otherwise be a risk of having the newly-added data reduce the effectiveness of any data searches, calling into question the efficacy of the entire system.

Summary

Accountants are likely to field queries from all over a business, as well as from outside parties, covering a massive number of topics. Report writing software will be sufficient for responses to the more common inquiries, while a database query language will be needed to plumb deeper into the underlying database for answers to more pointed, one-time questions. By structuring data into a database, the accountant can depart from reporting only in predefined formats, allowing for an enhanced reporting role that is more useful to the organization. Consequently, the accountant needs to have a strong operational knowledge of both report writing software and the applicable database query language.

Chapter 5
Systems-Related Fraud and Theft

Introduction

It is entirely possible, if not likely, that an organization's accounting information system (AIS) will be compromised at some point. There are many ways in which this can happen, including the following:

- Intentional acts – Including misappropriation of assets, cyber-attacks, unauthorized disclosure of data, sabotage, and terrorist acts.
- Natural causes – Including fires, floods, earthquakes, tornadoes, and hurricanes.
- System failures – Including software, hardware, and electrical failures.
- Unintentional acts – Including lost data, data entry errors or omissions, incorrectly following procedures, and misplaced documents.

Of the preceding items, our focus in this chapter is on the first item – intentional acts. Accordingly, we discuss the nature and types of fraud, computer-related fraud and computer attacks, fraud prevention and detection, and several related topics.

What is Fraud?

Fraud is the false representation of facts, resulting in the object of the fraud receiving an injury by acting upon the misrepresented facts. Stated somewhat differently, fraud is trickery used to gain a dishonest advantage over another person. The synonyms in the following exhibit can be used to gain a better understanding of the broad extent of fraud.

Fraud Synonyms

Blackmail	Double-cross	Ploy
Cheat	Extortion	Ruse
Con	Hoax	Scam
Confidence trick	Hoodwink	Sham
Deceit	Misrepresentation	Swindle

Fraud is proven in court by showing that the actions of an individual involved the following elements:

- A false statement of a material fact;
- Knowledge that the statement was untrue;

- Intent by the individual to deceive the victim;
- Reliance by the victim on the statement; and
- Injury sustained by the victim as a result of the preceding actions.

The key element in the preceding definition is *intent*. A company could make false representations in its financial statements simply because the accounting staff made a mistake in compiling certain financial information. This is not fraud (though it may be incompetence), since there was no intent to misstate the financial statements. Conversely, if a controller intentionally reduces the bad debt reserve in order to increase profits and thereby triggers a bonus for the management team, this *is* fraud, because a false statement was intentionally made.

Within a company, an employee can use fraud to steal assets, where facts are misrepresented in order to hide the theft. For example:

- A warehouse employee steals inventory and covers up the theft by recording the inventory in the warehouse tracking system as having been scrapped. The fraudulent action is recording a false transaction.
- A salesperson sells inventory to a customer, takes the cash payment from the customer, and never records the sale. In this case, the fraudulent action is *not* recording the transaction.

Most people who engage in fraud are company insiders. These people know how company systems function, understand where the controls are located, and where there are vulnerabilities that can be exploited. Given these advantages, they are far more likely to succeed in stealing assets than someone trying to penetrate the company from the outside.

Types of Fraud

There are a number of types of fraud that a business can experience. At the highest level, they can be broken down into two general categories, which are fraud committed *on behalf of* the organization and fraud committed *against* the organization. In the first case, employees alter the reported financial results of the business in order to make it look better than is really the case. This could be done in order to bolster the stock price, earn bonuses, or avoid a loan default. The benefit to the perpetrator may be indirect. In the latter case, employees are directly stealing from the organization, so they experience a direct benefit. We expand upon these concepts in the following sub-sections.

Financial Statement Fraud

In financial statement fraud, the management team alters the financial statements in order to reveal more sales, better profits, a more robust financial position, and/or better cash flows than is really the case. The range of possible alterations to the financial statements is impressive, including the inflation of sales figures, falsifying expenses, faking receivables and inventory, reclassifying cash flows, and even adjusting the disclosures that accompany the financial statements.

The victims of this fraud are investors and creditors. Investors are relying on the financial statements to judge the prices at which to buy or sell a company's shares, and so could make incorrect investment decisions. Creditors are relying on the statements to determine whether to loan funds or extend credit to the company, and could potentially lose these funds if the company turns out to be a poor credit risk.

Embezzlement

When embezzlement occurs, employees either directly take assets from the company for their own use, or assist in diverting assets from the company. For example, a warehouse person could walk out with finished goods inventory, a maintenance staffer could steal tools, and a sales clerk could steal cash from the cash register. When a person assists in diverting assets, this involves taking bribes or kickbacks from outsiders who are engaged in fraudulent activities. For example:

- *Supplier kickback.* A purchasing department employee accepts a 5% kickback from a supplier in exchange for approving its bid in a competitive bidding situation. The supplier bids at a higher price than would normally be accepted, so the company is losing funds as a result of the situation.
- *Supplier bribery.* A supplier bribes the receiving manager to overlook low-quality raw materials being delivered to the company. The company suffers from a higher failure rate in its production processes as a result of using the low-quality materials.

The level of embezzlement depends on the position occupied by the perpetrator, with more senior positions having a greater ability to embezzle. It is also possible that a person with a less-senior position can also embezzle a significant amount if they take advantage of a control weakness.

The Fraud Triangle

Under what conditions does someone commit fraud? There are three interlocking conditions, known as the *fraud triangle*, under which fraud is most likely to flourish. These conditions are:

- *Perceived pressure.* A person may be liable for significant liabilities, such as the cost of supporting sick relatives, college loans, car loans, and so forth. Or, they may have an expensive habit that requires ongoing funding. When the individual sees no way out of the situation, they may resort to fraud. However, there may only be a *perceived* level of pressure, such as earning comparatively less than one's friends. This latter situation can trigger expectations for a better lifestyle, perhaps involving a sports car, foreign travel, or a larger house. When a person does not see a clear path to meeting these expectations by honest means, he or she may resort to dishonest alternatives.

- *Opportunity*. When the preceding pressures are present, a person must also see an opportunity to commit fraud. For example, a maintenance worker may realize that there are no controls over checking out and returning tools; this is an opportunity for theft.
- *Rationalization*. An additional issue that is needed for fraud to continue over a period of time is the ability of the perpetrator to rationalize the situation as being acceptable. For example, a person stealing from a company's petty cash box might rationalize it as merely borrowing, with the intent of paying back the funds at a later date. As another example, a management team adjusts reported earnings for a few months during mid-year, in the expectation that sales will rise towards the end of the year, allowing them to eliminate the adjustments by year-end.

The issues noted here tend to interact. For example, if a person is under an intense amount of financial pressure and there is a serious opportunity for fraud, then the level of rationalization needed to justify committing fraud will be quite low. Conversely, if there is little pressure and only a modest opportunity to do so, then it will take a much higher level of rationalization to justify the fraud. Consequently, a good approach to proactively dealing with fraud is to work on all of these areas – reducing the financial pressure on employees and minimizing the number and size of opportunities for fraud.

We cover the pressure, opportunity, and rationalization issues in more detail in the following sub-sections.

Perceived Pressure

The most obvious type of pressure that may impact a person is financial pressure. While one might associate real financial pressure with someone living in a car or under a bridge, anyone can have a perceived amount of financial pressure even when they already earn a substantial amount of money. Consider the following situations:

- A person is living well beyond his means. For example, a production worker loves sports cars and is determined to have one, even though his hourly wage does not begin to qualify him for a car loan. Or, a corporate executive wants a private jet, so he will misrepresent his company's profits in order to sell shares at a higher price and then buy the jet.
- A person has incurred a large amount of debt. His current wage might have been sufficient under all normal circumstances, but the additional amount of debt payments renders his situation much less tenable. The same situation arises when a person's wages are being garnished.
- A person is suddenly confronted with a large expenditure. For example, a person's spouse is uninsured, and she must now undergo expensive radiation therapy to treat cancer.
- A person wants to be perceived as being successful. This calls for the acquisition of a large home, a cabin in the country, a fishing boat, and other

toys. This person is more concerned with the image being conveyed than having a low level of integrity.

Financial pressure can extend to the management team when they are trying to protect the viability of the company. For example, an entity's financial results have been gradually declining, and it is in danger of breaching its loan covenants, which will trigger a loan call by the bank. To avoid this situation, the management team adjusts the financial statements to keep the entity's reported results just higher than the thresholds stated in the loan covenants.

A type of behavior that can cause financial problems is any type of vice. For example, a person may be unable to stop gambling, and racks up enormous gambling debts. Or, an individual is addicted to hard drugs, and is always in need of cash to fund the habit. As another example, a person has a mistress and needs to support her lifestyle.

A different type of pressure is the desire to get even with an employer. For example, a person might have been denied a promotion, and so elects to commit fraud in order to make the employer "pay" for this decision. A person might feel the same way if he perceives his compensation to be unusually low, or if his contributions to the business have not been acknowledged.

Yet another type of pressure comes from the employer. This pressure usually comes in the form of a performance standard that must be met. For example, the senior management team imposes a very difficult commission plan on the sales staff; to meet their targets, the sales staff needs to sell more to customers than they really need. Similarly, if a very high profit goal has been set, the accounting staff feels that it needs to use subterfuge, such as keeping the books open into the following month in order to record additional sales.

Opportunity

A key factor contributing to fraud is the presence of a perceived opportunity to steal assets. These opportunities can come in many shapes and sizes. The opportunity for fraud is certainly enhanced when the environment within an organization is permissive, as would be the case in the following situations:

- *Absence of controls.* A key control might be missing that would otherwise prevent a theft from occurring, or at least detect it after the fact. This situation is more likely to arise when new systems are installed or existing ones are modified without paying attention to the underlying controls. In addition, a business that is not audited is less likely to have an independent review of its system of controls, and so may have no idea that it is lacking a key control. When any of the following types of controls are missing, it represents an opportunity for fraud to occur:

  o The presence of authorizations for transactions, so that a manager must issue an approval before a transaction can be completed, or employees are only authorized to engage in transactions up to a certain dollar limit.

- o Segregation of duties, so that it would require more than one person to commit fraud.
- o Independent reviews of a person's work, perhaps involving job rotations or supervisory reviews, so that a person could not keep up a fraud for a long period of time.
- o Controls over physical access to assets, so that someone would need to break into a controlled area in order to steal assets.
- o Proper supporting documentation for records, to identify the nature of a transaction and any related authorizations.

- *Accountability*. The level of accountability for all tasks should be quite clear within a business. When this is not the case, controls are significantly weaker, since no one is required to engage in preventive or detective activities.
- *Internal audit*. When there is an active internal audit department that is visibly examining transactions, this presents a significant deterrent. When there is no such group within a business, employees are more likely to engage in fraud, since there is no one in an oversight role.
- *Transitions*. Whenever there are layoffs, spin-offs, mergers, and plant closures, there is an increased risk that the control environment will break down, frequently because the key employees with a deep knowledge of controls are no longer working for the company.
- *Management example*. There may be a general environment of permissiveness within an organization. For example, if the management team is known to "play loose" with their expense reports, employees are more likely to follow their example. Or, if management is known to be creating fictitious customers in order to increase the reported sales level, employees will be more tempted to cheat the company and its investors in other ways. In this environment, the effectiveness of even a strong set of controls is weakened, since employees are more likely to work together to defeat the control system.
- *Management communication*. Ideally, management should be communicating constantly with employees regarding acceptable behavior, using training, a code of conduct, and other tools. If these communications are not present, employees do not have a clear indication of what is right and wrong, and so will be more inclined to step over the line and commit fraud.
- *Work environment*. In a negative work environment, employees have a vastly lower association with the business, and so are more likely to engage in fraudulent activities. Situations that can contribute to a negative work environment are:

- o A persistently high level of negative feedback from management
- o A strongly hierarchical management structure, where consideration is rarely given to suggestions from people lower in the organization
- o A widespread sense of job inequity, such as advancement being given to a small group of favored employees
- o Extremely difficult performance targets that are rarely attained

- o Minimal acknowledgement of good employee performance
- o Unusually low compensation and benefit packages

- *Vetting practices.* The human resources department must spend the time to research the backgrounds of all job candidates prior to hiring them. Otherwise, people with criminal backgrounds, questionable performances at prior employers, or falsified resumes will be hired, which leads to a higher incidence of fraud.

Rationalization

Someone committing fraud almost always needs to have some way to rationalize this conduct. There are many possible rationalizations, such as:

- I am taking the money from a corrupt organization
- I am using the money to help others
- The organization should have paid me this money
- This is only borrowing for a short time, and I will pay it back
- We will correct the books once we get through this rough patch and sales increase
- I have already paid enough income taxes
- If I pay more income taxes, the government will waste it anyways

With these kinds of rationalizations, a person can lie to himself that there is a good reason for engaging in fraud.

Fraud Perpetrators

There is no "classic" personality type that is more likely to engage in fraud. Instead, literally anyone can switch from being a completely reliable employee to someone who commits fraud on a regular basis. If the fraud triangle conditions noted earlier are present, then they can tip anyone over into being a fraud perpetrator. Further, someone can be a completely reliable employee for years and then suddenly commit fraud, if they are impacted by the fraud triangle.

If someone uses computer systems to engage in fraud, he or she is more likely to be younger and to have a relatively high degree of computing knowledge. Some are interested in the challenge of breaking into a system, and do not view doing so as bad behavior – they are simply beating the system. However, others engage in these activities specifically to make money. They use malicious software to break into systems and extract valuable data. They may sell data to outsiders for a profit, steal cash from financial accounts, or encrypt systems and threaten to leave them inaccessible unless they are paid off.

Given the problem with identifying potentially fraudulent employees, a business needs to enact strong preventive measures that impact *all* employees. We will return to this concept later, in the Fraud Prevention section.

Computer-Related Fraud and Theft

Many instances of fraud involve a company's computer systems in some way. For example, someone could access a computer in the treasury department to initiate an unauthorized wire transfer of company funds. Or, an employee could steal inventory from the warehouse and then cover up the theft by recording scrap transactions in the computer system for those items. And another possibility is for someone to download trade secrets from a company computer and sell them to the highest bidder. In every one of these cases, computers are being used as a point of access or tool for the commission of fraud or theft. Computer systems are an especially good entryway for those committing fraud for the following reasons:

- Funds can be shifted out of an organization within moments.
- Computer transactions involving fraud or theft can be difficult to find, sometimes not until months have passed.
- Computer files can be accessed by someone not physically located within the organization.
- Employee access rights into a computer system may represent thousands of points of potential access to company information.
- The theft of an employee laptop may allow for unauthorized access into a corporate system from that laptop from any location.

There are many ways in which a person can commit fraud or theft that are related in some way to computers. Consider the following general classifications of computer-related fraud:

- *False inputs.* There are many ways to obtain payments from a business by falsely entering requests for payment into a computer system. For example, an employee can file an expense report that contains fake expense claims. Or, a payables clerk can create a fake supplier, submit invoices into the system, approve them, and then intercept the outgoing payment. Another popular option is to create a fake employee in the payroll system and then have wage payments sent to an employee-controlled bank account.
- *Unauthorized data use.* There are many types of data breaches, such as selling customer data or trade secrets to competitors. As another example, an employee could use insider information about a business to buy or sell its shares, which is illegal insider trading. A variation is to demand a ransom after encrypting critical company data.
- *Unauthorized software use.* Employees may use company software in an unauthorized manner, alter its code, or copy it. The most common situation is buying a small number of licensed software copies and then making additional copies without paying for them.
- *Unauthorized system usage.* Someone may hack into a computer system to run processing activities that do not benefit the company, such as mining crypto currency on company computers.

Computer Attacks

There are many ways in which someone can engage in fraud or theft by attacking a computer system. In the following table, we note over a dozen ways in which this can be accomplished.

Methods of Computer Attack

Type of Attack	Description
Cyber extortion	The use of an attack or the threat of an attack in order to extort payments from a business. This is frequently combined with encrypting the victim's systems and offering to decrypt them in exchange for payment.
Hacking	Unauthorized intrusion into a computer or network, typically due to poor access controls or known flaws in operating systems.
Hijacking	Gaining control of a computer in order to carry out illicit activities (such as launching Internet attacks) without the knowledge of the computer's authorized user.
Identify theft	The fraudulent acquisition of another person's private identifying information, usually to obtain money or credit.
Malware	The insertion of malicious software onto a computer that damages the system or causes other unwanted actions, such as logging user keystrokes, extracting files, encrypting files, destroying files, changing file contents, inserting ads, and remotely controlling computers.
Man-in-the-middle attack	The placement of a hacker between a host and a client in order to intercept the network traffic passing between them, resulting in the loss of confidential data.
Pharming	The rerouting of Internet users to a phony website that looks just like a legitimate site in order to obtain personal information.
Phishing	The issuance of emails that appear to be from a legitimate source, frequently a financial institution, to obtain confidential information or distribute malicious links. These messages are designed to mimic authentic emails. Files linked to these emails purport to be related to the business or personal needs of the recipient, but instead contain malware.
Podslurping	Plugging a portable data storage device, such as a flash drive, into a computer in order to illicitly download confidential information.
Pretexting	The use of a pretext, such as conducting a survey or impersonating someone, to extract confidential information from the target. This information is then used for financial gain.
Spamming	The use of electronic messaging systems to send unwanted messages in bulk.
Spoofing	The issuance of an electronic message that is disguised to look as though it is from a party known to the recipient, with the intent of extracting confidential information from the recipient.
Typosquatting	The creation of a website that mimics a well-known site, which is accessed when a user incorrectly types in the URL of the well-known site. The bogus site is constructed to extract confidential information from the user or to download malware to the person's computer.
Zero-day attack	The use of a software vulnerability to attack a computer system until such time as the vulnerability is patched.

Fraud Prevention

A work environment in which employees feel a strong sense of buy-in to the mission of the organization is ideal for preventing fraud, since they are not likely to steal from an organization that they support. A sense of buy-in to a business can be particularly strong when management commits to a minimal level of employee turnover and couples it with a reasonable and fair compensation structure. In this environment, the key concerns of employees have been met, so there is no reason for them to engage in fraud. Additional adjustments to the work environment that can also reduce the incidence of fraud are:

- *Broad-based management.* The management team routinely asks employees for input on a variety of topics, which may include tactical and even strategic decisions. This likely means that the organization has a relatively flat management structure, with few levels of management. By doing so, employees have a better sense of contributing to the organization, and so are less likely to steal from it.
- *Employee interactions.* When there are issues, these items are addressed at once and openly, rather than being repressed. By doing so, it is more difficult for problems to fester, which could cause someone to "take it out" on the company by stealing from it.
- *Fair promotion criteria.* The company promotes based on the performance and abilities of its employees, rather than cronyism. When employees understand that they will be fairly considered for promotions, it is less likely that they will feel aggrieved if someone else is given a plum assignment or promotion.
- *Long-range planning.* The company focuses the attention of its employees on attaining long-term goals. Conversely, it does not force them to achieve short-term goals (such as quarterly sales figures) which are more likely to spawn a culture of financial statement fraud in order to meet those goals.
- *Orderly flow of business.* The business is well-designed to handle customer orders on a timely basis. This usually means there is a carefully controlled scheduling system that releases new jobs only when the system is able to handle the additional work load. Otherwise, purchases and overtime are handled on a rush basis, usually with scanty authorizations, which yields more opportunities for fraud.
- *Performance recognition.* The company routinely recognizes a job well done. This may involve public recognition, perhaps coupled with a system of minor rewards. This activity nullifies any feelings that might fester when a person believes she has made a good effort and yet has not been recognized for it.
- *Positive feedback system.* The feedback system used by the organization emphasizes giving positive feedback to encourage employees to engage in certain types of behavior, rather than employing negative feedback to punish employees if they do not follow the mandates of management. The use of

negative feedback tends to set employees against the company, making them much more open to the possibility of committing fraud.

- *Profit sharing.* When there is a generous profit sharing plan in place that makes significant payouts to employees, they will be more likely to watch over the company's operations and report suspicious activity, since fraud losses are cutting into their profit sharing payments.
- *Well-defined and robust systems.* In a business with well-defined systems, job descriptions and responsibilities are clear, as well as process flows. These systems should hold up well during times of duress, such as the handling of rush jobs for customers. This means there are no ambiguous areas in which someone can discern a weakness that can be exploited to commit fraud.

An anti-fraud work environment typically employs a viable open door policy that is actively encouraged by management. This policy states that employees are welcome to discuss any issues with management at any time. By encouraging this policy, employees are much more likely to bring up issues that could be indicators of fraud or theft.

Fraud and Theft Detection

Fraudulent activities can be quite difficult to spot directly, since they may be concealed and the proportion of fraudulent transactions is likely to be quite low. An alternative way to identify fraud is indirectly – by being alert for the symptoms of fraud. These symptoms can come in many forms, such as:

- *Accounting anomalies.* A key supporting document for a large expenditure is missing or has been altered.
- *Analytical anomalies.* A routine analysis of trend lines and ratios detects an odd spike or decline in the data.
- *Lifestyle symptoms.* An employee arrives at work one day with a sports car that he should not be able to afford.
- *Unusual behavior.* An employee starts working much longer hours.

In the following sub-sections, we explain the nature of these fraud symptoms.

Accounting Anomalies

The typical organization uses a certain set of accounting transactions that do not vary much over time, requiring roughly the same accounts and calling for the same types of supporting documents. When there are differences from these baseline transactions, there is a good chance that the anomalies are indicators of fraud. Here are a number of examples of accounting anomalies that could be symptoms of fraud:

- *Altered documents.* There may be an unusual number of instances in which accounting documents have been manually altered with crossed-out figures that have been replaced by different amounts. This could indicate that someone in the accounting department is modifying documents to hide the theft of assets.

- *High-volume credits.* When there are many credits in the accounts receivable records, it can indicate that the accounting staff is intercepting payments from customers and then covering their tracks by creating credits to reduce the balances in the customer accounts.
- *Increase in aged receivables.* When the collections department appears to be unable to collect on an increasing proportion of receivables, it is possible that some of those invoices are fakes. They may have been constructed internally to create sales that never actually occurred.
- *Increased expenses.* Someone could steal cash and then charge the amount to expense. This approach works well for fraud, since expense accounts are flushed out at year-end, so that the record of the theft does not persist in the account past year-end. When fraud occurs, charges are usually made to large-expense accounts, such as the cost of goods sold, so that a few thousand dollars of expense will not be detected through an analytical analysis.
- *Last-minute entries.* Management may be targeting a specific profit figure to report at the end of a reporting period. If so, they may mandate that a journal entry be created that ensures that the target figure is achieved. This journal entry is likely to be one of the last journal entries in a period, since all other entries must first be made before it is possible to determine the shortfall for which fake profits must be manufactured.
- *Missing documents.* There may be no supporting documents that explain why a transaction occurred. For example, there would normally be a customer purchase order associated with an internal sales order. If not, it is possible that an employee made up the sales order, with the intent of having goods shipped to a dummy corporation.
- *Rewritten records.* Employees may claim that they are rewriting records in order to eliminate errors or make the documents easier to read. What they may actually be doing is completely altering the documents in order to cover up a fraud.
- *Unsupported journal entries.* Someone could alter an account balance in order to bring the actual amount of assets on hand into agreement with the amount stated in the books. If so, they will have a difficult time creating any kind of supporting document that states the reason for the journal entry, and so may provide no supporting documentation at all.

The bulk of the issues underlying accounting anomalies have their origins within the accounting department, since few others have access to the accounting records. This means that someone within the department is engaged in fraud. Consequently, anyone investigating accounting anomalies will have to be exceedingly careful in their investigations, since the person engaged in fraud could be sitting next to them.

Analytical Anomalies

An excellent way to detect fraud is to keep track of a variety of financial and operational metrics over a long period of time. The activity level of almost any measure should not vary all that much over time, so when there is a sudden change in a measure, this is certainly grounds for an investigation. Here are several examples of analytical anomalies:

- *Budgeting perfection.* A company consistently budgets aggressively for more sales and profits, and has an amazing ability to almost perfectly meet those numbers, period after period. Further investigation reveals that the management team is using whatever type of reporting fraud it takes to meet the budgeted targets in every reporting period.
- *Commodity price differs from market.* A business uses a large amount of plastic pellets as direct materials in its plastic molding operations. A routine comparison of commodity market prices to the prices paid to the company's pellet supplier finds that there was a modest divergence between the market price and actual price paid, starting one year ago. This could indicate a kick-back situation between the supplier and the company's buyer assigned to the acquisition of plastic pellets.
- *Comparison of inventory value to volume.* The auditors of a wood products company evaluates the amount of finished boards that were supposedly in stock at year-end by calculating the approximate volume of boards that would be required to match the amount of ending inventory valuation that the client claims. This calculation reveals that the amount of inventory claimed would overwhelm the existing storage facilities. Clearly, management has been overstating the amount of ending inventory.
- *Fixed asset increases.* The auditors of a manufacturing firm routinely calculate the ratio of fixed assets to sales, to see if the proportion changes significantly from year to year. They discover that this proportion has spiked in the past year, indicating a surge in fixed assets. Further investigation reveals that the controller has been capitalizing expenditures that would normally have been charged to expense, resulting in an increase in profits just sufficient to earn the management team a hefty performance-based bonus.
- *Inventory count corrections.* A company uses an incremental daily inventory count (cycle count), which is resulting in a large number of adjustments to the book balance of the inventory. The preponderance of these adjustments are downward, and almost entirely in the area of finished goods; that is, counts are verifying that the book balances of raw materials items are accurate most of the time. The situation indicates that someone might be stealing finished goods from the warehouse.
- *Petty cash replenishment.* The controller is accustomed to replenishing the petty cash box in the production department about once every three months. Suddenly, the replenishment rate increases to once a month. Since the box holds $300 of cash, this means that the petty cash usage rate has jumped

from \$100 per month to \$300 per month. Some kind of fraud involving the use of petty cash seems likely.

- *Small amounts of overtime.* A review of overtime records finds that most employees incur overtime only at long intervals – except for one person, who routinely charges a half-hour of overtime, once or twice a week. This small amount falls below the overtime approval threshold for the business, so there is a possibility that the employee is reporting the overtime without actually working the extra hours.

- *Spike in expenses.* A trend line analysis of legal costs finds that legal expenditures jumped two years ago by 20%, and have stayed at that level since. There have been no unusual lawsuits or public company filings during that time, so it is possible that one or more law firms are overbilling the company.

- *Supplier billings too low.* A review of invoicing volumes by supplier finds that there are ten suppliers whose billings to the company never exceed \$99. Since the invoice approval threshold for the business is \$100, these smaller invoices are always paid automatically. Further investigation reveals that eight of the ten suppliers were added within the past year. The circumstances indicate that an employee might have set up a series of dummy corporations, and is using them to fraudulently bill the company at a level that will not be detected.

Analytical anomalies cannot always be detected if a fraud has been running for a long time. The reason is that a fraud auditor might be looking for unusual changes in a trend line, but if the fraud has been running for the entire duration of the trend line, the data will appear to be quite normal.

Another issue with analytics is that managers know these analytics will be run by their auditors, and so may alter the financial information to conform to the expectations of the auditors. Consequently, it may take a detailed analysis of analytics in multiple areas to discern whether there is a problem.

Lifestyle Symptoms

Employees who are engaged in fraud would require an immense amount of self-control to steal from their employer and not spend the money in some visible way. Instead, there is usually some evidence of a change in lifestyle. Here are several examples of lifestyle symptoms:

- Gambling trips to Las Vegas
- The replacement of an older car with a much nicer one
- Upgrades to an employee's house, or shifting to an entirely new one
- Taking up an expensive hobby, such as sailing or heli-skiing
- Stories of gifts made to friends and family

A common excuse given for a suddenly more profligate lifestyle is that a person has inherited wealth. If so, a reasonable question is why the person continues to work at the company. This is a particular concern when the individual refuses to take any vacation time or refuses to be promoted, which can indicate that they are covering up a fraud situation.

A change in lifestyle is one of the easiest indicators of fraud, and yet many people do not notice changes, or do not equate them to possible fraudulent activities. Consequently, it is necessary to include a discussion of lifestyle changes in fraud training for employees.

Unusual Behavior

When a person commits fraud, he will be under an increased level of stress. This can lead to changes in the person's behavior in the office, which may be extreme enough to be clearly visible to co-workers. Examples are:

- More variable mood swings
- A high level of suspicion of others
- Defensiveness
- Uses intimidation to keep others from investigating
- Using excuses to an excessive degree
- A higher level of security, such as locked filing cabinets or office doors
- Working longer hours
- Extensive amounts of drinking, smoking, and drug use

Combinations of several of the preceding items can be particular indicators that a person is engaged in some kind of fraud or theft activity.

Summary

There are many ways in which someone can commit fraud or steal assets through a company's AIS. Management needs to develop a cohesive and supportive employee environment to minimize the reasons for anyone to commit fraud, while also being constantly vigilant for any signs that fraud is occurring. There are also many ways in which a firm can be harmed by outsiders, especially via a broad range of computer attacks. The potential losses from these attacks can be mitigated somewhat by continually guarding against system intrusions and maintaining first-rate firewalls and virus detection systems. Nonetheless, there is still a good chance that an organization will be negatively impacted by fraud or theft at some point in its life.

Chapter 6
Systems of Control

Introduction

Someone intent on engaging in fraud will likely need access to a company's accounting system in order to both remove assets and cover his tracks. Without a comprehensive system of controls, it is not that difficult for a person to do so. The typical business contains many points of access to the accounting system in the form of personal computers, and may have dozens or even hundreds of processes that can be adjusted in an unauthorized manner. These weaknesses can open the door to massive losses, some so large that a business is financially crippled and may even be forced into bankruptcy. Despite these concerns, businesses routinely ignore the need for comprehensive controls, partially due to a limited understanding of the need for controls and partially because they do not want to incur the up-front expense of controls in exchange for a perceived low level of loss. In this chapter, we cover a number of control principles, the nature of internal controls and how they are constructed, related laws, several control frameworks, and various related topics.

Risk of Loss Concepts

When deciding whether a control is needed, one must first determine the potential monetary loss from a threat, which is considered to be the level of *exposure*. For example, the level of exposure associated with the process used to issue wire transfers could be massive, such as several million dollars when an unauthorized person cleans out a corporate bank account and sends the money to a foreign tax haven with strong banking secrecy laws. One must also determine the probability that a threat will occur, which is considered the *likelihood* of occurrence. The interaction of these two concepts results in the following possible scenarios:

- *High exposure, high likelihood.* When there is a strong probability of losing a significant amount of assets, a business should give the highest level of attention to the installation of a strong set of controls that mitigate the perceived risk.
- *High exposure, low likelihood.* When there is a high level of potential exposure but the probability of occurrence is low, the imposition of strong controls is still critically important, but ranks behind the controls needed for a high exposure, high likelihood threat.
- *Low exposure, high likelihood.* When there is a low level of expected monetary loss but a high likelihood of occurrence, the total amount of losses that may be experienced could be significant, so controls still need to be

imposed. These controls are more likely to be automated, so that their cost is minimal on a per-transaction basis.

- *Low exposure, low likelihood.* When there is a low probability of minimal losses, the accountant may choose to avoid the use of any controls, or to only impose the lowest-cost and most automated controls to minimize the threat.

In short, the combination of exposure and likelihood of occurrence drives the type and amount of controls imposed to mitigate a threat.

What is risk, and how does it relate to controls? *Risk* is the probability that events will vary from expectations. Examples of risk are:

- That competitors will alter the business environment
- That new technology will alter the business environment
- That new legislation will alter the business environment
- That a product failure will lead to a product recall
- That a customer will enter bankruptcy
- That a key raw material will increase in price

Of these sample risks, the first three are caused by external factors and the last three by internal factors. Controls can be used to mitigate internal risks. For example, if there is a risk of product failure, controls can be designed to test the quality of components as they enter the production process, and of finished goods before they are shipped to customers. Similarly, the risk that a customer will enter bankruptcy can be mitigated to some extent by the imposition of strong credit controls.

No matter how thoroughly controls are incorporated into an organization, it is impossible to use them to completely eliminate risk. Instead, there will always be some residual amount of risk that a business must accept. There is usually a tradeoff between imposing a really oppressive system of controls on a business in exchange for a lowered risk level, or a lighter system of controls that makes the business easier to manage, but at the cost of accepting a higher level of risk.

Control Principles

There are a number of principles to keep in mind when constructing a system of controls for a business. These principles are frequently the difference between a robust control system and one that appears adequate on paper, but which never seems to work in practice. The principles are:

- *Separation of duties.* The separation of duties involves assigning different parts of a process to different people, so that collusion would be required for someone to commit fraud. For example, one person opens the mail and records a list of the checks received, while a different person records them in the accounting system and a third person deposits the checks. By separating these tasks, it is much more difficult for someone to (for example) remove a check from the incoming mail, record a receivables credit in the accounting system to cover his tracks, and cash the check into his own account. Unfortunately, there is a major downside to the separation of duties, which is that shifting tasks among multiple people interferes with the efficiency of a process. Consequently, only use this control principle at the minimum level needed to establish the desired level of control – too much of it is not cost-effective.

- *Process integration.* Controls should be so thoroughly intertwined with business transactions that it is impossible for employees *not* to perform them as part of their daily activities. This level of integration substantially reduces the incidence of errors and the risk of fraud. An example of proper process integration with a control is running all produced items past a fixed bar code scanning station on a conveyor belt, to ensure that all completed goods are recorded. The information is collected without the staff having to do anything. An example of minimal process integration that will likely result in frequent control problems is requiring employees to record this information by hand on a paper form.

- *Management support.* The management team must make it abundantly clear to employees that it thoroughly supports the system of controls. This does not mean that a general statement of ethics is included in the employee manual. Instead, it means that management takes the time to explain controls to employees, is highly visible in investigating control breaches, and takes sufficient remedial action to make it clear to the entire staff that controls are to be taken seriously. Management also does not override its own controls, nor does it set performance standards that are so difficult to attain that employees would be forced to circumvent controls in order to meet the standards.

- *Responsibility.* No control system will work unless people are made responsible for it. This means that someone should be assigned responsibility for every control, and that they receive regular updates on the status of those controls. It would also be useful if the status of their controls are noted in their compensation reviews, and have a direct impact on changes in their pay.

- *Conscientious application.* Employees cannot simply treat controls in a perfunctory manner. Instead, there should be a culture that encourages the close examination of control breaches to determine what went wrong, and how the system can be adjusted to reduce the risk that the same issue will occur again. This level of conscientious behavior must be encouraged by the management team through constant reinforcement of the message that the system of controls is important. It also requires the availability of communication channels through which employees can anonymously report suspected improprieties.

- *Systems knowledge.* It is impossible to expect employees to conscientiously inspect controls unless they already know how systems operate. This calls for the ongoing training of employees to ensure that they thoroughly understand all aspects of the systems with which they are involved. This requires not only an initial training session for new employees, but also reminder sessions that are timed to coincide with any changes in processes and related controls, as well as thorough documentation of the systems. A good level of systems knowledge may call for the use of procedures, training materials, and a core group of trainers.

- *Error reporting.* It is impossible to know if a control is functioning properly unless there is a system in place for reporting control breaches. This may be a report generated by a computer system, but it may also call for open communications channels with employees, customers, and suppliers to solicit any errors that have been found. In this latter case, error reporting is strongly supported by a management group that is clearly interested in spotting errors and correcting them in a way that does not cast blame on those reporting the information. In addition, errors should be communicated all the way up through the organization to the audit committee and board of directors, who can enforce the establishment of enhanced controls.
- *Staffing.* There must be an adequate number of employees on hand to operate controls. Otherwise, there will be great pressure to avoid manual controls, since they take too much time to complete. This is actually a profitability issue, since a business experiencing losses is more likely to cut back on staffing, which in turn impacts the control system.
- *Outlier analysis.* Most businesses create control systems to deal with problems they have seen in the past, or which have been experienced elsewhere in the industry. They rarely create controls designed to mitigate outlier issues – that is, problems that occur very infrequently. The sign of a great control system is one in which employees take the time to examine the control system from a high level, and in light of the current and future business environment, to see if there are any outlier events that present a risk of loss in sufficiently large amounts to warrant the addition of controls. This outlier analysis requires excellent knowledge of the industry and a perceptive view of the direction in which it is headed.

Of the principles just noted, management support is the most crucial. Without it, a system of controls is like a building with no supporting framework – the entire structure crashes to the ground if there is any pressure placed upon it at all. For example, the control system may appear to have proper separation of duties, but this makes no difference if the management team ignores these separations for transactions that it has an interest in ramming through the system.

Internal Controls

Internal controls are the interlocking set of activities that are layered onto the normal operating procedures of an organization, with the intent of safeguarding assets, minimizing errors, and ensuring that operations are conducted in an approved manner. Another way of looking at internal controls is that these activities are needed to mitigate the amount and types of risk to which a firm is subjected.

Internal controls can be expensive in terms of both time and money, since control activities frequently slow down the natural process flow of a business, which can reduce its overall efficiency. Consequently, the development of a system of internal control requires management to balance risk reduction with efficiency. This process can sometimes result in management accepting a certain amount of risk in order to create a strategic profile that allows a firm to compete more effectively, even if it suffers occasional losses because controls have been deliberately reduced.

A system of internal controls tends to increase in comprehensiveness as a business increases in size. This is needed, because the original founders do not have the time to maintain complete oversight when there are many employees and/or locations. Further, when a company goes public, there are additional financial control requirements that must be implemented, especially if the organization's shares are to be listed for sale on a stock exchange. Thus, the cost of controls tends to increase with size.

Internal control comes in many forms, including the following:

- A board of directors oversees the entire organization, providing governance over the management team.
- Internal auditors routinely examine all processes, looking for failings that can be corrected with either new controls or adjustments to existing controls.
- Processes are altered so that more than one person is involved in each one; this is done so that people can cross-check each other, reducing fraud incidents and the likelihood of errors.
- Access to computer records is restricted, so that information is only made available to those people who need it to conduct specific tasks. Doing so reduces the risk of information theft and the risk of asset theft through the modification of ownership records.
- Assets are locked up when not in use, making it more difficult to steal them.

A key concept is that even the most comprehensive system of internal control will not entirely eliminate the risk of fraud or error. There will always be a few incidents, typically due to unforeseen circumstances or an exceedingly determined effort by someone who wants to commit fraud. In addition, even the best controls will occasionally fail. For example, even a seasoned accounting clerk will sometimes make a mistake in processing invoices and will under-bill a customer, or not issue an invoice at all. Or, a senior manager uses his authority to override the hiring process to hire an unqualified person. As another example, an automated control may not function because the underlying software was not designed to deal with a specific scenario.

The Failings of Internal Controls

A well-constructed system of internal controls can certainly be of assistance to a business, but controls suffer from several conceptual failings. They are:

- *Assured profitability.* No control system on the planet can assure a business of earning a profit. Controls may be able to detect or even avoid some losses, but if a business is inherently unprofitable, there is nothing that a control system can do to repair the situation. Profitability is, to a large extent, based on product quality, marketplace positioning, price points, and other factors that are not related to control systems.
- *Fair financial reporting.* A good control system can go a long ways toward the production of financial statements that fairly present the financial results and position of a business, but this is by no means guaranteed. There will always be outlier or low probability events that will evade the best control system, or there may be employees who conspire to evade the system.
- *Judgment basis.* Manual controls rely upon the judgment of the people operating them. If a person engages in a control activity and makes the wrong judgment call (such as a bad decision to extend credit to a customer), then the control may have functioned but the outcome was still a failure. Thus, controls can fail if the judgment of the people operating them is poor.
- *Determined fraudulent behavior.* Controls are typically designed to catch fraudulent behavior by an individual who is acting alone. They are much less effective when the management team itself overrides controls, or when several employees collude to engage in fraud. In these cases, it is quite possible to skirt completely around the control system.

Thus, the owners, managers, and employees of a business should view its controls not as an absolute failsafe that will protect the business, but rather as something designed to *increase the likelihood* that operational goals will be achieved, that financial reports can be relied upon, and that it is complying with the relevant laws and regulations.

Terminating Controls

Controls tend to slow down the flow of transactions within a business and result in extra costs, and so should only be used when there is a clear need for them. In addition, controls should only be retained for as long as the processes with which they are associated are unchanged. If a process is altered, the linked controls may no longer be needed, but are still retained because no one thought to remove them. The result is likely to be an excessive number of controls and a lower level of process efficiency than should be the case.

Another concern is that too many controls can restrict the ability of employees to take responsibility for their actions. Instead, there is a tendency to adhere to the rules, no matter what, in order to avoid taking responsibility. Eventually, an organization with too many controls becomes hopelessly bureaucratic and calcified, and nearly incapable of enacting any useful changes.

To avoid a burdensome number of controls, it is useful to periodically examine the current system of controls and see if any should be removed. This can be done in the following ways:

- *Review at process change.* Whenever there is a change to a process, incorporate into the process flow analysis a review of all controls built into the process. Doing so may point out that specific controls can be eliminated, or replaced by other controls that are more cost-effective.
- *Review on scheduled date.* Even if there have been no process changes, conduct a comprehensive controls review on a scheduled date, such as once a year. This review may pick up on minor process changes that have been implemented but not formally noted. This approach also allows for consideration of new, more technologically-advanced controls that were not available in previous years.

Tip: Never review a control in isolation from the other controls in a process, since the entire set of controls may provide backup coverage for each other. Deleting one control may weaken a control issue elsewhere in the business process.

No matter which approach is used, it may also make sense to bring in a controls specialist to review existing systems and recommend which controls can be terminated. By doing so, the company gains the benefit of someone who has seen a broad range of controls in many other companies, and who therefore has more experience upon which to base recommendations for changes. The report of this consultant can also be used as justification for changes to the system of controls.

If controls are to be terminated, be sure to discuss the changes thoroughly with the controller and chief financial officer, as well as the company's audit committee. These people may feel that a control should be retained, despite the dictates of efficiency, in order to provide some additional risk reduction. In addition, the termination of controls should be brought to the attention of the company's auditors, who may need to alter their audit procedures to account for the missing controls.

The termination of a control should not be a special event. Instead, it is an ongoing part of the alterations that a company makes as it changes its business processes to meet the demands of the market.

Types of Controls

When considering the proper balance of controls that a business needs, also consider the types of controls being installed. A *preventive control* is one that keeps a control breach from occurring, such as requiring an authorization before a purchase can be made. This type of control is highly prized, since it has a direct impact on cost reduction. Another type of control is the *detective control*, such as a bank reconciliation. This control is useful, but only detects a control breach *after* it has occurred; thus, its main use is in making management aware of a problem that must be fixed.

A control system needs to have a mix of preventive and detective controls. Even though preventive controls are considered more valuable, they also tend to be more intrusive in the functioning of key business processes. Also, they are installed to address specific control issues that management is already aware of. Management also needs a liberal helping of detective controls, which can be used to spot problems that management was not aware of. Thus, a common occurrence is to throw out a web of detective controls that occasionally haul in a new type of problem, for which management installs a preventive control.

In short, a mix of the two types of controls is needed, where there may be no ideal solution. Instead, there may be a range of possible configurations within which a controls auditor would consider a control system to be effective.

Manual and Automated Controls

If a control is operated by the computer system through which business transactions are recorded, this is considered to be an *automated control*. If a control requires someone to manually perform it, this is considered a *manual control*. Automated controls are always preferred, since it is impossible to avoid them. Conversely, manual controls can be easily avoided, simply by forgetting to enact them. Examples of automated controls are:

- A limit check in a payroll data entry screen that does not allow you to enter more hours in a work week than the total number of hours in a week.
- An address reviewer in the vendor master file that does not allow you to enter an address without the correct zip code.
- An error checker in the inventory database that does not allow an inventory deduction that would otherwise result in a negative inventory balance.

Continuous controls monitoring (CCM) is the use of automated tools to examine business transactions as they occur. A CCM system automatically pulls certain data elements from a database of transactions and reviews all of these data elements. The intent is to conduct a complete scan of the data for control breaches, errors, possible segregation of duties problems, and anomalies from what is expected. The review is conducted by comparing the data to a set of tables that contain permitted transaction authorizations, allowable boundaries for detecting anomalies, itemizations of fields that must be completed for a standard transaction, and so forth. These tables are set up for each major transactional area, such as for inventory, payroll, accounts payable, travel and entertainment, and customer orders.

By comparing the tables to the data, a CCM can spot potential control problems, which are then reported to management on a real-time basis. Here are several examples of CCM tests:

- For the proper authorization of supplier invoices for payment
- For the accuracy of inventory picking transactions

- For the completeness of customer orders
- For the issuance of customer invoices within __ hours of shipments to customers
- For the authorization of credit memos related to unpaid customer invoices

A CCM system is relatively expensive, so this approach to reviewing transactions is not typically available to a smaller organization. However, if implemented, the system can reduce the need for manual internal control reviews. In addition, external auditors can rely upon a CCM to some extent when designing their audit procedures, which reduces the cost of their audit. Thus, the net cost of a CCM is somewhat reduced when its full effects are considered.

Several examples of manual controls are:

- Requiring a second signature on a check payment that exceeds a certain amount.
- Requiring the review of the final payroll register by a supervisor.
- Requiring the completion of a monthly bank reconciliation.

The best controls are ones that are preventive (see the preceding section) and automated, since they actively prevent errors from occurring and are very difficult to avoid.

Constructing a System of Controls

The preceding discussion has revolved around the general concept of controls and the principles that should underlie them. But how do you actually create a system of controls? What are the nuts and bolts of building a system? The primary steps are:

1. *Understand the new system.* Work with the systems analysts who have designed the new system to understand what it is designed to do, and each step in the process flow. This may call for the use of flowcharts and walkthroughs of test transactions. The result may be a formal report describing the system, probably including a preliminary set of procedures.
2. *Explore possible control breaches.* Work with the internal and external auditors, department managers, and systems analysts to estimate where control breaches are most likely to arise in the prospective system.
3. *Quantify possible control breaches.* Estimate the number of occurrences of each type of control breach, the maximum and most likely amounts that a control breach would cost, and their impact on customers and other key company performance metrics.

4. *Design controls.* Based on the quantification of control breaches, design controls that will cost-effectively mitigate risks and be so thoroughly integrated into the underlying process that they will be as robust as possible. At this step, consider calculating the expected losses being avoided by installing a new control, which is expressed as:

$$\text{Impact} \times \text{Event likelihood} = \text{Expected loss}$$

A proposed control should only be installed if its cost is substantially lower than the associated expected loss that it is designed to minimize.

> **Tip:** When designing controls to avoid a potentially catastrophic loss, one way to evaluate their cost is to represent them as the cost of catastrophic loss insurance.

5. *Implement the controls.* Install the controls, along with all necessary documentation, forms, systems, and training, and oversee the initial rollout to ensure that it is operating as planned.
6. *Test the system.* A system of controls does not necessarily operate as planned, perhaps due to a misperception of how the underlying system operates, a bad control design, technology issues, poor employee training, and so on. To detect these issues, test the system of controls by feeding incorrect transactions into it, and see if the controls detect the transactions. If not, adjust the controls and repeat the exercise as many times as necessary.
7. *Conduct a post-implementation review.* All systems change over time, so expect control redundancies and gaps to appear as systems change. Review systems at least once a year, and more frequently if there have been major changes, to see if the existing system of controls should be adjusted. This task may be most easily handled by the internal auditing department, though the controller may want to take on this task instead.

In a larger company, it may be cost-effective to hire a controls analyst who deals with these matters on a full-time basis. In a smaller enterprise, it is more likely that this work will be handled by the controller, who might consider outsourcing it to a consultant.

Laws Related to Systems of Control

Two laws, passed 25 years apart, have a significant influence on the system of controls that should be present within a business. They are addressed in the following sub-sections.

Foreign Corrupt Practices Act

The Foreign Corrupt Practices Act, passed in 1977, prohibits the bribery of foreign officials in order to obtain business. The Act also requires organizations to maintain accurate accounting records, as well as a system of controls that is sufficient to provide reasonable assurance that assets are being used in accordance with the dictates of management. Companies that breach these requirements can be forced to disgorge any profits generated by bribery, while also paying significant fines. Individuals convicted of breaching the terms of the Act can face jail time.

Sarbanes-Oxley Act

The Sarbanes-Oxley Act, passed in 2002, was designed to improve the quality of financial reporting by publicly-held companies. It was written in response to the fraudulent reporting of Enron Corporation, WorldCom, and several other well-known businesses. Key provisions of the Act are as follows:

- The CEO and CFO must certify the accuracy of the financial statements (Section 302)
- It is illegal to improperly influence how an audit is conducted (Section 303)
- Material off-balance sheet items must be disclosed (Section 401)
- Management must establish internal controls and report on their scope and accuracy, while the company's auditors must certify the reliability of those controls (Section 404)
- Substantial fines are imposed on anyone falsifying, stealing, or destroying records (Section 802)
- Provides for the protection of whistleblowers from retaliation (Section 806)
- Sets criminal penalties when corporate officers do not certify the accuracy of the financial statements (Section 906)

For the purposes of this discussion, the most important topic within the Act was Section 404, which triggered significantly more in-depth systems of controls than had previously been the case. The higher cost of these controls also contributed to an ongoing decline in the number of publicly-held companies, since smaller firms could not afford the more oppressive system of controls that was now required by law.

Committee of Sponsoring Organizations (COSO)

The Committee of Sponsoring Organizations of the Treadway Commission (COSO) is a nonprofit organization that is a joint initiative of the following organizations:

- American Accounting Association
- American Institute of Certified Public Accountants
- Financial Executives International
- Institute of Management Accountants
- The Institute of Internal Auditors

COSO has developed a common internal control model that businesses can use as a standard against which they can assess their systems of control. The model was entitled *Internal Control – Integrated Framework*, and was originally issued in 1992, with several updates since then. This framework defines internal control as a process that is designed to provide reasonable assurance regarding the achievement of objectives in the following three areas:

- The efficiency and effectiveness of a firm's operations
- The reliability of a firm's financial reporting
- The compliance of a firm with applicable laws and regulations

The framework includes the following general concepts:

- Internal control is not an end in itself; rather, it is a process that is intended to support the requirements of a business.
- Internal control is impacted by individuals throughout a business; it is not simply a set of policies, procedures, and forms.
- Internal control can only provide reasonable assurance to an organization's management and board of directors; it cannot provide absolute assurance.
- Internal control is targeted at achieving specific objectives within a business.

The *Internal Control – Integrated Framework* is comprised of five components that are based on the manner in which a business is operated. COSO considers these components to provide an effective framework for describing a firm's system of internal controls. The five components are:

- *Control environment.* The control environment is the comprehensive set of actions taken by management that set the tone for how employees engage in their day-to-day activities. Taken as a whole, the control environment shows the level of support that management has for the system of internal controls. When there is a weak control environment, it is quite likely that the system of internal control will break down on a regular basis. A robust control environment typically includes the following:
  - o *Ethical values.* This is the values demonstrated by management, not only in what they tell the organization, but also as backed up by their actions. When management clearly follows its own rules, the rest of the organization is much more likely to behave in the same manner.
  - o *External influences.* Control requirements may be imposed by an outside agency, such as a regulatory agency or a stock exchange. A business must comply with these requirements in order to be allowed to operate by the outside party.
  - o *Goal stretch.* This is the extent to which management is trying to push the organization to increase its sales (or other metrics). The use of modest goals means that there is little reason for employees to fake transactions in order to enhance their reported performance.

- o *Human resources.* This is the use of well-designed recruiting, interviewing, onboarding, training, and evaluation systems to ensure that the best possible employees are hired. In addition, compensation levels and bonus plans should provide sufficiently high pay levels that employees do not feel resentment towards their employer. An essential process is being able to identify disgruntled employees and remove them from sensitive positions as soon as possible. In addition, the organization should obtain fidelity bonds on those employees working in sensitive positions, to protect it against losses from fraudulent behavior. When properly implemented, these systems eliminate those people from being hired who would otherwise have been tempted to engage in control breaches, and protect the business from the losses associated with any remaining bad hires.
- o *Linked authority and responsibility.* Employees should be given authority and responsibility in equal measure, so that they know they will be held responsible for their actions. This is accomplished with clear job descriptions, formal policies and procedures, and adequate training.
- o *Operating style.* This is the manner in which management deals with issues on a daily basis. An environment in which decision making is collaborative tends to result in a stronger adherence to controls than one in which management imposes its decisions on the rest of the organization.
- o *Organizational structure.* The manner in which a business is organized has a direct impact on the nature of the control system with which it is associated. For example, a firm that is organized by industry will have a somewhat different control structure than one that is organized by product line. A highly complex organizational structure is more likely to suffer control failures, since there are more opportunities to hide asset losses or modify transactions.
- o *Oversight.* This is the extent to which the board of directors and its agents (such as internal auditors) are overseeing the activities of the organization. When there is a high level of oversight, people are more likely to abide by the rules.

- *Risk assessment.* Every organization inevitably faces a number of risks that originate both internally and from outside the entity, each of which must be assessed. In order to assess risks, one must first establish objectives. The assessment of risk must be completed before one can determine how the various types of risk should be managed.
- *Control activities.* Control activities are the actions taken that enforce management directives, such as the imposition of policies and procedures. These activities are needed to ensure that actions are taken to mitigate targeted risks that might otherwise impede the achievement of a firm's objectives. Examples of control activities are:

○ *Approvals*. This is a required signature or digital approval before a transaction can proceed. It is intended to include some degree of management oversight in a transaction. However, it can slow down processes substantially, and so should only be incorporated into a process when there is a significant risk of loss. Approvals are typically avoided for more routine transactions.

○ *Asset protection*. A business needs to protect both its tangible and intangible assets. Tangible assets such as cash, blank checks, and computer servers are protected by storing them in secure locations. Intangible assets, such as customer lists and customer credit card information, are protected by user access controls.

○ *Document design*. Both paper-based and electronic documents should be designed to minimize data entry errors, as well as to simplify their use and ease their subsequent review. Document pre-numbering may be needed to make it easier to detect missing documents.

○ *Independent oversight*. There are a number of ways in which parties not directly associated with various processes can be called upon to review transactions for reasonableness. Several oversight alternatives are:

  ▪ *Analytical reviews*. This review is used to assess the reasonableness of account balances by comparing changes in account balances over time, as well as by comparing them to related accounts. For example, a 20% increase in sales should result in a similar increase in the accounts receivable balance. A proportionally larger increase in the receivables balance could indicate that the sales increased because credit was incorrectly extended to customers with lower credit quality, who then had difficulty paying the amounts due.

  ▪ *Reconciliations*. This is a process of matching two sets of records to see if there are any differences. Reconciliations are a useful way to ensure that accounting records are accurate, since they may uncover bookkeeping errors and possibly fraudulent transactions. An example of a reconciliation is the comparison of a bank statement to a firm's internal records of cash receipts and disbursements.

  ▪ *Verifications*. This is the use of various procedures to ensure the accuracy or truth of information. For example, internal auditors may compare source documents to a balance recorded in a company's general ledger to verify that the balance is correct and recorded within the correct date range.

○ *Project development oversight*. The development or purchase of accounting information systems can involve a substantial outlay of funds, so there should be controls in place to oversee every step of the process, to ensure that projects are examined at every major milestone, that change requests are properly investigated and authorized, and that post-implementation reviews are conducted to compare final cost and performance figures to original expectations.

o *Segregation of duties.* This is the separation of certain job tasks to ensure that one person cannot both commit fraud and conceal evidence of the crime. For example, the person who authorizes a transaction cannot also record it or have custody of any resulting assets. Similarly, a person who has custody of an asset cannot also authorize its purchase or record the purchase transaction. As an example of the latter situation, a warehouse staff person who also authorizes the purchase of inventory could authorize such a purchase and then steal it when the asset arrives. It is still possible for fraud to occur even when there is a proper segregation of duties, but it would require the collusion of two or more people, which is not common.

Control activities are prevalent throughout an organization, not just in its accounting department.

- *Information and communication.* A formalized system of communication is needed to ensure that both operational and financial reports are regularly generated and distributed to those responsible for running a business. There should also be systems in place to encourage communications across an organization, as well as up and down the corporate hierarchy, and with outside parties, such as suppliers and customers.
- *Monitoring.* A system of internal controls must be assessed on an ongoing basis in order to spot internal control deficiencies, which can then be reviewed and corrected. Internal auditors may engage in this assessment function. In addition, software can be used to detect viruses, phishing attempts, spyware, and so forth, while software audits can be conducted to determine whether installed software has been properly authorized and paid for. Ideally, the monitoring system should result in the continual improvement of a system of controls.

COSO issued a second control framework in 2004, entitled *Enterprise Risk Management – Integrating with Strategy and Performance*. As the name implies, this framework is targeted at supporting the ability of an organization to evaluate and improve its *enterprise risk management*[1]. By focusing on enterprise risk management, a business can obtain the following benefits:

- *Enhance opportunities*. By evaluating all opportunities and their associated risks, one can identify new opportunities, as well as the challenges associated with them.
- *Identify risks*. A formal process for risk identification may result in new risks being spotted that would otherwise have blindsided management.
- *Improve returns*. By properly managing risk, one can minimize losses, thereby improving overall returns.
- *Minimize performance variations*. Since losses are being minimized through risk mitigation, a business is more likely to achieve more predictable results.
- *Enhance resource positioning*. Resources may need to be deployed in order to deal with certain risks, so understanding risks can trigger a change in how assets are positioned within a business.
- *Improve organizational viability*. When risks are being properly managed, it is less likely that a business will unexpectedly falter, leading to its early demise. Instead, the firm is more likely to perform quite well over the long term.

This framework expands upon the internal control structure described in the earlier *Internal Control – Integrated Framework*, providing a more robust and wide-ranging focus on the larger category of enterprise risk management, where the focus is on risk, rather than controls.

The enterprise risk management model is still targeted at achieving an organization's business objectives, but the framework is now comprised of the following four categories:

- *Strategic*. This category includes high-level goals that are aligned with and support a firm's mission.
- *Operations*. This category addresses the efficient and effective use of an entity's resources.
- *Reporting*. This category focuses on the reliability of a firm's operational and financial reporting.
- *Compliance*. This category addresses a company's compliance with applicable laws and regulations.

---

[1] Enterprise risk management is a set of activities that are designed to mitigate or otherwise work with the portfolio of risk to which an organization is subjected. These activities are designed to alter some business activities in order to avoid the risk associated with them, offload some risk to other parties, and accept some risk as part of the strategic direction of the firm.

The enterprise risk management model includes the five components already described for the *Internal Control – Integrated Framework*, while adding three additional components, which are as follows:

- *Objective setting*. Management must set objectives for what it hopes to achieve before it can identify any potential events that could negatively impact their achievement. Consequently, there must be a process for developing objectives that are both supportive of the firm's mission and consistent with its level of risk tolerance. As examples of objectives, a firm might orient its activities toward minimizing the scrap rate in the production department, installing a company-wide enterprise resource planning system for all of its locations, and ensuring that it complies with every requirement imposed by a government regulator.
- *Event identification*. An organization must be able to identify those events that could negatively impact the achievement of its chosen objectives. Consequently, there should be a process for identifying these events, estimating which ones are most likely to occur, and understanding how they interrelate. This information is then incorporated into the firm's objective-setting process. For example, a business might be investigating whether to revise its warehouse management system. Possible related events are damage to IT equipment in the hazardous warehouse environment and the risk that wireless signals will be interrupted within the warehouse.
- *Risk response*. Management should have a standardized approach to avoiding, reducing, offloading, or accepting risk, where the actions taken align with their tolerance for risk. This step includes a review of identified events to determine which ones are susceptible to significant control problems when there are no internal controls, as well as those that are still susceptible to control problems even *after* internal controls have been implemented.

Neither of the COSO frameworks will provide ideal outcomes, because these control systems are dependent on human judgment, and so are susceptible to problematic decision making. Failures can also occur due to simple errors and mistakes, as well as through employee collusion and management overrides of the system. Given these potential failings, management and the board of directors cannot have absolute assurance that an organization's objectives will be achieved.

Another problem with these frameworks is that they are strongly oriented toward risk mitigation. A business that rigidly follows the requirements of these frameworks could work so hard to minimize its risks that it misses key business opportunities that it might otherwise have pursued if it had accepted a higher tolerance for risk.

Control Objectives for Information and Related Technology (COBIT)

A control framework for computer systems was developed by ISACA, which was formerly called the Information Systems Audit and Control Association. ISACA provides guidance, benchmarks, and other tools for any organizations that use information systems. The ISACA control framework is called Control Objectives for Information and Related Technology (COBIT). COBIT is defined by ISACA as follows:

> COBIT is a framework for the governance and management of enterprise information and technology, aimed at the whole enterprise. COBIT defines the components and design factors to build and sustain a best-fit governance system.

The framework defines a set of information technology (IT) processes, noting process inputs and outputs, significant process objectives and related activities, and performance metrics. In addition, COBIT sets forth a set of suggested best practices for the governance of IT systems. The COBIT process model is broken down into four domains, which are:

- Plan and organize
- Build, acquire, and implement
- Deliver, service, and support
- Monitor, evaluate, and assess

The essential components of the COBIT model are as follows:

- *Framework.* The model assembles IT governance objectives and best practices by IT processes and links them to business requirements.
- *Process descriptions.* The model provides a reference process model for all parties using IT systems. The processes map to the domains just described.
- *Control objectives.* The model provides a set of high-level requirements to be evaluated by management for the effective control of each IT process.
- *Management guidelines.* The model helps users to assign responsibility, agree on objectives, determine performance levels, and demonstrate relationships with other processes.
- *Maturity models.* The model assesses maturity and capability for each process and helps to evaluate gaps.

Processes and guidelines are stated at a high level, and have been aligned with the more detailed IT standards and best practices noted in more detailed control frameworks, such as the COSO model described in the preceding section.

When properly implemented, the COBIT framework can assist in complying with regulatory requirements, while minimizing the amount of wasteful information management. A well-implemented framework also provides assurance to auditors regarding the robustness of a client's system of internal controls.

> **Note:** ISACA is also well-known among accountants for its Certified Information Systems Auditor (CISA) designation, which is the default certification for anyone engaged in the auditing of information systems. It indicates that the holder has obtained a certain minimum standard of knowledge related to the assessment of system vulnerabilities, controls, and compliance reporting.

Summary

A key point to take away from this chapter is that there is no boilerplate system of controls that can be inserted into a company. Instead, the control system must be fashioned to meet the risk profile of a business, while accepting minor losses in areas where it is more important to pare back on controls in favor of having more efficient business processes. Consequently, it takes a deep knowledge of a company's processes to set up and continually tweak a system of controls that yields the proper blend of risk aversion and business performance.

Even if a correct set of controls is installed and they are designed to match the risk profile of a business, this does not mean that they will work properly; excellent control implementation demands a culture of conscientious examination of controls and control breaches by the entire organization. Only through a continuing and company-wide focus on the importance of controls is it possible to have a robust set of controls. Thus, a top-notch control system involves both the controls themselves and the commitment of the organization behind them.

Chapter 7
Information System Controls

Introduction

It is a rare organization that does not use a computerized accounting information system (AIS), instead relying on a manual one. While an AIS provides businesses with a massive improvement in processing power and data storage volumes, it also presents a number of challenges related to controls. In this chapter, we make note of the many controls that can be installed to enhance and protect an AIS system. These controls are classified as follows:

- *Security controls*. These controls confine access to the system and its data to authorized users, while also providing protection from any number of system attacks by outside parties.
- *Confidentiality controls*. These controls protect key business information from being accessed by unauthorized parties.
- *Privacy controls*. These controls are intended to protect personal information from unauthorized disclosure, as well as to ensure that it is collected and used only as specified by company policy and the requirements of regulators.
- *Processing integrity controls*. These controls are used to ensure that data are processed correctly and in a timely manner.
- *Availability controls*. These controls are intended to keep the system operationally available to meet the usage requirements of the business.

A full suite of these controls makes it much more likely that an organization will benefit from a highly reliable AIS.

Security Controls

The exact mix of security controls that an organization adopts will be driven by management's assessment of the risks to which the firm is subjected. This assessment will be based in part on the advice of information security specialists, but management also contributes its judgments concerning the likelihood and impact of each identified risk. This analysis will result in decisions to either accept information systems risks with no further action, or to impose controls to mitigate the risk. The resulting set of controls should be cost-effective, balancing the organization's appetite for risk against the cost of the controls and the burdens they place on the operating efficiency of the business.

Once the proper mix of controls has been decided upon, management needs to derive a set of information security policies that enforce these controls, noting the penalties that will be imposed if the policies are flouted by employees. These policies should then be communicated to all affected employees. This communication process should include the following:

- The ongoing support of management, not only through their direct participation in the process of communicating these policies to employees, but also by visibly following the policies themselves.
- Formal training classes that are tailored to the job functions of employees, so that employees are made aware of those policies that directly affect them. Thus, the information system policies communicated to the accounting staff could differ substantially from those provided to the sales department, which might interact with the AIS to a much lesser extent.
- Ongoing reminders of policies, perhaps involving a mix of written and in-person reminders, as well as a discussion of the policies in the employee manual.

Once these steps have been taken, management authorizes the expenditure of funds to acquire or build the tools needed to install the indicated controls. Some elements of this step may occur earlier than the communication of new controls to employees, on the grounds that the controls should be available for use as soon as employees are made aware of them – otherwise, employees will forget about the controls.

The final step in the process of developing security controls is to install a monitoring system that can be used to evaluate how effectively the controls are functioning. Management can use these monitoring reports to determine whether changes need to be made to the existing controls. In addition, and with the advice of information security specialists, management also needs to evaluate the possibility of new IT threats, and whether these threats call for the imposition of new controls, as well as changes to the existing set of information security policies.

Security Control Concepts

When deciding upon the types of security controls to install around and within an AIS, one should be cognizant of the need to employ overlapping controls. When there are multiple controls in place to address every risk, it is more difficult for someone to gain unauthorized access to the system simply by breaching a single control. Instead, they must navigate their way through a series of controls, thereby greatly reducing the probability of a successful attack. In the following sub-sections, we cover controls that are generally classified as preventive, detective, and corrective. Security controls tend to be more robust when two or more of these types of controls overlap each other. Though preventive controls act as the front line of defense against system attackers, the other types of controls are also needed to ensure that attacks are spotted, so that remedies can be constructed to prevent future attacks.

Another control concept is ensuring that the system of installed controls is sufficient to alert the organization that a preventive control has been breached, doing so in a sufficiently timely manner to prevent an attacker from stealing or destroying company assets. This may involve investments in additional preventive controls to minimize the probability of such a breach, or in detective or corrective controls to shorten the time needed to become aware of an attack and take corrective action.

Preventive Controls

As the name implies, preventive controls are designed to keep unauthorized access from occurring. There are far more preventive security controls than detective or corrective controls. The most essential types of preventive security controls are as follows:

- *Cultural reinforcement.* Management must create and maintain a strong culture of security awareness, so that employees are more likely to follow established system security policies. For example, managers can continually reinforce with the customer service staff the need to follow a specific protocol for handing out passwords to customers trying to access the company's systems. In addition, managers need to enforce sanctions against employees who break the rules, including the termination of their employment, in order to reinforce how critical it is that security policies be followed.
- *Employee training.* Employees need to have a clear understanding of safe computer usage practices, such as not openly posting passwords next to one's computer, never opening email attachments from unknown sources, and ensuring the physical safety of one's laptop computer when away from company premises. They should also be made aware of attacks taking the form of social engineering, and to handle these occurrences. This training tends to have a higher retention level among employees when it takes the form of role playing exercises. More specifically, those employees working in the area of system security should receive constant updates on the latest security threats and how to thwart them.
- *Authenticate access.* Authentication is the act of verifying the identity of a user, so that only appropriate users gain access to the AIS. Authentication can be conducted via a password, an ID badge, or a biometric identifier, such as a person's fingerprints or voice. The most secure form of authentication is *multi-factor authentication*, where two or more forms of evidence must be presented. For example, access to a website may involve entering a password and then also entering a code that is texted by the company to the user. If passwords are being used, it is critical to make them more difficult to replicate, preferably by mandating a minimum number of characters, and incorporating a mix of alphabetic, numeric, and special characters.
- *Authorize access.* Authorization involves the restriction of user access to specific parts of an AIS, as well as carefully defining the actions they are allowed to take within those areas. The level of authorization granted should closely match the requirements of a person's job, so that no excessive au-

thorizations are granted. For example, a payroll clerk should be allowed to enter the number of hours worked by employees into the AIS, but should not be able to enter journal entries in the general ledger, since modifications of the general ledger are outside of the area of responsibility of a payroll clerk. An AIS usually contains an authorization table, in which flags can be set that delineate the permissions granted to each user of the system. When an employee accesses any part of the system or attempts to perform a specific function, the AIS accesses the authorization table to see if the person is allowed to do so.

> **Tip:** Update the authorization table whenever an employee changes jobs within the company, since his or her authorizations will likely change. Of course, all authorizations should be terminated as soon as a person leaves the organization.

- *Control network access.* A *firewall* is part of a network that is designed to block unauthorized access to the system, while permitting outbound communications. It enforces a set of rules about which data packets will be allowed to enter or leave the network. This filtering process is most effective when deep packet inspection is used, which involves the detailed inspection of the contents of each data packet. An *intrusion prevention system* can also be used; this system monitors a network for malicious activity, blocks it, and reports it to the network manager. The malicious activity is identified by comparing it to a baseline of normal network traffic, or by comparing ongoing traffic patterns to a database of the traffic patterns associated with known methods of attack. These two access controls may be configured in multiple layers, possibly including additional firewalls at the level of individual departments, to make it more difficult for an attacker to gain unauthorized access to the system.
- *Protect endpoint devices.* An *endpoint device* is any computer hardware device connected to a network, such as a personal computer, printer, or tablet. To the greatest extent possible, each of these devices should have its own antivirus and firewall software, thereby minimizing unauthorized access to and corruption of these devices.
- *Control wireless access.* It is possible for someone to gain unauthorized access to a company's network by sitting just outside the building and hacking into the system through a wireless connection. This can be prevented by having inbound wireless traffic flow through the corporate firewall and intrusion prevention system. Also, turn on the security features built into the firm's wireless router, such as password access and encryption. A more targeted protection is to reduce the broadcast power of wireless routers, so that signals do not go beyond the walls of the building in which they are located.
- *Control physical access.* It is essential to control physical access to all parts of a network, including endpoint devices. Otherwise, someone could install a keystroke logger on a computer to track all keystrokes made on that de-

vice, download files, or simply steal the hard drive. Several ways to control physical access are as follows:

- o *Building access*. Provide only a single point of entry to the building, which is overseen by a receptionist. Opening any other door will trigger an alarm. The most secure environments call for the use of visitor sign-ins and personal escorts.
- o *Room access*. Access to those rooms containing computer equipment can be controlled with password-protected locks that can only be opened by authorized personnel. The entry of several incorrect passwords will trigger an alarm. A biometric locking system can be used that is based on the fingerprints or retinal scans of authorized users.
- o *Wiring access*. An attacker could engage in wiretapping if network cabling is easily accessible to them. Consequently, wiring should be routed through areas not accessible to outsiders. Further, wiring closets should be locked. For more redundant access control, protect the wiring in a wiring closet with a locked metal cage.

- *Scan for vulnerabilities*. Vulnerability scanning software can be used to assess an entire network for known weaknesses, as well as individual computers and software applications. The software is useful for detecting vulnerabilities caused by flawed programming or mis-configured settings. By making adjustments based on the findings reported by this scanning process, one can harden a system against external attacks.

- *Protect administrative access*. Administrative access to computers is needed in order to install and configure software. Given the essentially unlimited rights associated with administrative access, attackers are deeply interested in gaining access to them. To minimize the use of administrative rights, those users with such system access should also have another login that is associated with much more limited rights, which they are encouraged to use most of the time. By having these people use their more restricted accounts the bulk of the time (especially when reading email that may be compromised), attackers will be more likely to only gain access to their more restricted user accounts, not their administrator accounts.

- *Control system changes*. Whenever there is a proposed change to the system, perhaps in the form of a router replacement, software update, or the addition of new servers, these changes have to go through a formal change request process. This process involves documentation of the proposed change, an analysis of how the change impacts security, formal approval of the change, testing of the change in a controlled environment, and auditing of any control adjustments related to the change. These changes may also require updates to the systems documentation, so that ongoing employee training is adjusted. It may also be necessary to review the authorization table for affected employees, to see if any adjustments are needed.

- *Change default passwords.* Software is usually delivered to a company with a default password in place. This is also the case for the software built into network devices, such as routers. These defaults should be changed immediately, since they are publicly available. If they are not changed, an attacker can easily access the system with a default password.
- *Minimize laptop data.* It can be difficult to physically protect laptop and tablet computers when they are outside the office, so impose restrictions on the types of data that can be stored on them. If it is necessary to transport confidential information on one of these devices, then encrypt the data.

Detective Controls

In case an attacker is able to circumvent the preventive security controls just noted, an organization needs to also have detective controls, which identify the presence of the intruder. The following detective security controls are available:

- *Install logs.* An *access log* is typically available on many software packages, which logs the identity of every person accessing the system, as well as that person's subsequent activities within the system. Someone investigating an attack can use this log information to trace an attacker's actions within the system. These logs will only provide value to a business if someone routinely examines them for unauthorized activity. This analysis can be burdensome, since the amount of recorded log activity can be voluminous.
- *Install intrusion detection system.* An *intrusion detection system* is software that monitors a network for malicious activity or policy abuses by comparing actual network traffic to a baseline set of rules. Any issues detected will trigger an alert, after which the systems administrator needs to take further action.

Corrective Controls

Corrective controls that take action against an attacker usually require human intervention. There are several structures available for responding to attacks in a reasonably effective manner, which are as follows:

- *Formal response team.* There should be a designated group that is responsible for responding to system intrusions. This group must include technical specialists with sufficient knowledge to understand how to shut down intrusions and repair any damage caused. In addition, this group should have a direct line to senior management, which may need to make decisions when an attack has a significant negative impact on the business. For example, an interface into a company's production scheduling system that is provided to suppliers may need to be shut down; only a senior manager can properly estimate the impact this will have on the operations of those suppliers using the system.
- *Patch management system.* It is nearly impossible to create perfect software with no possible vulnerabilities, especially given the millions of lines of

code that may go into a software product. Consequently, software vulnerabilities and attacker exploits of those vulnerabilities are routinely being uncovered. As these exploits appear, software developers release software patches to erase the indicated vulnerabilities. A business must install these patches as soon as possible, but only after testing them to ensure that they do not alter the performance of its software in unexpected ways that could negatively impact the business. Managing the rollout of patches can be a major endeavor for a business, since developers may release a large number of patches each year.

The Nature of Directed Attacks

The bulk of the computer system attacks to which an organization will be subjected are not actually targeted specifically at that organization. Instead, they are more generic, such as viruses or malware linked to emails that are randomly issued to massive email lists. In effect, the receiving organization is only the unlucky recipient of a generic attack. In other cases, a firm may be subjected to a highly targeted attack, where the business is the sole focus of the attacker. In the latter case, the following steps are usually followed in order to gain unauthorized access to a system:

1. *Collect information.* The attacker first collects all possible information about the systems and controls used by the targeted business, using publicly available news sources, such as press releases by the business about its software and hardware purchases. The intent is to spot potential system weaknesses.
2. *Manipulate personnel.* The easiest form of unauthorized access is to manipulate company employees into giving up system access codes. Known as *social engineering*, this approach involves representing oneself as a valid user who has lost his user ID and password. For example, a hacker could pose as a company executive, asking for access to the system, or perhaps to a specific set of files within the system. Another common ploy is to call the company help desk and impersonate a new hire, who needs help logging in. There are many variations on how social engineering can be used.
3. *Conduct research.* If the manipulative approach does not work, the attacker can use automated tools to scan the company's computer systems and identify any computers that are subject to remote access, as well as the types of software running on those machines. One can then research whether there are any known vulnerabilities on the identified software, and determine how those vulnerabilities can be leveraged.
4. *Conduct the attack.* The attacker successfully takes advantage of the vulnerability to gain access to the system and download or destroy data, or take advantage of the target in some other way. In addition, the attacker may install a new form of access to the system that can be used in the future if the original software vulnerability is corrected. The more sophisticated hackers will also try to erase their activities from any monitoring logs used by the system, thereby making their attack invisible to the organization.

Confidentiality Controls

Much of the market value of today's organizations is based on their intangible assets, such as proprietary formulas, product cost information, customer lists, and bidding documents. These assets give a firm a competitive advantage, and so are essential to its long-term profitability. Consequently, it makes sense to enact confidentiality controls to keep these assets from being extracted from a business.

Before enacting confidentiality controls, one must first identify which assets require protection, where those assets are located, and who has access to them. For example:

- A candy company has developed a unique recipe for a sea salt caramel treat. Information about the recipe and the related production process are kept in the company safe, to which the owner, office manager, and production supervisor have access.
- A developer of software for automated cars has accumulated several million miles of driving data from the testing of cars that use its software. This database is located in a third-party data storage facility, and is accessible by all members of the company's development team.
- A consulting firm that specializes in services to the federal government has analyzed past bid packages and determined which combinations of words are most likely to lead to a successful bid. This information is contained in a binder in the sales support manager's office.

Once intangible assets have been identified, those responsible for them must decide how valuable the assets are to the business. The imposition of confidentiality controls can be expensive, so they must decide whether asset protection is cost-beneficial to the business. If an intangible asset is classified as warranting protection, then the following controls can be imposed:

- *Destroy targeted media.* When sensitive documents have been targeted for disposal, shred them prior to putting them in the trash. For example, old payroll registers may contain the social security numbers of employees, which are then made available to anyone willing to root through the company's trash. Similarly, computer media should be magnetically wiped and physically destroyed prior to disposal.
- *Encrypt data.* One can employ encryption to protect data. *Encryption* is a method by which data are converted from a readable form to an encoded version that can only be read by someone having access to a decryption key. Encryption is an especially useful tool for protecting information that is transmitted over the Internet or stored in a publicly-accessible location. This is not a perfect solution, since someone can still access the data if they can find the decryption key, which may be available if an attacker can log in as the legitimate user of a computer that contains this key. Consequently, encryption needs to be paired with strong access controls.

Note: A useful variation on the encryption concept is the *virtual private network* (VPN), which involves the creation of an encrypted connection over a less secure network (usually the Internet), where users must employ authentication methods such as passwords to gain access to the VPN server. This concept was developed to provide remote users with secure access to corporate resources, where they can exchange confidential information with other parties who also have access to the network.

- *Implement data loss prevention software.* Data loss prevention software detects and blocks attempts to move designated confidential data out of a network. It does so by searching for certain key words associated with the data being protected.
- *Implement digital watermarking.* A digital watermark is a marker that has been covertly embedded in a document or other file, such as a video or audio recording. It can be used to spot copyright infringements by third parties. It does not actively flag stolen files, but it will clarify their point of origination once they have been spotted. It acts as a detective control, spotting instances after-the-fact when documents have been stolen.
- *Implement information rights management software.* Information rights management (IRM) software protects documents containing sensitive information from unauthorized access. IRM is typically applied to spreadsheets, documents, and presentations, and protects them from unauthorized viewing, copying, forwarding, printing, and editing. The level of rights allowed can usually be specified by individual enterprise, department, group, or user. A downside of IRM is that a user must have specialized IRM software installed on her computer in order to open files having IRM protection. Also, a simple way to avoid this layer of protection is for someone to use a camera to take a picture of an on-screen image of a file that is IRM-protected.
- *Lock up documents.* When confidential information is only available on paper, be sure to store it in a secure location, such as a locking filing cabinet. Consider redundancy with this control, such as placing the locking filing cabinet in a locked room.
- *Minimize screen access.* Configure all computers to switch to screen saver mode after a few minutes of non-use, so that sensitive information is not displayed on screens. Computer screens can also be fitted with polarizers, so that the information on them will not be visible to a third party attempting to view them from an angle.
- *Train employees.* Employees should be made aware of which data are considered confidential, how to share data (or not) with outsiders, and how to protect it. They should have a particular awareness of which intangible assets are considered a competitive advantage by the company; with this understanding, they will be less likely to reveal it to outsiders, including competing firms. Beyond this basic training, employees should understand

how to use encryption tools, the company's document destruction policies and procedures, and how to identify new documents that fall within the firm's definition of confidential information. This training should be repeated over time, to ensure that everyone is aware of the need for confidentiality controls.

One of the preceding bullet points referenced the need for data encryption in certain situations. Encryption can be made more robust (that is, more difficult to decipher) by taking the following actions:

- Increase the length of the key, since this makes it harder for an attacker to identify patterns in the encrypted data.
- Use a tested, commercially-available encryption algorithm that has been proven through repeated testing to be difficult to crack.
- Impose strong access controls on cryptographic keys, to keep an attacker from stealing and using them to decrypt data. A key should be revoked as soon as the person using it leaves his or her position with the firm.

Encryption technology uses one of two methods to encrypt data. A *symmetric-key algorithm* uses the same cryptographic keys for both encryption and decryption. A *public-key algorithm* uses a public key, which is available to anyone, and a private key, which is retained by the company. These variations in usage result in the following differences between the two types of algorithms:

- *Processing time.* Public-key encryption requires more time to complete than symmetric-key encryption, so symmetric-key encryption is more useful for the encryption of large amounts of data.
- *Key transmission.* The recipient of encrypted data that uses a symmetric-key algorithm needs access to the secret key, which can be difficult to securely transmit to the recipient. This is not a problem with a public-key system, where the key may even be posted on the company's website for anyone to access. The problem can be resolved for the users of a symmetric-key algorithm by using public-key encryption to e-mail encrypted keys to them.
- *Key theft.* Loss of the private key used in a public-key algorithm allows an attacker to impersonate the company, perhaps committing it to contracts with a digital signature.
- *Number of keys.* Each recipient of data that uses a symmetric-key algorithm needs a separate key, whereas anyone can use a public-key algorithm to communicate with the company. This can present a problem for the user of a symmetric-key algorithm when it transacts business with many other parties, since it must maintain a large number of keys.

An associated risk is that cryptographic keys must not be lost, since such an event would make it impossible to recover encrypted data. This risk can be mitigated by ensuring that all keys used within a business are stored securely in escrow.

Privacy Controls

An organization needs to protect the personal information of its employees, customers, and suppliers. If this information is released, outsiders could use it in ways that harm individuals. For example, someone could extract an employee's name and social security number from unprotected documents and use it to file a fraudulent claim for a tax refund with the Internal Revenue Service. Or, someone could use this information to apply for a loan and then abscond with the cash, leaving the employee with a black mark on her credit record that could be difficult to expunge. Given these concerns, the American Institute of Public Accountants and the Canadian Institute of Chartered Accountants worked together to construct a framework for the management of privacy risks, which is called the Generally Accepted Privacy Principles (GAPP). The 10 privacy principles encompassed by GAPP are as follows:

1. *Management.* The business needs to define, document, communicate, and assign accountability to specific individuals for its privacy-related policies and procedures.

2. *Notice.* The business provides notice about its privacy-related policies and procedures, and states the purposes for which personal information is collected, used, retained, and disclosed.

3. *Choice and consent.* The firm should obtain the consent of individuals prior to collecting or using information related to them, describing to them the options available. It is recommended that companies use the opt-in policy, where individuals must specifically give the business permission to use information about them.

4. *Collection.* The firm commits to collect only that personal information stated in its notice to individuals, and only uses it for the purposes stated in the notice.

5. *Use, retention, and disposal.* The business minimizes the use of personal information to the purposes noted in its notification, and for which individuals have given their consent. The firm will only retain this information for as long as needed to fulfill the purposes it has stated to the individuals, or as required by law, after which it disposes of the information.

6. *Access.* The organization provides individuals with access to their personal information, which they can review, update, and delete.

7. *Disclosure to third parties.* The firm can only disclose personal information to third parties for the purposes stated in its notice, and with the consent of the individual. These disclosures should only be to third parties that provide a similar level of privacy protection to confidential information.

8. *Security for privacy.* The business is obligated to protect personal information against unauthorized access or loss.

9. *Quality.* The organization is obligated to maintain accurate, complete, and relevant personal information about individuals, for the purposes stated in the notice. This requirement can be achieved by giving individuals access to the information for review and update purposes.

10. *Monitoring and enforcement.* The firm is able to monitor compliance with its privacy policies and procedures, and also has enacted procedures to address any complaints and disputes related to privacy.

By following the dictates of the GAPP framework, a business should be able to properly manage the collection, use, retention, and disposal of all data that requires some degree of privacy protection.

In order to follow the requirements of GAPP, it is likely that a business will need to appoint someone to the role of information compliance officer, who acts on behalf of individuals to ensure that the firm properly collects, uses, protects, and disposes of their confidential information.

As was the case for confidentiality controls, one must first identify the nature of any personal information being collected, whether this information needs to be protected, where it is located, and who has access to it. For example:

- An on-line mortgage company stores client mortgage applications in the servers located at its home offices. After one year, these applications are downloaded to storage at an off-site location. During the initial year of use, all credit review staff have access to these records.
- A retail establishment retains the credit card information of its online customers. This information is stored in a secure server at an off-site location. Only the IT manager has direct access to this information. Credit card information is deleted from the system if a customer has not placed any new orders within the past two years.
- A custom clothier maintains the personal measurements of its clients. This information is maintained on index cards in a filing cabinet at the shop. Access to the cards is not controlled. The cards are reviewed at the end of each year, and the cards associated with inactive customers are thrown in the trash.

When reviewing the need for controls in this area, one should consider whether there are relevant local laws that require a business to contact all impacted parties when there has been a data breach. When this is the case, the contact cost, as well as the associated negative publicity, should be considered when deciding upon the extent of the controls that are adopted.

The controls associated with data confidentiality can also be applied to privacy issues. In addition, the following controls can be used:

- *Restrict programmer access.* Programmers should not be allowed direct access to personal information, even when developing applications that will use this information. For software development purposes, they can instead use a set of fake test data that contains information that is similar to actual personal information.
- *Train employees.* Employees should be made aware of which data are considered to be personal, as well as how to both use and protect it. They

should also be made aware of the financial and reputational impact on the company if confidential information is incorrectly used.

Processing Integrity Controls

A business should have controls in place to ensure that data are processed correctly and in a timely manner. These controls can be subdivided into the general categories of input controls, processing controls, and output controls, which are described in the following sub-sections.

Input Controls

If there are not solid controls over the data being input into a system, then its output will likely be incorrect and therefore not usable. The following input controls can be useful for enhancing input quality:

- *Cancel source documents.* Stamp or deface all source documents that have already been entered into the system, thereby reducing the probability that they will be entered again. For example, a stamp can be applied to the face of a supplier invoice that states the date on which data entry occurred, and which leaves room for the initials of the person who completed the related data entry.
- *Impose completeness checks.* Configure the software to only allow an entry to be completed if all designated fields contain data. For example, the entry of an employee timesheet into a payroll module will only be accepted if the employee number, date, and hours worked fields have been completed.
- *Impose field checks.* Configure the software to only allow entries of the correct type, such as a field that only accepts alphabetic values for the entry of a state in an address field.
- *Impose limit checks.* Configure the software to only allow entries for numerical amounts that reside within a predetermined high-low value range. For example, the number of hours worked by a person cannot exceed 168 hours per week.
- *Impose reasonableness checks.* Configure the software to compare the relationships between two data items. For example, an employee cannot charge more billable hours to a customer project than he has been paid by the company over the same period of time.
- *Impose validity checks.* Configure the software to compare key entries to master file data for verification purposes. For example, if a customer number is entered into the system by an order entry clerk as part of the creation of a customer order, the system should match the entered customer number against the customer master file to see if the customer already exists in the system.
- *Require sequential numbering.* All source documents from which data are input into the system should be prenumbered in sequential order. By doing so, one can determine whether any data are being entered twice (or more),

and whether any source documents are missing. Further, configure the system to automatically flag any duplicate data, such as when a clerk attempts to enter a supplier invoice that has already been entered into the system.

Processing Controls

An organization should have a sufficient number of controls to ensure that its systems process data correctly. The following controls can have a positive impact on processing activities:

- *Conduct data matching.* The system can compare information in different files before completing a transaction. The most common example is three-way matching, where the system verifies that there is an authorizing purchase order and a corresponding receipt of goods before allowing the payment of a supplier invoice.
- *Cross-foot totals.* When data are stored in a spreadsheet, calculate the totals for each column and then add the totals to see if they match the grand total. The grand total and the cross-footed totals should always match. If not, there is an error in the spreadsheet.
- *Prohibit concurrent updates.* It is quite possible that two users will attempt to update the same record at the same time, resulting in either an error or one update being erased by the other update. For example, two warehouse employees could attempt to alter the on-hand balance of an inventory item at the same time. This situation can be resolved by blocking access to one of the parties until the other party has completed its update activities.

Output Controls

A firm should monitor the information being generated by a system, to ensure that the output is reasonable. The following controls may be of use:

- *Reconcile output.* The totals generated by a system should be periodically reconciled to the underlying source documents. For example, the ending balance in the fixed assets account can be reconciled to records of asset purchases and disposals. Similarly, the total of all individual customer invoices should be compared to the ending balance in the accounts receivable account. Whenever a variance is found, one should investigate it; a possible outcome is an adjustment to the records in the system.
- *Verify output.* Have a knowledgeable user verify the output before releasing it for general use. For example, the company controller routinely examines a preliminary version of the payroll register before authorizing the printing of paychecks, to ensure that the amounts to be paid are accurate.

EXAMPLE

Aphelion Corporation processes payroll for its employees once every two weeks. When timesheets are entered into the system, the payroll clerk initials and dates each one to indicate that it has been entered (input control). Further, the payroll software will not allow a time entry to be entered unless the employee number has been entered (input control). It will also limit the number of hours entered to 24 per day (input control). In addition, the system verifies that each employee number entered matches an employee number in the employee master file (input control).

Once initial processing is complete, the clerk prints a listing of hours worked by all employees and compares it to the totals on the individual timesheets (output control). Finally, the controller must review and initial the final payroll register before paychecks can be issued (output control).

Availability Controls

A company cannot function properly unless its systems are operational with a high degree of regularity. Otherwise, its key processes will degrade or fail entirely, resulting in the eventual demise of the business. The following controls can be rolled out to reduce the risk of significant system downtime:

- *Use multiple backups*. Maintain several copies of key data, preferably stored in different locations, so that the destruction of the firm's primary systems will not also destroy the associated data. This calls for a tightly-managed process to ensure that backups are conducted. In addition, if management is not willing to reenter the data that could potentially be lost between the date of the last backup and the present period, then it should commit to very frequent backups. Several variations on the backup concept are as follows:

  - *Full backup*. This is a complete backup of the entire database. It can be quite time-consuming, and so is usually only conducted at longer intervals, such as once a week.
  - *Incremental backup*. This is a backup of just those data items that have changed since the last full backup. The result is an ongoing series of partial backups. To restore an entire database, one would have to first restore the latest full backup, and then layer on each subsequent incremental backup. The main advantage of an incremental backup is a greatly reduced period of time needed to conduct each backup.
  - *Differential backup*. This is a backup of all data items that have changed since the last full backup. The result is just one backup in addition to the full backup, so that restoration of an entire database would require the restoration of the latest full backup, followed by restoration of the latest differential backup. This backup takes less

time than a full backup, but the time required will increase as more time passes since the last full backup.

> **Note:** It can be useful to periodically practice how to restore a database from backup, not only to minimize the total time required to do so, but also to ensure that the backups actually contain data.

- *Use redundant components.* Install systems that are comprised of redundant components, so that they will continue to function even when a single component fails. These systems are significantly more expensive than normal computing equipment, and so are typically reserved for the most critical systems. For example, airline reservation systems are designed to be redundant, so that system downtime is extremely rare. A common redundancy for data storage is a *RAID system* (redundant arrays of independent drives), where data is written to multiple storage devices at the same time. Then, if one of these devices fails, the data is still available. A more advanced system for businesses that cannot afford to have any downtime is *real-time mirroring*, where identical copies of a database are maintained at two different data centers, and those databases are continually updated in real time. This level of redundancy allows one data center to continue if the other one suffers a failure.
- *Protect data centers.* It is critical to protect data centers to minimize the risk of damage to them. The following options may be employed:
  - o *Access controls.* Install strong controls to limit access to the data center, only allowing in authorized personnel.
  - o *Air conditioning.* Install sufficient air conditioning equipment to keep temperature and humidity levels within the design parameters of the computer equipment.
  - o *Fire suppression.* Install fire suppression systems that will not damage the computer equipment when it is activated.
  - o *Height.* Construct data centers away from flood plains and perhaps on higher floors, to minimize the risk of water damage.
  - o *Location.* Build data centers away from business locations, so that a natural disaster impacting the organization will not impact the data center.
  - o *Power management.* Install an uninterruptible power supply to compensate for power shortages, as well as surge-protection equipment to guard against power spikes.
- *Impose operator training.* Systems operators should be thoroughly trained in how to recover from system failures. This training should include the use of standard procedures and ongoing simulations of system failures.
- *Develop a disaster recovery plan.* A disaster recovery plan is a set of instructions for how to respond to a major incident. The intent behind the plan is to bring the organization's operations back to full functionality as

soon as possible. It is most commonly targeted at an organization's technology assets, where the main options are real-time mirroring with a second data center (as discussed earlier), a cold site, or a hot site. A *cold site* is a separate business location that is rented as a backup to the normal data center. It does not necessarily contain the required computing equipment, so there will be a time delay while the necessary equipment can be brought in and installed. A *hot site* is also an off-site location, but it is maintained with all necessary equipment needed to support company operations, and so will result in a very short downtime for the business. A cold site is significantly less expensive than a hot site to maintain on an ongoing basis.

> **Note:** A disaster recovery plan must be constantly updated to reflect ongoing changes to the operations of a company's computer systems. Otherwise, the documentation for a system restart may not match how the systems actually function.

The use of a cloud storage solution will shift data storage off-site, to (hopefully) redundant data storage sites located well away from the company's facilities. While it is likely that the use of cloud storage will minimize the risk of data loss, it is still possible that the destruction of a supplier's data storage facilities will leave a business with few options for recovering its data, other than to continue making its own backups. Another concern with cloud storage is the bankruptcy of the supplier offering this service. Consequently, one should routinely review the financial condition of this supplier to minimize the risk of an unexpected shutdown in data access.

The extent of the availability controls discussed here will be highly dependent upon the ability of an organization to remain in operation for an extended period of time without access to its most critical data. If this period is estimated to be quite short, then it makes sense to invest a significant amount of time and training effort in availability controls. The evaluation of this problem should include consideration of the firm's *recovery time objective*, which is the targeted time period within which a business process must be restored in order to avoid any unacceptable consequences related to a break in the continuity of business operations and service levels.

Digital Signatures

A final topic related to information system controls is the use of digital signatures, which are needed to sign electronic documents in an enforceable manner. A *digital signature* is a mathematical approach to verifying whether a digital document is authentic. A valid digital signature gives the recipient of the document reason to believe that it was sent by a known party, that the document was not altered in transit, and that the sender will not repudiate having sent the document. Thus, a digital signature ideally has the following characteristics:

- *Authentication.* A digital signature authenticates the source of a document, since it is linked to a specific party. This feature is especially important for financial transactions, such as a request to initiate a wire transfer.
- *Integrity.* A digital signature provides high confidence that a document was not altered during transmission to the recipient. Any change in the document will invalidate the signature.
- *Non-repudiation.* A digital signature indicates that the entity signing a document cannot later deny having signed it. This is a critical characteristic in many jurisdictions, where digital signatures are legally binding.

Three algorithms are employed in the construction of a digital signature. These algorithms are:

- *Key generation algorithm.* This algorithm randomly selects a private key from a set of available private keys. Its output is the private key and a related public key.
- *Signing algorithm.* This algorithm uses the message that will be linked to the digital signature and the selected private key to produce a digital signature.
- *Signature verifying algorithm.* This algorithm either accepts or rejects a message's claim to authenticity, based on the message, the public key, and the digital signature.

These three algorithms are needed, as a group, to ensure that a digital signature has been properly constructed and can be verified.

Summary

Clearly, an AIS requires a broad array of security controls to prevent access to the system, detect any intrusions, and repair and improve the system on an ongoing basis. Security controls are primarily the responsibility of the IT department, rather than the accounting department, since these controls address the underlying network, hardware, and software used by the entire organization, not just the accounting department.

The core confidentiality control is the training of employees, who need to understand which documents are considered confidential and why that is the case, as well as how to identify and treat these documents. There are other controls over confidential assets, several of which are automated, but a proper internal understanding of the need for confidentiality forms the basis for an effective set of controls in this area.

Privacy controls are largely similar to those used for confidentiality controls; in addition, management must be careful to minimize internal access to personal information. This is a particular concern with programmers, who will need to run test records through their software to see if the software functions properly. In these cases, management should only allow the use of fake test data that have the characteristics of the actual records for individuals.

The bulk of the controls associated with processing integrity are installed on the front end, where data entry occurs, and are mostly designed into the system. The accountant is more involved on the output side of these controls, where ongoing reconciliation and verification activities are needed to ensure that the information produced by the system is correct.

The controls related to system availability attack the problem from multiple directions. The use of RAID systems, real-time mirroring, and data center protection are all incorporated into the initial construction of computer systems. Ongoing backups protect data, while the use of training and disaster recovery plans are needed to assist in the reconstruction of damaged or destroyed systems. A mix of these controls results in a high level of system availability.

Chapter 8
Auditing Accounting Information Systems

Introduction

Auditing primarily involves the examination of financial records to determine whether they are accurate and have been compiled in accordance with the applicable accounting standards. The concept can also be applied to the collection of evidence regarding assertions about any type of performance. Larger organizations employ internal auditors to conduct reviews of internal processes and report their findings to management, typically with recommendations for improvements and corrections. Internal auditors also assist in the design of information systems, in order to create a balance of processing efficiency and relevant controls. External auditors are usually hired to review a company's financial statements and the underlying system of controls. Their audit opinions are highly valued by members of the investment community and creditors, who need an independent appraisal of the financial statements of the business.

In this chapter, we review the types of audits that may be conducted, the various steps involved in an audit, and the specific auditing activities associated with an accounting information system (AIS).

Types of Audits

There are a number of types of audits that an auditor can conduct, including the following:

- *Compliance audit*. This is an examination of the policies and procedures of an entity or department, to see if it is in compliance with internal or regulatory standards. This audit is most commonly used in regulated industries or educational institutions.
- *Financial audit*. This is an analysis of the fairness of the information contained within an entity's financial statements. It is conducted by a CPA firm, which is independent of the entity under review. This is the most commonly conducted type of audit.
- *Information systems audit*. This involves a review of the controls over software development, data processing, and access to computer systems. The intent is to spot any issues that could impair the ability of IT systems to provide accurate information to users, as well as to ensure that unauthorized parties do not have access to the data.
- *Investigative audit*. This is an investigation of a specific area or individual when there is a suspicion of inappropriate or fraudulent activity. The intent

is to locate and remedy control breaches, as well as to collect evidence in case charges are brought against someone.

- *Operational audit.* This is a detailed analysis of the goals, planning processes, procedures, and results of the operations of a business. The audit may be conducted internally or by an external entity. The intended result is an evaluation of operations, likely with recommendations for improvement.

Of the audits described here, the information systems audit is the one most directly targeted at accounting information systems, though an operational audit may also touch upon certain aspects of an AIS. This work is most likely to be conducted by an internal auditor, though an external auditor may explore those aspects of an AIS pertaining to systems of control.

The Audit Process

When an auditor is asked to audit an AIS, the process followed typically involves the establishment of an overarching audit strategy, which is then used as the basis for a detailed audit plan. Once the types of evidence outlined in the audit plan have been collected, the auditor uses it to come to a conclusion and derive recommendations to management and company directors. We expand upon these topics in the following subsections.

Audit Strategy

A significant amount of planning is required for an audit, in order to focus on those activities most likely to generate an audit finding with a high degree of confidence. This planning process begins with the audit strategy document. The *audit strategy* sets the direction, timing, and scope of an audit, and is the foundational document for the more detailed audit plan. The strategy document is based on the following considerations:

- The characteristics of the engagement[2]
- Reporting objectives
- Timing of the audit
- Nature of communications
- Significant factors in directing engagement team efforts
- The results of preliminary engagement activities
- The knowledge gained on other engagements
- The nature, timing, and extent of resources available for the engagement

The audit strategy document could be relatively short for a minor audit, perhaps in the form of a brief memo.

---

[2] Such as reviewing the controls for the accounts payable module in the accounting software.

The strategy used could be based on whatever investigation is requested by management or the board of directors. Or, it could be based on an analysis of the key threats faced by a business, such as a heightened risk of fraud in a particular area. In the latter case, the strategy will focus on the identification of those controls specifically targeted at the designated threat, whether the controls are adequate, and whether there are any control weaknesses requiring correction.

Audit Plan

The *audit plan* states the detailed steps to be followed in the conduct of an audit. The plan includes risk assessment procedures, as well as additional procedures to be followed based on the outcome of the risk assessment. The contents and timing of the plan will vary from year to year, depending on changes in the circumstances of the business, and the scope and nature of the audit. By creating an audit plan at the start of an audit, an auditor is in a better position to anticipate problems that may arise during the audit, while also conducting the audit in an efficient manner.

At its most detailed level, an audit plan contains a checklist of the audit procedures that must be followed. The auditor signs off on each checklist item as it is completed, and then inserts the checklist in the audit working papers as evidence that the audit steps were completed. The plan also contains a time budget, stating the amount of time allocated to each auditor position for each assigned task. This time budget is monitored over the course of the audit to see if additional resources must be allocated to the various procedures outlined in the plan.

Risk Assessment

The focus of the activities in an audit plan is heavily dependent on those aspects of an engagement with the highest perceived risk factors. *Audit risk* is the risk that an auditor will not detect errors or fraud while examining a target area. Auditors tend to increase the number of audit procedures in order to reduce the level of audit risk. There are three types of audit risk, which are:

- *Control risk*. This is the risk that potential material misstatements would not be detected or prevented by a client's control systems. When there are significant control failures, a business is more likely to experience undocumented asset losses, resulting in incorrect financial statements. A system of strong internal controls tends to result in a low level of control risk.
- *Detection risk*. This is the risk that the audit procedures used are not capable of detecting a material misstatement. This situation is especially likely when there are several misstatements that are individually immaterial, but which are material when aggregated. There will always be some amount of detection risk in an audit, since audit procedures do not comprehensively examine every business transaction – instead, they only review a sampling of them.
- *Inherent risk*. This is the probability of loss based on the nature of an organization's business, without any changes to the existing environment.

Within an AIS, inherent risk is mostly associated with transactional errors or fraud. It is more likely in the following situations:

- o *Judgment.* A high degree of judgment is involved in business transactions, which introduces the risk that an inexperienced person is more likely to make an error.
- o *Estimates.* Significant estimates must be included in transactions, which makes it more likely that an estimation error will be made.
- o *Complexity.* Transactions are highly complex, and so are more likely to be completed or recorded incorrectly. For example, an AIS that employs advanced technology has a relatively high inherent risk.

Collection of Evidence

Audit evidence is the documentation collected by an auditor as part of a review of the accounts, internal controls, and other matters needed to certify a company's financial statements or achieve some other goal. The amount and type of audit evidence collected will vary by engagement, depending on the type of industry, the condition of the company's financial system, and the type of audit. The amount of evidence collected must provide a reasonable basis for the auditor's conclusions.

The following methods are common techniques used for the collection of audit evidence:

- *Conduct a process walkthrough.* For example, step through the documented controls associated with the processing of payroll.
- *Conduct an analytical review.* For example, if sales increase by 20% during a review period, then the accounts receivable balance should increase by about the same amount.
- *Confirm information with third parties.* For example, send confirmation letters to customers, asking them to verify the amount of receivables outstanding.
- *Examine supporting documents.* For example, see if there is a purchase order or manager approval signature associated with a payment to a supplier.
- *Inspect assets.* For example, conduct an on-site inspection of fixed assets to ensure that they are present and in reasonable operating condition.
- *Interview employees.* For example, talk to the employees engaged in a physical inventory count, addressing all aspects of how they conduct the count.
- *Issue questionnaires.* For example, distribute a questionnaire to the credit department, probing for any issues they have encountered with credit being granted in an unorthodox or unapproved manner.

- *Observe selected activities*. For example, watch how the order entry staff enters customer purchase orders into the order entry system.
- *Recalculate numeric amounts*. For example, manually compile the total amount of amortization expense associated with intangible assets.

The collection methods used will vary by audit. For example, a review of a company's billing controls will likely place an emphasis on a process walkthrough, employee interviews, and the observance of selected activities, while an audit of a new automated commission calculation system would be more likely to focus on the recalculation of numeric amounts.

Evaluation of Evidence

Once all evidence has been gathered, the auditor examines it to see if the outcome is sufficient to form a conclusion. If not, additional evidence may be gathered, perhaps with an emphasis on a different type of evidence, to see if doing so will allow for a more conclusive outcome. Reaching a conclusion may depend upon whether any errors found are material. One should assume that misstatements are material if they could, either individually or in aggregate, reasonably be expected to influence the economic decisions of users. Further, judgments about materiality are made in light of surrounding circumstances and are affected by the size or nature of a misstatement or a combination of both factors.

There are several issues to consider when deciding whether uncorrected misstatements are material. Consider the following:

- The nature, amount, and cause of the misstatement.
- The possible effect of the misstatement on future reporting periods.
- Whether the accumulation of material misstatements in the balance sheet could contribute to more misstatements in future periods.
- Whether the existence of an offsetting misstatement is appropriate.
- Whether the misstatement originated in a prior year.

It is not cost-effective for an auditor to achieve complete assurance that a system is functioning properly, for this would require a massive investment in the analysis of every transaction passing through the system. Accordingly, the auditor tries to obtain reasonable assurance that there are no material errors in the system, which may call for the use of incremental increases in the amounts and types of evidence obtained.

Communication of Findings

Once the auditor has collected and evaluated all audit evidence, she summarizes this information and states her conclusions in a formal report, along with any recommendations for improving the system. Depending on the arrangement, this report may be issued to management, the board of directors, and the audit committee. If authorized to do so, the auditor may revisit the topic at a later date, to see if any recommendations were implemented.

AIS Audits

The central focus of an AIS audit is to review the efficacy of the controls associated with the system. Some of these controls are built into the software, while others take the form of policies, procedures, and forms that are associated with the system. When engaged in an AIS audit, the auditor is primarily concerned with the following issues:

- *Change and acquisition authorization.* Software is being developed, modified, or acquired with the express approval of management.
- *Confidentiality.* Access to data is strictly observed, so that confidentiality policies are not breached.
- *Exceptions.* Incorrect or unauthorized data are promptly identified and dealt with in a consistent manner.
- *Processing.* Transaction processing is conducted correctly.
- *Protection.* The system's hardware, software, and data are protected from malicious access.

The audit activities associated with each of these issues are described in the following subsections.

Change and Acquisition Authorization

A multitude of system-related errors and control weaknesses can be introduced whenever software is modified or acquired. Accordingly, the auditor should be positioned in the role of independent reviewer, testing these systems and reporting any negative findings or recommendations back to management. The auditor should not be directly involved in the design or acquisition of systems, since doing so could remove the objectivity needed to conduct an impartial evaluation. The auditor can engage in a mix of the following activities to detect problems and form an opinion about how well the controls function:

- Conduct a review of the general systems development and modification process, including all related policies and procedures, authorization controls, and the standards that apply to the evaluation of programming activities. This review may include interviews with those employees involved in systems development and modification activities.
- Verify that management has authorized all software development activities, software modifications, and purchases, noting their approvals when development milestones have been completed. Also examine any documentation of approvals by users for system changes.
- Review the existence of approval documentation for the programming specifications being used.
- Verify that the development staff is maintaining separate development and production versions of software. Also, test whether there is a procedure in

place for replacing the production version with the development version once the development version has been approved for use.

- Verify that a complete suite of tests were conducted for all software used prior to its rollout for general use. This should include a review of test data and test results, as well as the policies and procedures that govern these tests. Also, make note of how the team resolved any unusual testing outcomes.
- Test for unauthorized program changes by using a source code comparison program to compare the most recent version of software to the original source code, and then verifying that each change made was properly authorized.
- Review systems documentation to see if it accurately reflects the capabilities of the software, as well as any changes to modified software.

The auditor should be particularly cognizant of the risk of programming errors occurring when software is modified. These changes are typically made years after the original design work, and by programmers who were not involved in the original system design. Their unfamiliarity with the software increases the risk of having flawed software updates.

Confidentiality

A business that stores crucial intellectual property or confidential customer or supplier information online has to be concerned with its confidentiality. The following activities can be of assistance in formulating an opinion about confidentiality-related controls:

- Review all policies and procedures related to the storage of and access to data.
- Review all policies and procedures related to the assignment and updating of passwords.
- Review the access controls granted to all system users to see if there are any access rights that seem excessive or that go beyond the needs of an employee's current position.
- Investigate the extent to which encryption is used to protect data, both on the premises and as part of data transfers beyond the premises.
- Review the security procedures associated with backed up files, including backups stored in off-site locations.

Exceptions

An AIS will inevitably encounter exception records that do not meet its input criteria, possibly many times a day. The system should be able to log these exceptions as they occur, while also providing procedures for their correction, which are consistently applied. Since exception records are much easier to correct at the point of data entry, the auditor should be concerned with the ability of the business to spot these errors as they enter the data entry system. A mix of the following activities can be used to detect problems and form an opinion about how well exception-related controls function:

- Investigate whether installed controls are functioning properly. Examples of these controls are cross-footing, visual inspections, field checks, validity checks, limit checks, and completeness checks.
- Determine whether only authorized personnel are entering data into the system, and whether approvals are required once batches have been entered into the system.
- Verify whether batch control totals are being prepared, and errors reconciled.
- Discuss with employees the procedures in place for dealing with exception records, as well as the presence of any undocumented controls.
- Verify that the error log is being updated and reviewed on a regular basis.
- Trace any identified exceptions to see how they were resolved. Compare these resolutions to the documented procedures for doing so.

Processing

The auditor should verify whether transaction processing is being conducted correctly. An AIS might accept erroneous or incomplete input data, incorrectly process data, or generate incorrect reports. Processing errors can cause significant problems, so the auditor needs to engage in especially detailed efforts to detect issues in this area. A mix of the following activities can be used to detect problems and form an opinion about how well processing-related controls function:

- Review the policies and procedures governing data processing activities, looking for complete coverage of all situations. Discuss them with employees to see if actual usage varies from the documentation.
- Observe IT employees as they engage in data processing activities, with a particular emphasis on processing and output controls.
- Recalculate the processing accuracy of selected transactions. Alternatively, run test data through the system and compare the results to expectations; the test data should include both valid and invalid[3] data. The intent is to spot instances in which the system does not flag invalid data, or processes valid data incorrectly. The use of test data can be a problem when they are subsequently incorporated into a company's files, so be sure to reverse these transactions in the system.
- Investigate any errors reported by the system, focusing on how they were dealt with by employees.

---

[3] Examples of invalid data are records containing fields with no entries, with excessively high or low quantities, and alphabetic entries in numeric fields.

- Manually recreate selected reports and compare them to output automatically generated by the system.
- Compare the actual distribution of system outputs to the documented distribution lists, and investigate any differences.

Concurrent audit techniques can be an especially effective way to examine system processing. These techniques involve the ongoing automated examination of processes. This is achieved by embedding audit sub-routines into the application systems used by employees to process transactions. The system then flags unusual transactions for review by the audit staff. This approach has the advantage of providing a complete review of *all* transactions, rather than the small sample sizes that auditors normally examine. Concurrent audit techniques are especially useful when there is a heightened need to spot errors and irregularities immediately.

Protection

A large part of the controls built into and around an AIS are concerned with protecting the system from malicious access. Such access could result in damaged hardware, modified or destroyed programs, and lost or stolen data, any of which could halt company operations. The auditor can engage in a mix of the following activities to detect problems and form an opinion about how well the controls function:

- Conduct a walk-through of the data processing area.
- Discuss documented and undocumented security procedures with employees.
- Examine the policies and procedures related to physical access to computer systems. Observe their application to actual attempts at gaining physical access.
- Examine the policies and procedures related to user access to data. Test the functionality of these policies and procedures. Observe how attempts at unauthorized access are handled. Also, note the extent to which data encryption is used, both on the premises and for data transmissions. In addition, investigate the extent to which firewalls and virus protection software are incorporated into the system.
- Review data backup and data recovery policies and procedures. Observe the backup process and whether backups are sent offsite.
- Review system access logs, and investigate the extent to which unauthorized access records are investigated.
- Review the firm's disaster recovery plan, as well as the results of any simulations based on the plan.

- Review the history of software patches and updates, as well as hardware updates.
- Verify the extent to which preventive maintenance activities are employed. Also note whether surge protectors and uninterruptible power supplies are being used.

The best auditing technique involves active attempts to penetrate the system, both physically and online, to see if the existing controls are adequate. The auditor should take the view that a determined attacker would pursue similar steps to gain access to the system.

Computer-Assisted Auditing

An auditor can employ audit software to examine large data files for specific types of exceptions. These exceptions can represent control problems, and so are worthy of additional examination by the auditor. The software can also summarize or sort data in different ways, standardize the formatting of disparate files, and perform statistical and analytical analyses. These operations can highlight suspicious transactions or indicate trends that would not otherwise be apparent to a casual observer.

The use of computer-assisted auditing allows the auditor to examine a complete data set, rather than just a sample, as is common when using more traditional auditing methods. For example, audit software can be used to highlight any billings to customers for which offsetting credit memos were created that exceed a certain threshold amount. These highlighted billings could represent situations in which an accounting clerk has intercepted incoming payments from customers and hidden the theft with a credit memo.

The proper use of audit software requires one to have a detailed knowledge of the layouts of the files to be reviewed, as well as how to set up commands to search for specific issues within the data. The software then uses the criteria input by the auditor to create a search program, which combs through a copy of the live data and extracts any exceptions found. This software can assist in locating the proverbial "needle in a haystack" that more traditional sampling activities would be much less likely to find. However, the auditor still needs to interpret what the results mean, which calls for a detailed knowledge of the functions of the business and how it uses data in its operations.

Computer-assisted auditing is especially valuable within larger firms, where there may be massive transaction volumes, operations situated in distant locations, unusually intricate operations, or some combination of these factors.

Summary

In this chapter, we have outlined the general process flow for the conduct of an audit of an AIS. This process will likely be followed by a firm's internal auditors, and to some extent by the firm's external auditors as part of their annual examination of its financial statements and related systems of control.

A particular concern in the design of an audit plan is the risk assessment. When there appear to be significant control, detection, or inherent risks, it may be necessary to expend far more effort in expanding sample sizes and employing additional audit procedures in order to gain additional assurances regarding the adequacy of the controls under review.

Chapter 9
The Sales Cycle

Introduction

The sales cycle is the set of activities related to the provision of goods and services to customers. These activities include the receipt of customer orders, the shipment of goods, billings to customers, and cash collections. An accounting information system (AIS) is designed to support each of these activities, so that there is a smooth transactional flow that minimizes the risk of introducing errors or preventing customers from being serviced in a timely manner. In this chapter, we discuss the information system flows associated with each set of activities that comprise the sales cycle, including the most essential controls associated with each one.

Sales Cycle Overview

The sales cycle is comprised of several distinct components, involving order receipt, order fulfillment, billing, and cash receipts. Though these are all distinct activities that are usually completed by different people within a company, it is useful to see how the overall process flows. In this section, we provide an overview of all four parts of the sales cycle, indicating how information flows between them. The full sales cycle for an AIS contains the following activities:

1. Examine the initial customer order to ensure that all mandatory fields have been completed correctly. The order does not proceed further into the system until correct entries have been made in the indicated fields.
2. Verify inventory availability. If the customer has ordered goods (as opposed to services), the system checks the on-hand balance of finished goods that are available to ship and which have not yet been reserved for other customer orders. If there are not enough units available, the system examines the production schedule to see if there will be enough units available within the planning horizon of the production department. If not, the system may search for similar units that are in stock; this information can be relayed back to the customer, in case the individual wants to switch the order to the units that are currently available. If not, the system calculates an expected inventory availability date for the customer, or simply states that the units being ordered will have to be backordered.
3. Verify customer creditworthiness. If the customer is requesting delayed payment for the order, the system routes the amount of the credit request to the credit department. The system then provides the credit department with the customer's historical ordering and payment history (if available) and may also download a credit report about the customer from a credit reporting agency. Once the credit department has had time to review this infor-

mation, it accepts or rejects the credit request, setting a credit amount in the prior case.

4. If the customer has paid in advance or has been approved for credit, the credit department sets a flag in the system, indicating its approval for delivery of the indicated goods to the customer. If the customer has instead ordered services, the applicable department is notified by the system that it can schedule the service in its work calendar.

5. If goods are to be shipped, they appear on a picking list, sorted by warehouse location, which is used by the warehouse staff to pick items from stock in the most efficient manner. Once goods are shipped, they are flagged in the AIS, which notifies the accounting department that an invoice can be prepared and issued to the applicable customer.

6. If services are to be provided, the service staff completes the indicated work order and then flags it in the AIS as being complete. This triggers a request to the accounting department to prepare and issue an invoice to the applicable customer.

7. Once a customer order has been flagged for billing, the billing clerk reviews whether all parts of the order have been completed, or if only a portion has been completed, which results in a partial billing. In addition, the clerk checks the AIS to verify that goods have been shipped or services provided. If so, an invoice is prepared and issued to the customer. This invoice may be delivered by mail, as an email attachment, through a direct interface to the customer's computer system, or manually entered through the customer's web portal.

8. Once the customer pays the amount indicated on the invoice, the cash arrives either at the company's bank lockbox or at its accounting department. In the first case, the bank overseeing the lockbox compiles the payment information into a remittance file, which it sends to the accounting department. This remittance file may be input directly into the AIS through an interface, or transferred manually into the AIS. In the latter case, the accounting department logs all received checks into the accounting system, offsetting outstanding invoices.

The preceding activities are the primary components of the sales cycle. The AIS is a key component of the cycle, since it is the main repository of the data used in each step of the process. Consequently, the AIS needs to be protected from a number of threats in order to keep the cycle from being corrupted with incorrect data. When there is incorrect data in the system, a business could be subject to any of the following failures:

- Customer orders are accepted that have not been authorized by the customer.
- Customer orders are not fully or accurately loaded into the system.
- Credit is issued to customers who are unable to pay.

- Delivery dates are promised when there is not sufficient inventory on hand to fulfill orders.
- Incorrect items are picked and shipped to customers.
- Goods are shipped to the wrong address.
- Duplicate shipments are sent to customers.
- Customers are not invoiced for goods or services.
- Billings sent to customers are incorrect.
- Credit memos are either not issued to customers or are issued incorrectly.
- Employees steal incoming cash from customers.
- Confidential information is used by an unauthorized party.
- Data are destroyed within the system, and there is no backup.

The preceding failures could easily result in the loss of customers, along with the lifetime revenues that might have been earned from them.

Order Entry Activities

Order entry is an area in which customer orders are examined, translated into the format used by a company to process orders, and eventually sent on to other parts of the company for credit checks and fulfillment.

The order entry function is usually managed by the sales department, though it is sometimes found within the accounting department, on the grounds that order entry processes have a major impact on the data used by the accounting department. Nonetheless, the sales manager usually wants control over order entry, to ensure that new customer orders are properly entered into the AIS. The main activities conducted by the order entry function are described in the following sub-sections, after which we cover the controls usually associated with the function.

Initial Order Receipt

A customer order may arrive in a company through several different avenues, which are as follows:

- *From a salesperson.* A salesperson could take the order, writing it down on an in-house company order form. If so, the salesperson is aware of the data required to process an order, and so is likely to have supplied everything needed for data entry. Even so, the order entry staff must transfer this information to the order entry system, looking for any missing or incorrect data. An alternative is for the salesperson to enter the order directly into the system via a network connection, perhaps using a wireless tablet computer that has a direct link into the AIS. If so, the system will perform most data checks automatically, requiring little or no additional input from the order entry staff.
- *From a purchase order.* The customer may create a purchase order and send it to the company. If so, the data on this document needs to be manually transferred to the order entry system. It is quite possible that the purchase

116

order will not contain every data item needed, so the order entry staff may need to make inquiries with the customer.

- *From customer entry into a web page.* If the company provides a web page to its customers, they can fill out the online form to place an order, bypassing any need for the manual transfer of data to the AIS. These online forms can be a powerful sales tool for a company if they are designed to allow customers to create customized product configurations, or to suggest that associated products be purchased at the same time. For example, a camera store's AIS may see that a customer has selected a particular type of camera, and then suggests that the person also buy various filters, batteries, and memory cards to go along with the camera.

Note: An added advantage of allowing customers to make customized orders directly through an online form is that the company is justified in charging for payment in advance. Doing so greatly improves the organization's cash flow, since money is now available to acquire inventory and pay for processing costs. When orders are placed for standard products, customers are much more likely to demand delayed payment terms.

When orders are entered directly into the system, either by customers or salespeople, the system can be configured to automatically review all data entered and require changes as needed at the point of data entry. When the system is more manual, data are usually transferred only from a standard sales order form, such as the one that appears in the following exhibit. The form should always be assigned a unique identification number, so that it can be tracked. If the company pays commissions, there should also be a space on the form to state the name of the person who is being credited with the sale.

Sample Sales Order Form

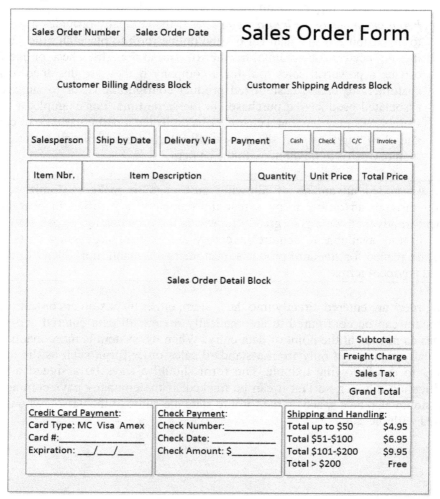

The sample form includes a considerable amount of payment information, which is only needed if the order entry staff is also responsible for accepting payments from customers. In situations where customers are always invoiced, there is no need for this information on the sales order form.

If multiple copies of a sales order are to be issued, it may not be wise to include credit card information on the sales order, since this information will be spread throughout the company. An alternative is to use a stamp on just the order entry department's copy of the sales order, on which are noted the credit card payment details.

When customer order data are instead being entered directly into a computer, the fields appearing in the preceding sales order form are approximately replicated on the screen, with some variations to increase the efficiency of the data entry process.

In general, an AIS should be designed to emphasize the error-free entry of customer orders into the system. An additional enhancement is to configure the system so that customers can enter their orders directly into the system; if this is made available, a further enhancement is to present customers with additional purchasing opportunities as they place their orders, thereby increasing sales.

Credit Investigation

When a company is selling standardized goods to another business, it is quite likely that the sales will be made on credit. If so, there is a significant probability that some customers will not pay, resulting in bad debts. The risk of bad debts can be controlled to some extent through the AIS, but a large part of it is a judgment call for management. They can choose to grant more credit to weak customers in order to generate more sales (though at the risk of a significant increase in bad debts) or grant credit only to the most qualified customers in order to reduce bad debts (which will reduce the amount of sales generated). Granting more credit to weak customers is most viable in a robust economy where many companies are doing well, but can be increasingly risky when the economy becomes weaker, making it more difficult for poor performers to pay their bills.

For the purposes of this discussion, we will focus only on the ways in which an AIS can be employed in the credit granting process. When a customer is new, and so is applying for credit the first time, the AIS should be configured so that any credit amount requested by the customer will be automatically forwarded to the credit department for review. Until a credit review has been completed and a credit amount entered into the system, the customer's order is put on hold. To avoid an excessive amount of work, the credit department may set the AIS to automatically grant a small amount of credit, such as $1,000, to every new customer without any review. Doing so improves the flow of small orders through the system and concentrates the attention of the credit department on larger credit requests, where the company is at greater risk of incurring significant bad debt losses. Once a review has been conducted, the credit staff enters an authorized maximum amount of credit into the system. The AIS then compares the outstanding order amount to this maximum credit level, and flags the order for further processing if it is for less than the authorized amount of credit. If the order amount is for greater than the authorized credit level, then the system will notify the order entry staff to contact the customer and request advance payment for the difference.

When an order comes from an existing customer with an established credit limit, the system automatically subtracts any unpaid receivable balances for the customer from the credit limit to see how much credit is still available, and then compares this amount to the total for the new order. If there is still sufficient credit remaining, then the order is flagged for further processing. If not, the order is forwarded to the credit department to see if they want to grant a one-time credit waiver to allow the order, or to permanently increase the credit limit to cover the amount of the order, or to deny the order. In the latter case, the order entry staff needs to contact the customer to request advance payment for the amount by which the order exceeds the available credit limit. A variation for the order entry staff is to encourage the customer to pay down any outstanding receivable balance, rather than making an advance payment, thereby increasing the amount of available credit.

To ease the task of granting credit, the AIS can aggregate key information about each customer and present it to the credit staff. This information may include:

- Current credit limit
- Payment terms
- Amount of receivables within payment terms
- Amount of receivables more than 30 days overdue
- Trend line of average days to pay
- Internal credit rating (compiled by the system)
- External credit rating (imported from an outside credit rating service)

A more detailed form of analysis available from the system is the *accounts receivable aging report*, which lists unpaid customer invoices and unused credit memos by date ranges. A perusal of this report can direct attention to specific overdue invoices. A sample aging report appears in the following exhibit.

Sample Accounts Receivable Aging Report

Angus Corp.	Amount	Current	1-30 Days Past Due	31-60 Days Past Due	61+ Days Past Due
Invoice #3552	$10,400.20	$10,400.20			
Invoice #3472	5,678.50		$5,678.50		
Invoice #3310	7,825.25			$7,825.25	
Invoice #3291	2,058.40				$2,058.40
Totals	$25,962.35	$10,400.20	$5,678.50	$7,825.25	$2,058.40

Inventory Status Review

When a customer places an order for the delivery of goods, the order entry staff checks the system to see if there are enough units on hand to deliver to the customer. The AIS does so by calling up the amount of finished goods on hand and subtracting out any units that have already been promised to other customers, but which have not yet shipped. In addition, if there are more units scheduled for production or to be acquired from suppliers, then the system adds these units to the availability total (adjusted for the dates on which they are expected to be available for shipment). With this information in hand, the order entry staff can then give customers a reasonably firm expected ship date. This process can be automated, so that customers entering their own orders through an online form can also access an expected shipment date.

In cases where there not enough units available for shipment, the system can present the customer with alternative products that are similar to the ones being ordered, and which are currently available for shipment. By doing so, the company may be able to preserve a sale that would otherwise be lost to a competitor.

When a customer order is finalized, the units committed to that order are then subtracted from the remaining available balance for the affected units, which reduces the amount available for subsequent orders from other customers.

If the customer is told that the requested units are not available and will be back ordered, then the system notifies the production scheduler that the units should be added to the short-term production schedule. If the goods are instead ordered from a supplier, then the system routes a purchase request to the purchasing department, which issues a purchase order to the relevant supplier(s).

Customer Inquiries

Customers can be expected to routinely contact the order entry staff about the status of their orders, or to make changes to those orders. Employees should be able to give accurate responses to customers within a very short period of time, or else there will be a risk of losing repeat business from them. The system can be configured to present customer information to the order entry staff that is most likely to be asked about by customers, such as the following:

- Order status
- Remaining credit limit balance
- Unpaid receivable balance

The system can also be configured to allow customers direct access to it, so that they can look up this information themselves, and possibly make modifications to unfulfilled orders. The customer portal may also include a frequently asked questions page that will resolve the majority of the questions that customers may have.

Order Entry Controls

The most critical controls related to the order entry function are as follows:

- *Order authorization.* In rare cases, a customer may deny that it ever authorized the purchase of goods or services, and so will not pay for them. This risk can be averted by enforcing the use of digital signatures on electronic purchase orders, or by keeping the signatures of authorized persons on file (which can be matched against the signatures on purchase orders) or by contacting customers to confirm the receipt of orders.
- *Data completeness.* The system should be configured to scan data entry fields to ensure that all required fields have been completed before an order is accepted. The system can also pull in some data that it already has on file, thereby reducing the amount of data entry required. For example, entering a customer number will access the related account information for that customer in the customer master file, eliminating the need to enter ship-to and bill-to addresses. A more advanced AIS can also compare the ordered amount to a customer's order history, to see if the unit quantity in the current order is reasonable. Without these automated actions, it may be neces-

sary to spend more time entering an order into the system, and may require additional contacts with customers, which delays the fulfillment process and annoys customers.

- *Access restrictions.* Tightly control access to the customer master file, since data are being pulled from this file and inserted into sales orders by the system. If the data in this master file are corrupted, it can have a major impact on downstream operations in the sales cycle, which rely on the existence of a perfectly accurate order entry system on the front end of the cycle.

- *Credit authorization.* A credit department is made responsible for monitoring the amount of credit granted to customers. The warehouse is not allowed to ship goods to customers without the prior approval of the credit department. This usually means that a credit flag or stamp is associated with each customer order when it has been approved for shipment. When a new sale will exceed the preset credit limit for a customer, the approval of the credit manager is required before the order can ship. The sales staff should *not* be given the power to grant credit, since they have an incentive to grant credit to everyone in order to earn a commission.

- *Chain of command.* The credit manager should not work for the sales department, since the sales manager will likely try to pressure the credit manager into granting credit to financially weak customers in order to secure sales. A better approach is to have the credit manager report to the treasurer, chief financial officer, or controller; these individuals are more focused on cash flow and profits than sales, and so will be more supportive of the credit function.

- *Receivable monitoring.* A collections group within the accounting department is responsible for routinely monitoring overdue receivables, following up with customers to secure payment, and notifying the credit department of any problems encountered. Doing so may result in adjustments to the amount of credit granted to customers.

- *Reporting.* The AIS can be configured to generate a number of status reports related to the order entry function, which are primarily designed to detect variances from historical trends. For example, reports can show the trend of orders by salesperson, product line, product, region, and distribution channel. A variation is to issue these same reports for the gross margins of orders. In either case, management can gain insights into how sales are changing over time.

Shipping Activities

The shipping function involves picking goods from stock, aggregating them into a completed customer order, and shipping them to the customer. The beginning of this process is the *picking ticket*, which is generated by the system and printed out in the warehouse. This document states the items, quantities, and inventory locations of the items that have been ordered by a customer. The ticket may be sorted in an order that minimizes the travel time of the person assigned to take the items from the warehouse shelves. A warehouse employee then walks through the warehouse and picks the designated items, noting on the ticket which items have been picked. A wireless bar code scanner may be used to scan these items as they are picked, thereby removing them from the relevant warehouse locations in the system and tagging them as being ready to ship. Alternatively, the information on completed picking tickets can be manually entered into the system, thereby reducing the on-hand inventory balances.

There are more efficient ways to engage in picking. For example, *zone picking* involves combining groups of customer orders into a master batch, so that multiple orders are picked at the same time. Doing so vastly reduces the travel time required to pick goods for orders. Inventory pickers then forward their picked items to a central packing location, where the items are separated and matched to specific customer orders. Not only does this approach reduce travel time, but it also reduces the number of inventory transactions to be recorded, since picks are being conducted for multiple units at the same time.

The person responsible for packing and shipping orders to customers will first ensure that the items delivered from the warehouse match the amounts stated on the picking ticket. She then enters the ticket number into the system, which automatically calls up the sales order number, item numbers, and unit quantities to be shipped. After verifying that this information is correct, the shipper then prints a packing slip and bill of lading for the shipment.

A *packing slip* describes the contents of a delivery of goods to a customer. It is usually attached to the outside of a shipment, so that the receiving staff at the customer can easily access it. The packing slip identifies each item delivered, as well as the quantity shipped, and may also note any items that are still on backorder. The document should also refer to the order number under which the customer originally ordered the goods. A sample packing slip format follows.

Sample Packing Slip

A *bill of lading* documents the type and quantity of goods being sent from a seller to a buyer. It is included with the shipment. The document also details the method of shipment and how it will be routed, and can be used as a receipt for the cargo. A bill of lading can be used as proof of ownership of the goods being moved. A sample bill of lading appears in the following exhibit.

Sample Bill of Lading

STRAIGHT BILL OF LADING - SHORT FORM		
Carrier Name: Carrier Address: City State and Zip: SAC	Phone Date DUNS	SHIPMENT IDENTIFICATION NO. FREIGHT BILL PRO NO.
		TRAILER/CAR NUMBER
TO: Consignee Address City State and Zip	ROUTE	
FROM: Shipper Address City State and zip	SPECIAL INSTRUCTIONS	
FOR PAYMENT SEND BILL TO: Name Address City State & Zip	SHIPPER'S INTERNAL DATA SID NO.	

Number Shipping Units	*HQ	Kinds of Packaging, Description of Articles, Special Marks and Exceptions	Code	Weight Subject to Correction	Rate	Charges

REMIT C.O.D. TO Address City State & zip	**COD** AMT: $	C.O.D. FEE		
	Subject to Section 7 of conditions, if this shipment is o be delivered to the consignee without recourse on the consignor, the consignor shall sign the following statement:	PREPAID ☐ $ COLLECT ☐ $ TOTAL CHARGES $		
NOTE - Where the rate is dependant on value, shippers are required to state specifically in writing the agreed or declared value of the property. The agreed or declared value of the property is hereby specifically stated by the shipper to be not exceeding	The carrier shall not make delivery of this shipment without payment of freight and all other lawful charges.	FREIGHT CHARGES ARE PREPAID UNLESS MARKED COLLECT		
$ per	Signature of Consignor	CHECK BOX IF COLLECT ☐		

RECEIVED, subject to the classifications and lawfully filed tariffs in effect on the date of the issue of this Bill of Lading, the property described above in apparent good order, except as noted (contents and conditions of contents of packages unknown), marked consigned and destined as indicated above which said carrier (the word carrier being understood throughout this contract as meaning any person or corporation in possession of the property under the contract) agrees to carry to its usual place of delivery at said destination, if on its route, otherwise to deliver to another carrier on the route to its destination. It is mutually agreed as to each carrier of all or any of the said property, over all or any portion of said route to destination and as to each party at any time interested in all or any of said property, that every service to be performed hereunder shall be subject to the bill of lading terms and conditions in the governing classification on the date of shipment. Shipper hereby certifies that he is familiar with all the bill of lading terms and conditions in the governing classification and the said terms and conditions are hereby agreed to by the shipper and accepted for himself and his assigns.

SHIPPER PER	CARRIER PER

* Mark "X" or "RQ" if appropriate to designate Hazardous Materials as defined in the Department of Transport Regulations governing the transportation of hazardous materials. The use of this column is an optional method for identifying hazardous materials on bills of lading per Section172.201(a)(1)(iii) of Title 49, Code of Federal Regulations. Also, when shipping hazardous materials the shipper's certification statement prescribed in Section 172.204(a) of the Federal Regulations must be indicated on the bill of lading, unless a specific exemption from this requirement is provided in the Regulations for a particular material.

The most critical controls related to the shipping function are as follows:

- *Perpetual inventory.* There should be a *perpetual inventory* record keeping system in place, so that all inventory transactions are immediately updated in the inventory record file. Doing so ensures that the book inventory matches the actual inventory, so that delivery promises are made to customers based on reliable on-hand quantities.
- *Cycle counting.* There is an ongoing cycle counting program, where a small portion of the inventory is counted every day. Any errors found are used to correct the inventory record file, thereby enhancing the accuracy of the file.
- *Bar coding.* Inventory items and locations are stored on bar codes, which are scanned whenever there is an inventory transaction. Bar codes are much more accurate than manual data entry, thereby lowering the risk of errors creeping into the inventory record file.
- *Warehouse fencing.* Access to the inventory is restricted by constructing a fence around the inventory storage area, with access controlled through a single warehouse gate.
- *Packing verifications.* At the point where picked items are packed for shipment to the customer, someone can compare the amounts stated on a picking ticket to what is being inserted into a shipping container, to ensure that what the customer ordered is actually being shipped.
- *Shipping verification.* The system should automatically compare the ship-to address stated on the sales order to the ship-to address for which a bill of lading has been created, and flag any instances in which the two addresses are different. Any variances should be investigated, to ensure that deliveries are made to the correct addresses.
- *Reconciliations.* The internal audit staff periodically reconciles shipping documents with the originating customer purchase orders, in-house sales orders, picking lists, and packing slips to see if errors occurred anywhere in the sales cycle. Any errors found are reviewed to see if additional controls or training should be implemented to minimize the risk of a recurrence.
- *Sales order cancellation.* If a company is manually processing its sales orders through the picking and shipping stages, it is possible that a sales order will be erroneously fulfilled and shipped more than once. To prevent this, sequentially number all sales orders and staple a copy of the shipping documents to it once a shipment has been issued. Doing so prevents the sales order from being fulfilled again.
- *Reporting.* An AIS can be configured to report on variances between actual and book inventory quantities, which can focus attention on the process failures causing these variances to occur. The reporting can be summarized for specific locations within the warehouse, or by product, or even by inventory picker, which may be useful for researching the reasons for variances.

The main emphasis for shipping controls is to ensure that there are no inventory stockout situations, where a customer is informed that inventory is not actually available, and so will be delivered (if at all) later than expected. The avoidance of stockout situations requires extremely accurate inventory records that properly reflect the actual unit quantities on hand.

Billing Activities

The billing function involves issuing an invoice to the customer as soon as possible after goods have been shipped or services provided. Rapid issuance is needed in order to accelerate cash flow, since the customer will pay the invoice within the payment terms stated on the invoice, which begins as of the invoice date. For example, if the payment terms state that the customer will pay in 30 days, and the invoice date is March 1, then the customer can be expected to issue payment by the end of March. However, if the billing clerk delays issuing an invoice until March 11, then the customer's payment back to the company will be correspondingly delayed by 10 days. This delay reduces the amount of cash that the company has on hand to deal with its own liabilities, which increases its risk of defaulting on its obligations.

The billing preparation process uses a selection of the data associated with a customer's sales order, as well as data about the items shipped to the customer. All of the information needed for an invoice can be extracted from the AIS. The invoice states the amount to be paid and where to send payment, along with a variety of other information that is intended to assist the customer in processing payment.

The AIS always contains a standard invoice template, which most businesses use with only minor adjustments to bill their customers. The typical invoice contains the following information:

- *Header section*. Itemizes the billing address of the seller and customer, as well as the invoice number, invoice date, and payment due date. There may also be space for the name of the salesperson (if any), which is used for contact information and calculating salesperson commissions.
- *Billing detail block*. Lists each item sold to the customer, including the description, unit price, quantity, and extended price.
- *Summary section*. This is an extension of the billing detail block, in which all items sold are summarized. A freight charge and sales tax may be added, to arrive at a total invoice amount.

It may be useful to make a few modifications to the template to reduce the time required to receive payments from customers, as well as to reduce the number of customer payment errors. Recommended modifications are noted in the following exhibit.

Invoice Format Changes

Credit card contact information	If customers want to pay with a credit card, include a telephone number to call to pay by this means.
Early payment discount	State the exact amount of the early payment discount and the exact date by which the customer must pay in order to qualify for the discount.
General contact information	If customers have a question about the invoice, there should be a contact information block that states the telephone number and e-mail address they should contact.
Payment due date	Rather than entering payment terms on the invoice (such as "net 30"), state the exact date on which payment is due. This should be stated prominently.

The goal in creating an invoice format is to present the minimum amount of information to the customer in order to prevent confusion, while presenting the required information as clearly as possible. The following sample invoice template incorporates the invoice format changes that we just addressed.

An alternative to the issuance of invoices when goods are shipped is *cycle billing*, where invoices are issued to customers on a rotating basis. For example, customers whose last names begin with A through G are billed during the first week of the month, followed in the next week by those customers whose last names begin with H through M, and so forth. By engaging in cycle billing, a business can flatten the volume of billing work to be completed on any given day. This practice is most commonly used by organizations that have many customers and massive billing operations, such as utilities.

A more efficient variation on the billing process is to send an electronic notification straight into the computer system of the customer or via an intermediary electronic mailbox that is regularly polled by the customer's computer system. The most common methodology is called *electronic data interchange* (EDI), where one trading partner creates a transaction in a standard format and sends it to an electronic mailbox, from which another trading partner downloads the information for its own use. Ideally, these transactions are automatically created and read by the sending and receiving parties, respectively. The result is a paperless exchange of information at high speed, since there is effectively no transit time between the parties. The transactions most commonly used in an EDI system are purchase orders and invoices. These systems are mostly used by larger organizations, since they are better able to afford the installation and integration of an EDI module into their in-house systems.

Sample Invoice Template

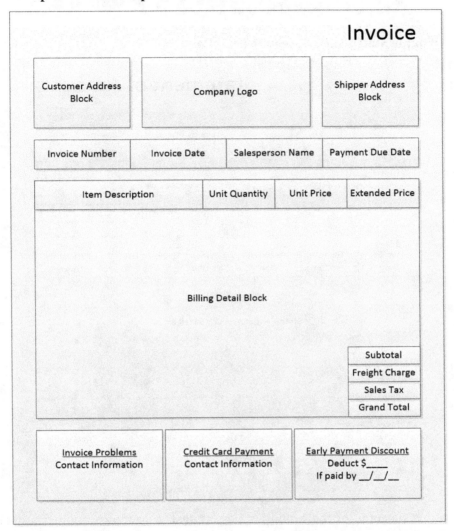

In addition to the issuance of invoices, the billing staff is also responsible for issuing periodic statements of account to customers. The *statement of account* summarizes all open invoices remaining as of the statement date. It is also quite useful to include any customer payments that have not yet been assigned to an invoice, since this may prompt a contact from the customer, informing the accounting staff of how to assign a payment. There may be time buckets at the bottom of the statement, showing whether any invoices are overdue for payment; customers can glance at these time buckets to see if any invoices are overdue, and will then be more likely to delve into the statement in greater detail. Finally, the statement should be constructed to have a tear-away section that can be used as a remittance advice (see the next section), so that customers can pay directly from the statement. A sample statement of account template follows.

Sample Statement of Account Template

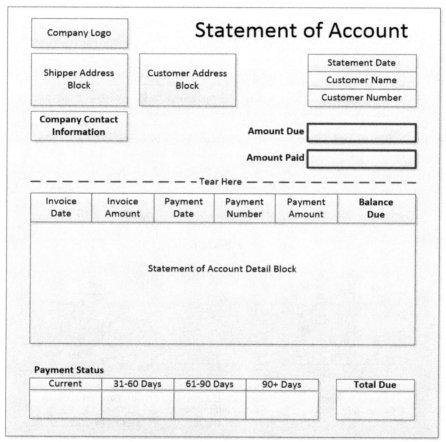

A possible outcome of the billing process is that a customer complains about a specific problem, resulting in the issuance of a credit memo to reduce its outstanding receivable balance. A *credit memo* is a contraction of the term "credit memorandum," which is a document issued to the customer, reducing the amount that the buyer owes to the seller. A credit memo may be issued because the customer returned goods to the company, or there is a pricing dispute, or a marketing allowance, and so forth. The seller records the credit memo as a reduction of its accounts receivable balance.

There are several varieties of credit memo, each one serving a different purpose. They are:

- *Specific credit.* A credit may be granted for a specific product return, price adjustment, or other reason related to the contents of an invoice. If so, the customer may be waiting for a detailed credit memo that it will refer to in its payment of an invoice. This type of credit memo calls for a format that states specifically what happened. It must contain a unique identifying number, which the customer can reference when it uses the credit as a deduction from a payment. The credit should also contain a field for a reason code, as well as the number of units returned. In all other respects, other than payment information and freight charges, the credit memo format is the same as the invoice format. A sample credit memo template follows.

Sample Credit Memo Template

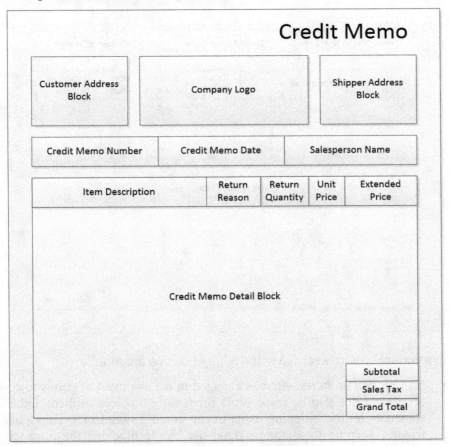

- *Internal credit memo.* Whenever the company writes off an account balance due to customer nonpayment, it should still create a credit memo, but it does

131

not mail the document to the customer. Otherwise, the customer may use the credit to offset some other payment. Many accounting systems provide for an internal credit memo, along with a separate form that clearly states the nature of the transaction. In this case, the key point is that the form state that it is an internal credit memo, and that it is not to be mailed to the customer. A sample template follows.

Sample Internal Credit Memo Template

Internal Credit Memo

Customer Address Block	Company Logo	Shipper Address Block

Credit Memo Number	Credit Memo Date	Salesperson Name

Item Description	Return Reason	Return Quantity	Unit Price	Extended Price

Credit Memo Detail Block

Do Not Mail

	Subtotal
	Sales Tax
	Grand Total

The most critical controls related to the billing function are as follows:

- *Segregation of duties*. Anyone engaged in the shipment of goods to customers should not also be responsible for issuing invoices to them. Otherwise, someone in the shipping department could fraudulently ship goods to friends, keeping them for personal use, while blocking the issuance of a related invoice or being able to issue an offsetting credit memo.
- *Authorizations*. A supervisor should approve all credit memos issued above a certain threshold level. By doing so, an accounting clerk cannot intercept

incoming payments from customers and then hide the theft by issuing a credit memo.

- *Automatic credit memo blocking.* The system may be configured to automatically block the processing of credit memos unless the receiving department has processed an offsetting returned product delivery from the customer. Once blocked, a credit memo must be authorized by a supervisor, thereby concentrating management attention on those cases in which the customer is being allowed to retain goods while still being issued a credit.
- *Automatic price posting.* The system is configured to automatically enter prices in the pricing fields on invoices from the pricing master file. Doing so eliminates the risk that prices will be incorrectly entered into invoices. Further, access to the pricing master file should be strictly controlled, to minimize the risk of unauthorized pricing changes. In addition, set up a change log for this file and review it regularly, to determine whether prices have been altered.
- *Statement issuance.* The accounting department issues month-end statements to all customers that have an outstanding balance. If customers compare these statements to their own records, they may spot discrepancies that indicate the presence of fraud or mistakes within the company. The contact information listed on these statements should route inquiries to someone other than the billing clerk, since this clerk is the person most likely to be engaged in fraudulent activities.
- *Reconciliations.* The internal audit staff periodically reconciles the invoices issued with customer purchase orders, sales orders, and shipping documentation to ensure that all goods delivered and services provided have also been invoiced. Any errors found are reviewed to see if additional controls or training should be implemented to minimize the risk of a recurrence. A useful tool in this process is to configure the AIS to periodically report on any deliveries for which there is no associated invoice.
- *Additional fee review.* An invoice may have sales taxes and/or shipping and handling charges associated with it. The internal audit staff can periodically review these amounts on invoices to see if they have been properly calculated.

The most crucial of the preceding controls is the periodic reconciliation process, to ensure that all shipments are invoiced. If any deliveries do not trigger an invoice issuance, then the company will lose the revenue that would otherwise have been generated.

Cash Collection Activities

The process used to collect cash from customers can follow one of two paths. The most prudent approach from a control perspective is to have customers send their payments either electronically or to a lockbox that is operated by the company's bank. This direct routing keeps cash off the company's premises, thereby eliminating the risk of theft by employees. The alternative is to process all incoming customer payments through the company's mailroom. The mailroom staff opens the mail and forwards all payments to the cash receipts clerk, who logs them into the AIS. More specifically, the clerk matches cash receipts against the individual invoices being paid, so that the cash asset increases in the general ledger and the accounts receivable asset declines by a comparable amount. This identification process is made easier if the customer includes a remittance advice with its payment. A *remittance advice* provides details about which invoices are being paid by the customer, and also identifies the customer. This advice usually comes in the form of a tear-away document that is attached to a check, but can also arrive within an email, especially when the payment being made is electronic. A more basic variation on the concept is for the company to issue two copies of each invoice to its customers, with a request to return one copy along with the payment, in order to identify the invoice with which the payment is paired.

Once all payments have been recorded in the system, the cash receipts clerk prepares a bank deposit slip for the cash to be transported to the bank, and then delivers a copy of the deposit slip and the cash to a courier, who transports it to the bank. A more efficient approach involves *remote deposit capture*, where the clerk uses a special check scanner and scanning software to create an electronic image of each check to be deposited. The clerk then transmits the scanned check information to the bank, instead of making a physical deposit. The bank accepts the electronic information, and posts funds to the company's account. Remote deposit capture is useful for eliminating the physical delivery of checks to the bank, which also makes it possible to use a bank located anywhere – it no longer has to be physically close to the company.

Several issues that can arise during the cash collection process are as follows:

- *Early payment discounts*. Customers may take a discount from the stated amount of an invoice, because they paid early. This discount must be charged to a discounts taken account, so that the full amount of the affected account receivable is removed from the aged receivables report.
- *Unidentified payments*. It is quite common for some customer payments to not be clearly traceable to a specific receivable. If so, the cash receipts clerk initially charges the cash to a receivables suspense account. When additional research identifies the relevant invoice being paid, the payment is shifted out of the suspense account and charged to the accounts receivable account instead.

The most critical controls related to the cash collection function are as follows:

- *Segregation of duties*. Anyone engaged in the receipt of customer payments should not also record these receipts or issue credit memos. Otherwise, the person could use these additional activities to hide the theft of cash. In addition, the person who performs periodic bank reconciliations should not be the cash receipts clerk, to ensure that a third party has oversight over the activities of the clerk.

- *Lockboxes.* Customers should be encouraged to send their payments to a bank lockbox, so that their payments never appear on the premises of the company. Instead, the bank operating the lockbox deposits the cash directly into the company's account and sends an electronic notice to the accounting department that details the amounts deposited. Doing so eliminates the risk of employee theft of customer payments.

- *Check listing.* Have two mailroom staff open all mail and create a listing of all checks received. Having two people perform this function minimizes the risk of cash being stolen in the mailroom. In addition, the check listing can be compared to the cash receipts posting later made by the cash receipts clerk, to see if the clerk removed any cash.

- *Cash registers.* If the company operates a retail store, enforce the use of cash registers, which are designed to document the receipt and disbursement of cash. Cash registers make it more difficult for sales clerks to steal cash.

- *Batch totals.* Customer payments are frequently delivered to the cash receipts clerk in a single batch from the mailroom, and so are processed by the clerk in a single batch. The total dollar amount of the checks processed should match the total resulting reduction in accounts receivable. If not, the decline in receivables will probably be less than the dollar amount of the checks processed, indicating that some of the cash received was not applied.

- *Restrictive endorsement.* As soon as checks are received from customers, stamp them as being for deposit only to the company's bank account. Doing so keeps them from being diverted and deposited into a different bank account.

- *Daily deposits.* Send someone to the bank every day with the day's cash receipts. Doing so removes the cash from the premises, thereby eliminating the risk of overnight cash theft.

The optimum method for processing cash collections is to have customers send their payments to a bank lockbox. Doing so completely eliminates the risk of having cash stolen from the company premises, since it is never there. In addition, remittances straight to a lockbox typically reduce the delay before these payments are made available for use by the company, since the intermediate routing through the company is eliminated.

Summary

The sales cycle needs to be designed for a high degree of efficiency and effectiveness, since it absorbs a significant amount of staff time to operate properly. In addition, all sales cycle processes need to be configured with a full set of controls, to ensure that customer orders are fulfilled, invoices are issued both correctly and in a timely manner, and the related cash receipts are processed correctly. The controls used should also deter fraudulent activity, since there would otherwise be a significant risk of asset loss.

The data collected during the sales cycle is routinely used to trigger transactions elsewhere in a business, such as the expenditure cycle that is discussed in the next chapter. Thus, the sales cycle is usually considered the foundation transaction cycle upon which all of the processes in a business are based.

Chapter 10
The Expenditure Cycle

Introduction

The expenditure cycle is the set of activities related to the acquisition of and payment for goods and services. These activities include the determination of what needs to be purchased, purchasing activities, the receipt of goods, and payments to suppliers. Much of the input to the expenditure cycle comes from the sales cycle that we discussed in the last chapter, where purchasing requirements are driven by the volume and type of customer orders. An accounting information system (AIS) is designed to support each of these activities, so that there is a well-planned purchasing process that minimizes the risk of interruptions in the production process and the delivery of goods to customers. In this chapter, we discuss the information system flows associated with each set of activities that comprise the expenditure cycle, including the most essential controls associated with each one.

Expenditure Cycle Overview

The expenditure cycle is comprised of several distinct components, including the requisition of goods and services, supplier selection, the ordering of goods and services, their receipt, and subsequent payment for them. Though these are all distinct activities that are usually completed by different people within a company, it is useful to see how the overall process flows. In this section, we provide an overview of every part of the expenditure cycle, indicating how information flows between them. The full expenditure cycle for an AIS contains the following activities:

1. Determine which goods and services need to be ordered. Most goods to be ordered are needed by the production process. To do so, the system calculates the components that need to be on hand for scheduled production and subtracts out on-hand and unallocated raw materials to arrive at the amounts that must be acquired. Alternatively, if goods or services are needed for a selling or administrative function, the user fills out a requisition form that details her requirements and forwards it to the purchasing department.
2. When goods are being purchased for ongoing production, the system will present the purchasing staff with a preliminary purchase order, using the preferred supplier stated in the inventory master file for each item to be purchased. The purchasing staff reviews and approves these orders, which are then either sent electronically direct to suppliers, or printed and mailed to them.

3. When non-standard goods and services are being requested, the purchasing staff investigates possible suppliers, selects the best one, and issues them a purchase order.
4. As goods are received, the receiving department accesses open purchase orders in the system and enters the quantities received.
5. When supplier invoices are received, they are logged into the system by the accounts payable staff. The system then compares these invoices to the authorizing purchase orders and receiving information to determine whether the invoices can be paid. There can be a significant amount of manual reconciliation work at this stage. The outcome is a set of invoices that have been approved for payment.
6. The system schedules payments to suppliers based on the predetermined payment terms with each one. When a scheduled payment date arrives, the system processes a batch of payments, which will either be in the form of electronic funds transfers or checks.

The preceding activities are the primary components of the expenditure cycle. The AIS is a key component of the cycle, since it is the main repository of the data used in each step of the process. Consequently, the AIS needs to be protected from a number of threats in order to keep the cycle from being corrupted with incorrect data. When there is incorrect data in the system, a business could be subject to any of the following failures:

- Purchases could be placed with unapproved suppliers.
- Goods may be ordered that are of substandard quality.
- Goods may be delivered to the wrong location or on the wrong date.
- Goods may be ordered in excessive quantities.
- Unordered items are accepted by the receiving staff.
- Payments could be made to fictitious suppliers.
- Supplier invoices are paid more than once.
- Supplier invoices with incorrect unit prices or quantities are paid.
- Available discounts are not taken.
- Available credit memos are not used to reduce payments.
- Confidential information related to banking information is revealed to unauthorized parties.
- Data are destroyed within the system, and there is no backup.

The preceding failures could easily result in significant overpayments or problems with goods that result in delayed or substandard finished products.

Purchasing Activities

The purchasing function is comprised of multiple activities, including ordering systems, supplier analysis, competitive bidding processes, procurement card management, and much more. These activities are described in the following subsections.

Materials Ordering Systems

The most significant input to the purchasing process for a manufacturing business is the materials ordering system. This system compiles the number of units that must be ordered so that the production system can meet its due dates. There are several ways in which material requirements can be compiled, as noted in the following bullet points:

- *Two-bin inventory control*. This system involves the storage of goods in two bins, one of which contains working stock, while the other contains reserve stock. The amount of inventory kept in the reserve stock bin equals the amount the company expects to use during the ordering lead time associated with that item. One should reorder goods as soon as the working stock bin is empty, so that replacement parts arrive before the reserve stock bin is empty. The calculation for the amount of inventory to keep in the reserve stock bin is:

  (Daily usage rate × Lead time) + Safety stock = Reserve bin quantity

  In the preceding calculation, *lead time* is the sum of the time required to place a replenishment order and for the supplier to deliver the ordered goods. *Safety stock* is excess inventory that acts as a buffer between forecasted and actual demand levels. This inventory is maintained so that a company has sufficient units on hand to meet unexpected customer and production demand. The safety stock formula is:

  (Maximum daily usage – Average daily usage) × Lead time = Safety stock

---

EXAMPLE

Vegas Manufacturing Corporation experiences weekly usage of 500 units of its micro cell phone battery, so the daily usage rate is 100 units. The lead time to acquire the battery is three days. The reserve storage bin should contain at least 300 batteries, to cover expected usage during the three-day lead time. In addition, the company assumes that usage levels can vary by as much as 25% from the average usage rate. Consequently, 75 additional batteries are kept in the reserve storage bin. This is calculated as 300 reserve units × 25% safety stock allowance. Thus, the total reserve stock is 375 units.

Two-bin inventory control is commonly used for low-value items that can be purchased and stored in bulk, and for which stocks are maintained in the production area, rather than the warehouse. This system tends to result in a larger investment in inventory, but can be operated manually. A potential risk when using it is that parts may be re-ordered even when there is no further need for them.

- *Material requirements planning (MRP).* This system uses bills of material[4], inventory records, and a production schedule[5] to forecast and order materials, so that the materials needed for scheduled production are available in the correct quantities and on the correct dates. The process begins with a forecast of units expected to be sold, from which are subtracted the unit quantities of unallocated finished goods currently on hand, to arrive at the number of additional units of finished goods needed. These unit counts are then multiplied by their associated bills of material to arrive at the exact number of each type of raw materials needed to produce the required units. The on-hand balances of raw materials are subtracted from the calculated raw material requirements to arrive at the unit quantities of raw materials that must be purchased from suppliers. This system requires extremely high data accuracy in order to function properly, but can result in a significant reduction in the amount of inventory on hand. It works best in an environment where there are predictable demand patterns that can be incorporated into scheduled production.

EXAMPLE

Green Lawn Care produces electric lawn mowers. In its most recent sales forecast, the sales department projects that it will sell 1,000 units of its 40-volt cordless electric lawn mower. Green currently has 200 completed units of this product in stock, so an additional 800 units must be produced. According to the bill of materials for the product, each unit comes with four 8" plastic wheels, so 3,200 of these wheels will be needed to construct the required units. The system reviews the current parts inventory, and finds that there are 1,200 wheels currently in stock that have not been assigned to any current production jobs. When these 1,200 wheels are subtracted from the 3,200 required wheels, the company finds that it needs to order 2,000 additional wheels from a supplier. Further, the supplier has a 10-day lead time before it can deliver the wheels, so the production of the 800 needed units is set up in the production schedule for 10 business days from the current date.

- *Just-in-time (JIT).* This system is specifically designed to minimize inventory levels, and does so based on a cluster of lean manufacturing activities that are designed to only produce enough products to meet immediate

---

[4] A bill of materials is the record of the raw materials, sub-assemblies and supplies used to construct a product. It may also include an estimate of the scrap that will occur during the production process.

[5] A production schedule identifies in detail the work orders that will be processed through a manufacturing system, including unit quantities and production start dates.

customer demand. The system does so by pulling demand through a production facility, where each step in the process is only authorized to manufacture a limited amount of inventory. The system requires implementation of the following concepts:

- o *Pull concept.* Under JIT, each step in the production process is triggered by a notification, or *kanban*[6], that is provided to it by the downstream workstation that is a request for a specific quantity of an item. A workstation is only allowed to produce the exact amount of the authorization. This approach massively reduces the amount of work-in-process inventory.
- o *Lot sizes.* JIT advocates the use of very small production lot sizes, preferably of just one unit. This means that inventory moves through the production process in very small, discrete batches. As each lot is completed, it is immediately passed along to the next downstream workstation, thereby minimizing the amount of inventory between workstations.
- o *Machine setups.* JIT advocates small lot sizes, but this is impossible when it takes a long time to set up a machine for each production run. Consequently, there are many tools and concepts available for shortening machine setup times, which makes it cost-effective to quickly re-set a machine to manufacture even a single unit.
- o *Inventory movements.* When inventory lot sizes are small (as just described), it makes more sense to place them in small transport containers and move them to the next workstation via a conveyor belt. This eliminates a great deal of materials handling labor and equipment. This arrangement tends to result in workstations being positioned close together, to reduce the amount of travel time on the conveyors.
- o *Just-in-time deliveries.* A JIT system does not require much on-site inventory. Instead, a company using JIT requires its suppliers to make a large number of small deliveries, sometimes directly to where the parts are needed in the production process. This concept can nearly eliminate a firm's investment in raw materials inventory.

The JIT system can strip much of the inventory investment out of a business, but it can fail if supplier deliveries do not arrive when expected. Since the system does not use an inventory buffer, the production operation will stop if there is any hiccup in the supply chain that feeds it raw materials. The system works best in an environment where it is difficult to predict the demand for products, as is frequently the case when products have a short life cycle. In this situation, the system can rapidly ramp up to meet unexpected demand, while also being able to curtail production quickly to deal with sudden drops in demand.

---

[6] A kanban is an authorization to produce goods or withdraw goods from a supply bin. A kanban can take many forms, such as a colored card, an email, or a bin.

The key difference between the MRP and JIT systems is that an MRP system is designed to "push" production through the system in order to meet a forecast of estimated demand, while a JIT system is designed to "pull" production through the system based on actual customer orders. While the concepts underlying these systems are quite different, the end result in both cases is a substantial reduction in a firm's investment in inventory.

Non-Materials Ordering

The preceding discussion of ordering systems was focused on the ongoing purchase of goods related to the production process. In addition, employees may need to acquire other items, such as computer equipment or office furniture. In these situations, they complete a *purchase requisition* form to request that the purchasing department acquire goods and services. The form is designed to give the purchasing staff specific information about what is being ordered, including the suggested supplier, the catalog number used by the supplier for the item being ordered, and the price offered by that supplier. The form also includes space for a due date for each line item, which allows the requesting department to set different due dates for different items in the form. There is also space for a charge code for each line item, which keeps the purchasing staff from having to guess at where each purchase should be charged. Finally, the form contains a number of spaces for approval signatures, depending on the expense level of the item(s) being ordered. The budget approval signature is designed to ensure that there are sufficient funds in the budget to pay for the items being ordered. A sample requisition form appears in the following exhibit.

Sample Purchase Requisition

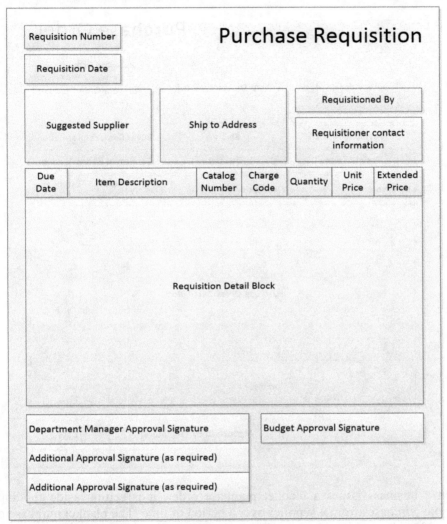

The Purchase Order

A *purchase order* is the primary document used by the purchasing department to order goods and services. A sample purchase order is shown in the following exhibit. It should specify a considerable amount of information in order to avoid confusion with the supplier. In addition to the usual itemization of items to be purchased and their price, the following sample purchase order also states the due date, both freight and payment terms, and a phone number to call to confirm receipt of the order.

Sample Purchase Order

Bill To Address Block		**Purchase Order**
Supplier Address Block	Ship To Address Block	Purchase Order Date
		Purchase Order Number

Payment Terms	Ship Via	Buyer Contact Information
Freight Terms	Due Date	Confirm to Phone Number

Item No.	Item Description	Quantity	Unit Price	Extended Price
	Purchase Order Detail Block			

Comments		Subtotal
		Sales Tax
		Grand Total

Authorized By: [signature]	Date

When a business issues a blanket purchase order, it is setting aside funding for multiple purchases from a supplier over a period of time. The blanket purchase order release form is used to order specific goods and services within the funding block set aside in the blanket purchase order. In the following sample release form, we see that it is quite similar to a standard purchase order form. However, standard contract terms (such as payment terms) are removed, with a reference back to the blanket purchase order, where the contract terms are located. Also, the release references the blanket order upon which it is based.

Sample Blanket Purchase Order Release

Blanket Order Release		

Bill To Address Block

Supplier Address Block	Ship To Address Block	Blanket Order Number
		Release Number
		Release Date

| Ship Via | Due Date | Buyer Contact Information | Confirm to Phone Number |

| Item No. | Item Description | Quantity | Unit Price | Extended Price |

Blanket Order Release Detail Block

	Subtotal
	Sales Tax
Blanket order terms and conditions apply to this release	Grand Total

| Authorized By: [signature] | Date |

Supplier Analysis

When a company operates a closely-coordinated production or fulfillment process, it depends on its suppliers to deliver goods and services exactly as needed. Otherwise, the company's reputation with its own customers suffers. This means that a business cannot afford to have low-quality suppliers – which it likely has if the historical approach to purchasing has been to award contracts to the lowest bidder. Instead, the purchasing department needs to evaluate suppliers based on many other criteria than just price. This evaluation may involve a lengthy process of examining, evaluating, and scoring each supplier before the best group of suppliers has been located. Once this selection process has been completed, a company can work on building long-term relations with its supplier base. Eventually, the core group of suppliers will be so closely associated with the business that there will be little chance of their being replaced by other suppliers. Thus, the supplier selection process should be viewed as the start of a long-term marriage.

What criteria are used when deciding whether to accept the services of a new supplier? There are many possibilities, some of which are specific to a particular industry. However, the following three general classifications of criteria will apply to most situations:

- *Finances*. A supplier must be not only solvent, but also have sufficient funding to pay for its own ongoing research programs and the capital spending needed to expand its production capacity as needed.
- *Capability*. A supplier must be able to service the company's needs after an order has been placed. One should consider a supplier's historical capacity levels, any plans to add capacity, its ability to fulfill rush orders, and whether it is hampered by a production bottleneck.
- *Responsiveness*. A supplier must be able to perform the tasks required by the company. This is the most difficult of the criteria to evaluate, since the related information is the most difficult to collect. A particular focus should be placed on the ability of the supplier to consistently deliver in a dependable manner. Responsiveness is an especially important criterion when a company is using a JIT system, and so needs to have frequent, timely deliveries from its suppliers.

Once suppliers are certified, orders are routed to them on a routine basis, possibly bypassing competitive bidding situations.

Competitive Bidding

When goods or services are being ordered for the first time and the purchase amount is quite high, it may be cost-effective for the purchasing staff to initiate a competitive bidding process. Under this arrangement, the department prepares a request for proposals (RFP) bid package that contains the specifications of the required goods or services, as well as delivery requirements, and issues it to a group of qualified suppliers. Once a bid package has been created, the purchasing department manages a tightly-choreographed bidding process. This process is intended to conclude the bidding process within a reasonable period of time, while also treating all participants in a fair and equitable manner. The process flow may include the following steps:

1. *Pre-bid conference*. A notice is issued to all suppliers likely to be interested, stating a time and place at which a pre-bid conference will be held. This meeting is used to go over the specifications and bidding requirements, as well as to discuss any other issues with the members of the company's bidding team.
2. *Bid package issuance*. The bid package is issued to all suppliers that have indicated an interest in receiving the documentation.
3. *Response receipts*. Those suppliers choosing to participate submit their proposals to the purchasing department. Their responses are logged in, so there is an official record of receipt.

4. *Bid opening*. No further bids are allowed after the predetermined bid closing date has passed. Shortly thereafter, all bids are opened, and their key contents are transferred to a summary sheet.
5. *Bid evaluation*. The detailed information from each bid is transferred into a summary comparison sheet, where the answers provided by suppliers are scored and multiplied by a weighting factor for each answer or aggregation of answers given. Based on the weighted results, a winning bidder is chosen.
6. *Contract creation*. The winning bidder is contacted, and the parties mutually craft a contract that is based on the terms stated in the successful bid.

Reverse Auctions

When the focus of a purchase is primarily on price, a company may set up a *reverse auction* with a pre-qualified group of suppliers. This is an on-line bidding situation in which suppliers can repeatedly bid their prices lower on a predefined set of criteria in order to obtain the lowest bid. The identities of the participating suppliers are kept confidential. Because of the nature of the process, it can result in substantial price reductions for the buyer.

Depending on the type of reverse auction system used, the following information will be available to all bidders:

- Actual bid prices that have been submitted; or
- The relative rankings of the bidders, based on their prices submitted

Bids will continue until no one is willing to bid any lower, or until a predetermined expiration time is reached.

Reverse auctions are usually confined to situations in which the items needed are fully commoditized, with no differentiating features by supplier, and with industry-standard specifications.

A reasonable concern posed by suppliers is that reverse auctions excessively focus on price. When a supplier prefers to compete on other factors than price (such as fast order turnaround), it is at a disadvantage in a reverse auction. Also, the use of reverse auctions sends the message that there will be no attempt by a company to build relations with a specific supplier – it just wants the best price.

Procurement Cards

Companies have found that the traditional use of purchase orders is not cost-effective for many smaller purchases, so they have instituted a procurement card system for these purchases. Procurement cards are company credit cards, and are given to a small number of authorized users to purchase low-cost items. When fully rolled out, a procurement card program can be used to deal with a substantial number of purchases, removing them from the purview of the purchasing department. However, use of the cards should be strictly controlled, to keep employees from using them to make excessive or inappropriate purchases.

Supplier-Managed Inventory

A company may choose to have a few suppliers take over the management of certain inventory items, such as all fittings and fasteners. To do so, these suppliers are given access to the warehouse area in order to review and replenish the inventory. This approach eliminates the cost of purchase order preparation, since suppliers handle replenishment tasks on a scheduled basis, with no further authorization by the company. However, the supplier may find ways to increase its prices, since it is incurring the additional cost of visiting the warehouse on a regular basis. An additional problem is that these inventory items may not be tracked within the company's inventory database.

Spend Management

Spend management is the process of collecting spend information, aggregating it to discern possible purchasing opportunities, acting on this information, and monitoring compliance with the new, better-managed purchasing process.

One aspect of spend management involves the aggregation of information about a company's expenditures into a database, which can then be sorted in a variety of ways to uncover opportunities for cost reductions, primarily through the concentration of purchases with a smaller number of suppliers. The spend management database lies at the center of the spend management system. Information from the purchasing departments in a company's subsidiaries is pulled into the database. Once the information is assembled, it is cleaned up with the following techniques:

- *Name linkages.* It is extremely likely that each subsidiary uses a different supplier identification code for its suppliers, so the aggregated information probably contains information about purchases from a single supplier that are listed under several different names. A table must be constructed for the database that links all of these name variations to a single supplier name. Thus, purchases from ATT, AT&T, and AT&TWIRELESS would all be linked to the same phone company.
- *Description linkages.* As was the case for supplier names, the descriptions of items purchased may vary wildly from each other at the subsidiary level, and so must be standardized in the spend database.
- *Commodity code linkages.* Every purchase made should have attached to it a standard *commodity code*, which assigns a spend category to the purchase. This information is useful for aggregating purchases by commodity type, which can then be used to concentrate purchases with preferred suppliers for volume discounts. It is best to have all subsidiaries record purchases using the same standard commodity code system, such as the North American Industry Classification System (NAICS).
- *Credit rating linkages.* The database should include a data feed from a third party credit rating service, which contains the credit rating for each supplier.

This information is useful for determining which suppliers may be in financial difficulty, so that spending can be shifted to more reliable suppliers.

A spend database can be enormous, which means that all of the preceding data cleansing and enhancement activities must be performed through automated routines. It is not even remotely cost-effective to engage in these activities manually.

Once information has been fully aggregated into the spend database, the information is sorted by commodity code to determine spend levels for all of the various types of commodities. The resulting reports can be used to drive down costs by any of the following means:

- *Consolidate suppliers*. While each subsidiary may proudly point out that it has already consolidated its supplier base, each one may have consolidated around a different group of suppliers. The database can reveal that the subsidiaries have few suppliers in common at the commodity code level, which represents an opportunity for *all* of the subsidiaries to consolidate their purchases with the same group of suppliers. The net result can be a remarkable decline in the overall number of suppliers from which purchases are made. For example, if there are five subsidiaries and each one purchases from five suppliers, of which only 20% are commonly used by all subsidiaries, this means a total of 20 suppliers could potentially be stripped away from a pool of 25 suppliers, which is an 80% reduction.
- *Consolidate professional services*. There is a tendency for each department or subsidiary to hire their own professional services firms, such as consultants, tax accountants, attorneys, and auditors. The spend report will aggregate professional services, so that management can see the overall extent of purchasing in this area, and especially the large number of services firms used. A likely outcome is a general retrenchment of the purchasing function in this area, where work can be centralized with a much smaller number of services firms. Doing so may also result in the discovery that some services were being duplicated in several company locations.
- *Source through distributors*. The spend report may reveal that the company is spending a relatively small amount with a large number of suppliers in certain commodity code categories. When this is the case, the easiest solution may be to locate a single distributor through which all of the items can be purchased. The result could be a massive reduction in the number of suppliers, which reduces the administrative and accounting burden of the purchasing and accounting departments.
- *Source overseas*. If certain commodities have high labor content, there may be an opportunity to source them from overseas locations where labor rates are extremely low, which can yield significant cost reductions.

It can take a long time to gradually work through the information provided by a spend database, shifting purchases to a smaller and smaller pool of suppliers. Over time, the categories of unaddressed commodity codes will shrink, in which case the emphasis should always be on the next largest remaining spend by commodity code. It is possible that the lowest-spend commodity codes will never be addressed, because the potential savings are so small that they are not worth investigating.

Purchasing Controls

The most critical controls related to the purchasing function are as follows:

- *Purchase requisition approvals.* When an employee fills out a purchase requisition form, it must be approved by the manager who will be charged with the related expense. Doing so keeps expenditures under control.
- *Purchases from approved suppliers.* Once suppliers have proven themselves to be reliable, they are designated in the system as approved suppliers. As such, the purchasing staff is authorized to buy from them, frequently on a sole-source basis. Purchases from other suppliers are not allowed by the system.
- *Price oversight.* The prices at which goods and services are purchased may be higher than the market rate, so buyers can be required to consult standard price lists and catalogs before placing orders. Reasonable pricing can be assured for high-priced items by requiring the use of a competitive bidding process.
- *Buyer rotations.* Buyers should be periodically assigned to a different group of suppliers. Doing so reduces the risk of *kickbacks*, where suppliers pay a buyer to route purchase orders to them.
- *Change log.* There should be a change log that records all changes to the vendor master file, which is monitored regularly for unusual changes. Otherwise, someone could gain access to the file, add unapproved suppliers, and then process invoices for those suppliers without the knowledge of anyone.
- *Procurement card receipts.* Procurement card users should be required to obtain receipts for all purchases made, and attach them to the monthly statements issued by the credit card processor, so that their purchases can be validated.
- *Reports.* The system can prepare several reports that can be used to monitor the purchasing function. Examples of these reports are:
  - *Scrap and rework tracking.* When the purchasing department tries to save money by buying substandard materials, the scrap and rework rate experienced by the production department will likely increase. A report that tracks scrap and rework information can be used to judge purchasing performance.

○ *Budget versus actual.* Budget versus actual reports are distributed for each department, so that managers can spot any variances from their expectations for expenditures.

○ *Supplier scorecard.* The company can keep track of a number of performance measurements for its suppliers and aggregate them into a scorecard. Examples of these measurements are on-time delivery performance, the product defect rate, and the billed price variance.

Receiving Activities

The second major function in the expenditure cycle is receiving, where employees examine incoming deliveries to see if goods are properly authorized and meet the company's specifications. This department also logs all received goods into the AIS.

A larger organization that deals with significant volumes of inbound goods may require its main suppliers to issue an electronic notification, known as an *advance shipping notice*, when they ship goods to the company, including an estimated date and time of arrival. This information can be used to schedule which receiving dock to use for a specific delivery, as well as to plan for an adequate amount of available manpower to process receipts.

Once goods arrive at the receiving dock, the receiving staff looks for an identifying bar code that the supplier has placed on the outside of the shipping container or in a packing slip. This bar code identifies the authorizing purchase order number. Scanning this bar code brings up the relevant purchase order information on a computer terminal in the receiving area. The receiving staff then inspects the goods and enters the quantity received in the terminal, along with their condition. This log-in process accomplishes the following:

- It notifies the system that requested goods are now available, so they can be routed either into the warehouse for later use, the production area for immediate use, or to the requesting person.
- It notifies the accounting department that the supporting receiving documentation is now available for the related supplier invoice.
- It warns of any missing, damaged, or out-of-specification goods detected by the receiving staff, which will have to be returned to the supplier and replaced.

All received goods are itemized in a *receiving report* that is generated by the AIS. The following information is typically included in the report:

- The date and time on which the delivery was received
- The name of the shipping company that delivered the goods
- The authorizing purchase order number
- The item number, name, and quantity of each item received
- The condition of the items received, which may be completed only when there are damaged or sub-standard goods

When the receiving department notes a variance from the original purchase order, such as too few units delivered or damage to the goods, the purchasing department contacts the supplier to discuss either a reduction in the invoiced amount or a replacement delivery to fulfill the remainder of the order.

Receiving Controls

The most critical controls related to the receiving function are as follows:

- *Purchase order requirement*. Deliveries will not be accepted at the receiving dock unless there are authorizing purchase orders on file for them. This policy minimizes purchases from unauthorized suppliers.
- *Block quantity information*. There is a tendency for the receiving staff to simply check off the amount stated on a purchase order as having been received, without actually counting the number of units in a delivery. This behavior can be eliminated by not showing the purchase order quantity in the computer screen presented to the receiving staff.
- *Receiving signature requirement*. The person who logs in a supplier delivery must sign off on the receipt. Doing so allows for the tracing of incorrect receipts back to the responsible party.
- *Services inspection*. A particular problem is verifying whether contracted services were ever provided to the company. This may call for a detailed review of the services by someone competent to evaluate them.
- *Reports*. There should be a reporting system in place for evaluating the delivery performance of suppliers. The system can track whether deliveries were made within designated time frames, whether quality levels meet or exceed the company's requirements, and whether the full amounts ordered were delivered. These reports may take the form of a report card that is shared with suppliers, and which is used as the basis for routing additional orders to suppliers or dropping nonperforming ones.

Though an essential control over receiving is the requirement that all received goods have an authorizing purchase order, this can be difficult in practice. People outside of the purchasing department may initiate orders without a purchase order, so it is likely that some deliveries will arrive without them. These exceptions should be viewed as opportunities to instruct employees about the need to use purchase orders.

Payment Activities

The payment function is designed to process and pay for incoming supplier invoices and employee expense reports as expeditiously as possible, while flagging any suspect invoices for further review. Smaller organizations still use a largely manual process to make payments, but larger organization that have to deal with massive invoice volumes have adopted more automated approaches, as we will point out in this section.

The standard manual approach to setting up supplier invoices for payment is to match all received supplier invoices to their authorizing purchase orders, as well as evidence of receipt. If there are any discrepancies between these documents, the payables staff must resolve them before payment can proceed. If the amount to be paid differs from the amount stated on the supplier invoice, the payables staff may send an adjustment letter to the supplier, stating the amount of and reason for the difference. This can keep the supplier from charging late payment fees and pestering the payables staff with questions about the unpaid difference. A sample adjustment letter appears in the following exhibit.

Sample Adjustment Letter

Adjustment Notification

Supplier Address Block	Company Logo	Company Address Block

To whom it may concern:

[Company name] has short-paid your invoice number _____ by the amount of $_____, for the following reasons:

- ☐ Damaged goods
- ☐ Incorrect items delivered
- ☐ Incorrect quantity delivered
- ☐ Items delivered after requested due date
- ☐ Price on invoice does not match purchase order
- ☐ Quality test failed

Additional Comments Block

If you would like to discuss these issues with us, please contact the accounts payable department at [phone number].

When there is an authorizing purchase order, there is no need to obtain any additional payment approval, so these invoices can be entered into the system and processed for payment. When an invoice does not have an associated purchase order, the payables staff ascertains which manager's department will be charged the amount stated on the invoice, and sends the invoice to that manager for approval.

Since managers have a habit of losing these invoices, an alternative approach is *negative approval*, where managers are notified that payment *will* be processed unless they state otherwise.

A variation on the approval concept is to automatically approve all smaller invoices that are lower than a predetermined threshold level. Doing so reduces the work associated with obtaining manager approvals, but also presents the risk that some invoices will be paid that should have been rejected. Employees can also game the system by telling suppliers to issue a number of small invoices that are less than the approval threshold, rather than one large invoice that will require manager approval.

A more efficient approach is to have suppliers submit electronic invoices to the company that are ported directly into the AIS. Doing so eliminates the need for manual data entry by the payables staff.

A larger organization may have arranged with its suppliers to schedule payments to them as soon as goods are delivered, rather than going through the additional effort of processing a supplier invoice. In this situation, known as *evaluated receipts settlement*, the AIS multiplies the number of units received by the standard unit price stated in the authorizing purchase order to arrive at the amount to be paid, and then pays this amount on the date required under the payment terms negotiated with each supplier. Not only is this system fully automated, but it also eliminates the need to process any supplier invoices.

The payment process must also deal with employee expense reports. These documents contain requests for reimbursement for expenditures made by employees on behalf of the company. There may be a detailed review process of each expense report submitted, or the company can use a software package that automatically walks employees through the process of submitting an expense report, which greatly reduces the amount of required review work. There may also be an accounting policy that allows for the automatic approval of expense reports for those employees who have a record of submitting perfectly documented expense reports, along with a few random audits to ensure that these people are still performing at a high level.

Irrespective of the method of approval used, the system will automatically schedule invoices for payment, based on the payment terms negotiated with each supplier. The system then processes either an electronic payment (usually an Automated Clearing House [ACH] payment) or a check on the indicated payment date. Once these payments are made, the system reduces the cash balance and the payables balance in the general ledger to reflect the reduction in payables. In addition, the system flags the related purchase orders as having been paid. When ACH payments are made, the system usually sends a remittance advice to the supplier as a separate email, noting exactly what was paid and which discounts were taken. When a check is issued, the remittance advice takes the form of a tear-away page that is part of the check.

When checks are issued, an authorized check signer reviews the supporting material for each check before signing it, to verify that there are no issues. When the amount to be paid exceeds a certain amount, company policy may mandate that a second check signer also sign the check. The checks are then mailed to the indicated suppliers.

A separate payment system that may be used is the petty cash fund. *Petty cash* is a small amount of bills and coins that are kept on the premises to pay for minor expenditures. There may be a petty cash fund in each major department. A petty cash custodian is responsible for this fund, and maintains an up-to-date reconciliation of the amount of bills and coins remaining in the fund. It is typically replenished by the accounting department once a month. Examples of the items that may be paid for from the petty cash fund are food, office postage, and office supplies. Petty cash funds can be a convenient alternative to the slower check payment process, but the funds are subject to theft, and so are being replaced by procurement cards and employee expense reporting systems in many companies.

Payment Controls

The most critical controls related to the payment function are as follows:

- *Supplier master file access*. Lock down access to the supplier master file, so that only an authorized person can create and revise records for approved suppliers. Otherwise, someone could create a record for an unapproved new supplier in the system and process invoices against it.
- *Segregation of duties*. The person who signs checks and approves electronic payments should not be associated with the payables function. Otherwise, someone could set up a payment in the system to himself and then approve it.
- *Three-way matching*. Either the AIS or an employee should match purchase orders to receiving documents and supplier invoices, to ensure that the supplier invoices are for the authorized prices and for the number of units received, which is called *three-way matching*. Document matching is usually avoided for smaller invoices, since it can be a painstaking process.
- *Procurement card reconciliation*. The users of company procurement cards should retain all purchase receipts, and then use them to complete a reconciliation of the monthly credit card statement, to verify that all purchases can be supported.
- *Expense report reviews*. Require employees to submit receipts for all expense reimbursements claimed on their expense reports. An even better control is to require the use of a corporate credit card for most travel expenditures, which greatly reduces expense report totals.
- *Freight charge analysis*. The internal audit staff should examine a selection of freight invoices on an ongoing basis to see if the rates charged were correct, and whether the company or the supplier should have been charged by the transport company.
- *Accelerated processing*. The payment system should be configured so that all invoices are entered into the system on an expedited basis. Doing so provides the company with enough time to take advantage of any early payment discounts offered by suppliers.

- *Corporate credit card usage.* A business that has experienced ongoing problems with employee expense reports can require that larger expenditures, such as airlines and hotels, be made using a corporate credit card. Doing so greatly reduces the amount of money being spent on expense report reimbursements.
- *Duplicate invoice rejection.* The system should be configured to automatically reject any supplier invoices for which the same supplier invoice number has already been paid. This control is designed to prevent situations in which a supplier sends several copies of an invoice to the company, and more than one is submitted for payment.
- *Blank check security.* All blank checks should be stored in a locked location, as should the signature stamp (if used). Doing so keeps someone from accessing the checks and preparing their own payments.
- *ACH account blocking.* Set ACH debit blocks on all company bank accounts, so that an outside party cannot use the ACH system to extract funds from the account. This control can be modified by the bank to allow ACH debits from pre-authorized suppliers.
- *Positive pay.* The company enters into a *positive pay* arrangement with its disbursing bank, under which the company periodically sends a file to the bank, containing information about the checks it has issued. The bank then compares its records of these checks to the checks actually being submitted for payment, to detect any fraudulent checks.
- *Electronic payment oversight.* The ability to issue electronic payments should be restricted to a very small number of employees, with all payments requiring additional management approval before they can be finalized. Additional controls should include daily limits on the amounts of electronic transfers the bank is allowed to process, as well as password access to the payment software.
- *Supporting document cancellation.* Once an invoice has been paid, the payables staff should stamp the associated receiving report line item(s) and purchase order as having been paid. In a more automated system, the AIS will automatically flag these documents as having been paid.
- *Reconciliations.* The internal audit staff periodically examines supplier invoices and supporting documents to ensure that they were properly authorized, and that goods were actually received. Any anomalies found are examined to see if there are process improvements to be made that could keep these issues from arising again. In addition, the checking account should be reconciled every day, so that payment anomalies can be spotted and investigated at once. Unannounced reconciliations should also be conducted occasionally on petty cash funds, to see if they are being managed properly.

There are many ways in which the payments function can fail, so management should install most of the preceding controls. The exact number and types of controls installed will vary, depending on how the underlying system is configured.

Summary

The expenditure cycle should be oriented toward the dual goals of keeping costs low while also ensuring that goods and services are made available to the organization in a timely manner. Unless expenditures are properly managed, there is a good chance that inventory shortages will cause sales and profits to decline. There is a significant risk of loss in this cycle, unless purchases and payments are closely controlled, so a full suite of controls should be installed throughout the purchasing, receiving, and payment functions.

The expenditure cycle shares some data with the production cycle, which is targeted at the acquisition of raw materials in order to support the manufacturing process, along with other activities. We deal with the production cycle in the next chapter.

Chapter 11
The Production Cycle

Introduction

The production cycle is the set of activities related to the manufacture of finished goods. These activities include product design, production scheduling and operations, and cost accounting. An accounting information system (AIS) can support some of these activities to achieve a smooth flow of well-designed products into the manufacturing process, with sufficient cost information to make product pricing decisions. The main input to the production cycle is customer order information from the sales cycle, to which it sends back updates concerning the amount of finished goods produced and available for sale. The production cycle also generates a multitude of requisitions for raw materials that are processed by the expenditure cycle, which sends back status updates about the arrival of raw materials that are loaded into the production scheduling function.

In this chapter, we discuss the information system flows associated with each set of activities that comprise the production cycle, including the most essential controls associated with each one.

Production Cycle Overview

The production cycle is comprised of several distinct components, involving the design of products, their incorporation into a production schedule, manufacturing activities, and a cost accounting feedback loop. These four areas are usually managed by four different departments – the engineering, materials management, production, and accounting departments, respectively. In this section, we provide an overview of these four components of the production cycle, indicating how information flows between them. The full production cycle contains the following activities:

1. The engineering department uses an iterative process to develop product designs. This process requires input from the accounting department concerning the costs of proposed product components, while the marketing department advises on the product features needed. The industrial engineering group provides input about how new products can be designed to make them easier and less expensive to manufacture. The engineering staff incorporates a targeted selling price and profit margin into its design work, in a process called *target costing*, to design new products that will be assured of earning a reasonable profit.

2. Once a product design has been finalized, the engineering staff creates a bill of materials (of which an example for a desk phone appears in the following exhibit), which itemizes every component in the product. It also works

with the industrial engineering group, typically through several production runs, to develop a labor routing, which states the estimated amount of labor that will be required at each production workstation in order to complete the product.

3. A sales forecast from the sales department is used as an input to the development of a production plan, which states the number of units to be produced, as well as the timing for when each batch of the product will be initiated. Based on this schedule, the system issues purchase requisitions to the purchasing department to obtain the necessary raw materials (as described earlier in the Expenditure Cycle chapter).

4. The materials management staff releases job orders into the production department in accordance with the requirements of the production plan, and schedules direct labor staffing based on the labor routing information for each product on the shop floor. Completed goods are either shipped immediately to customers or stored in the warehouse as finished goods.

5. The cost accounting staff compiles cost summaries for each batch completed by the production group, which it provides to both the engineering manager and production manager. This information is needed to spot variances from expectations, which could lead to design changes or alterations in the work instructions used on the shop floor.

Sample Bill of Materials

Part Number	Description	Quantity
PH-124A	Base	1
PH-400A	Keypad	1
PH-718C	Microphone	1
PH-032H	Cord	1
PH-620J	Shell	1
PH-900D	Speaker	1

The preceding activities are the primary components of the production cycle. The information system supporting these activities needs to be protected from a multitude of threats in order to keep the production cycle from failing to generate goods on a consistent basis and within cost expectations. When there is incorrect data in the system, a business could be subject to any of the following failures:

- Product designs are poor.
- Raw material purchases are inadequate or excessive for production runs.
- Labor staffing is inadequate or excessive for production runs.
- Incorrect costing results are issued for production jobs.
- Confidential information is used by an unauthorized party.
- Data are destroyed within the system, and there is no backup.

The preceding failures could result in delayed deliveries to customers, or excessive investments in raw materials or finished goods inventory, which can threaten a company's solvency.

Product Design Activities

The product design process tries to balance the conflicting goals of providing sufficient features and quality to justify a targeted price point, while also generating an adequate profit. The outcome is more likely to succeed when target costing is used by the product design team. The basic steps in the process are:

1. *Conduct research.* The first step is to review the marketplace in which the company wants to sell products. The team needs to determine the set of product features that customers are most likely to buy, and the amount they will pay for those features. The team must learn about the perceived value of individual features, in case they later need to determine what impact there will be on the product price if they drop one or more of them. It may be necessary to later drop a product feature if the team decides that it cannot provide the feature while still meeting its target cost. At the end of this process, the team has a good idea of the target price at which it can sell the proposed product with a certain set of features, and how it must alter the price if it drops some features from the product.

2. *Calculate maximum cost.* The company provides the design team with a mandated gross margin that the proposed product must earn. By subtracting the mandated gross margin from the projected product price, the team can easily determine the maximum target cost that the product must achieve before it can be allowed into production.

3. *Engineer the product.* The engineers and purchasing personnel on the team now take the leading role in creating the product. Buyers are particularly important if the product has a high proportion of purchased parts; they must determine component pricing based on the necessary quality, delivery, and quantity levels expected for the product. They may also be involved in outsourcing parts, if this results in lower costs. The engineers must design the product to meet the cost target, which will likely include a number of design iterations to see which combination of revised features and design considerations results in the lowest cost.

4. *Ongoing activities.* Once a product design is finalized and approved, the team is reconstituted to include fewer designers and more industrial engineers. The team now enters into a new phase of reducing production costs, which continues for the life of the product. For example, cost reductions may come from waste reductions in production (known as *kaizen costing*, which is the process of continual cost reduction after a product has been designed and is being produced), or from planned supplier cost reductions. These ongoing cost reductions yield enough additional gross margin for the company to further reduce the price of the product over time, in response to increases in the level of competition. Kaizen costing does not generate the

160

size of cost reductions that can be achieved through initial design changes, but it can have a cumulatively significant impact over time.

EXAMPLE

SkiPS is a maker of global positioning systems (GPS) for skiers, which they use to log how many vertical feet they ski each day. SkiPS conducts a marketing survey to decide upon the features it needs to include in its next generation of GPS device, and finds that skiers want a device they can strap to their arm or leg, and which does not require recharging during a multi-day vacation.

The survey indicates that skiers are willing to pay no more than $150 for the device, while the first review of costs indicates that it will cost $160 to manufacture. At a mandated gross margin percentage of 40%, this means that the device must attain a target cost of $90 ($150 price × (1 – 40% gross margin). Thus, the design team must reduce costs from $160 to $90.

The team decides that the GPS unit requires no display screen at all, since users can plug the device into a computer to download information. This eliminates the LCD display and one computer chip. It also prolongs the battery life, since the unit no longer has to provide power to the display. The team also finds that a new microprocessor requires less power; given these reduced power requirements, the team can now use a smaller battery.

Finally, the team finds that the high-impact plastic case is over-engineered, and can withstand a hard impact with a much thinner shell. After the team incorporates all of these changes, it has reached the $90 cost target. SkiPS can now market a new device at a price point that allows it to earn a generous gross profit.

Product Design Controls

The most critical controls related to the product design function are as follows:

- *Restricted access.* Passwords and encryption should be used to block unauthorized access to product design information that could be used by competitors, including the bills of material and labor routings.
- *Raw material shortfalls and overages.* Any request by the production staff for additional parts should be routed to the engineering department, since this signals that the associated bill of materials may contain too few parts. Similarly, documentation of any excess parts returned to the warehouse should be copied to the engineering department, since it indicates that the unit quantity stated on the bill of materials is too high.
- *Overtime requests.* Any request by the production staff for overtime that can be traced to a specific production job should be routed to the engineering department, since this signals that the associated labor routing may designate too few labor hours.
- *Common parts analysis.* A company can miss the benefits of volume discounts by not standardizing the components used across its product line.

Devising a standard set of components and requiring its use by design teams can mitigate this problem.

- *Accountant involvement.* An accountant should be assigned to each product design team, and provides assistance by reviewing the costs incurred by similar products in such areas as rework, warranty claims, and product re-calls to reduce the risk that these issues will be experienced with new product designs.

Of the preceding controls, the involvement of an accountant in the design process can be considered a highly effective preventive control, while the examination of raw materials shortfalls and overages can be quite useful as a detective, after-the-fact control.

Production Scheduling Activities

The creation of a production plan, usually referred to as the *master production schedule* (MPS), can be quite difficult, since the scheduler has to balance the conflicting goals of producing enough for actual customer orders, while also producing sufficient additional inventory to cover anticipated customer demand. The scheduling chore is further complicated when there are raw material shortages, lengthy ordering lead times for raw materials, bottlenecks in the production process, equipment failures, and reduced staffing situations. When an MPS is being properly managed, it can minimize both finished goods shortages and the expediting of orders through the production process, while also minimizing overtime, machine usage, and expedited freight charges. A well-managed MPS should be able to do the following:

- Act as the guiding document for the management of the manufacturing function.
- Be the link between overall business planning and detailed production operations.
- Allow for the issuance of reliable delivery commitments to customers.
- Enhance the efficiency of the manufacturing process.
- Assist in the planning of how available production capacity will be used.

An MPS is presented in tabular format, and contains the following information:

- *Demand forecast.* This is the company's best estimate of the amount of customer demand for its products.
- *Allocated.* This is actual customer orders that have been accepted into the system.
- *Reserved.* This is production slots reserved by management, on the expectation that actual customer orders will be received.
- *Unplanned.* This is production slots for unexpected customer orders that were not included in the demand forecast.

- *Net demand.* Within the time fence (explained later in this section), this is a subtotal of the allocated, reserved, and unplanned line items. Outside of the time fence, this is the demand forecast.
- *Firm planned orders.* This is orders that have already been released to the production floor, and so only appear near the beginning of the MPS.
- *Planned orders.* This is orders that have been automatically calculated by the planning system, or which have been manually entered into it. They usually appear in the MPS for periods after which firm planned orders have already been stated. The formula for a planned order is:

Safety stock + Net demand – Projected available balance (prior period)
– Firm planned orders

= Planned orders

- *Projected available balance.* This is the projected number of available units. The formula for the projected available balance is:

Projected available balance (prior period) + Planned orders + Firm planned orders
– Net demand

= Projected available balance

- *Available to promise.* This is the number of units available for new customer orders.

A sample MPS for a single product appears in the following exhibit.

Sample Master Production Schedule

Safety stock: 40	Week 0	Week 1	Week 2	Week 3	Week 4	Week 5	Week 6
Green Widget Product							
Demand forecast				80	70	90	50
Allocated		70	50	30	20	10	
Reserved				10	20	40	20
Unplanned			10		10		
Net demand			70	60	80	70	90	50
Firm planned order		20					
Planned order			40	80	70	90	50
Projected available balance	110	60	40	40	40	40	40
Available to promise		40		40	20	40	30

The main issues associated with the management of an MPS are as follows:

- *Planning horizon*. This is the future time period covered by the MPS, and is used to both plan production work and determine material requirements. The planning horizon should be long enough to encompass the cumulative lead times associated with all items listed in the MPS.
- *Time fence*. The first week or so of the MPS may be frozen, with no changes allowed during this period of time. The time fence is imposed because it would not otherwise be possible to gather the raw materials for new orders, due to the lead time constraints imposed by suppliers.
- *Accuracy*. The accuracy of the MPS is quite high within its first few weeks, and then becomes increasingly subject to change as near-term actual orders are replaced by forecasts.
- *Feasibility analysis*. The unit quantities in the MPS should be matched to the capacity of the work centers in which jobs will be completed. This can be done by estimating the labor hours and machine capacity required for each work center, to spot bottlenecks that will keep the MPS from being achieved. If bottleneck issues cannot be resolved, then either additional resources (such as more staffing or outsourcing) are added, or the MPS is revised.
- *Multi-location planning*. The planning chore becomes much more complex when a business needs to coordinate manufacturing activities across a number of production facilities, since the output of some facilities needs to be routed to other locations, which can result in the build-up of inventory between the facilities if their schedules are not closely coordinated.

The MPS is a constantly evolving document, with numerous updates outside of the designated time fence, likely on a daily basis.

In a material requirements planning system (as described in the preceding Expenditure Cycle chapter), the planned quantities stated in the MPS are multiplied by the raw material quantities stated in their associated bills of material to determine the total raw material requirements for production. These requirements are then subtracted from on-hand and in-transit raw materials to arrive at the amounts of raw materials that must be acquired in order to produce the units stated on the MPS. For example, we provided a simple bill of materials for a desk phone earlier in this chapter. If 1,000 of these phones were planned for production on the MPS, the required raw materials, less on-hand inventories, would be calculated as noted in the following exhibit.

Sample Calculation of Raw Materials Requirements

Part Number	Description	Unit Quantity	Required Production Quantity	Less: On-hand Inventory	Raw Materials Purchase Requirement
PH-124A	Base	1	1,000	100	900
PH-400A	Keypad	1	1,000	--	1,000
PH-718C	Microphone	1	1,000	400	600
PH-032H	Cord	1	1,000	650	350
PH-620J	Shell	1	1,000	250	750
PH-900D	Speaker	1	1,000	50	950

When there is sufficient production capacity on hand and all required raw materials are available, an item scheduled on the MPS is authorized for production by the issuance of a production order. A *production order* states the number of units to be manufactured, the date when the order is released to the production floor, and where the units should be delivered once they have been completed. It also itemizes the work center operations that need to be completed and the number of units to be produced by each operation. The work center operators then add information to the production order as they complete required tasks, stating the number of units produced and the in-and-out dates and times. It is possible that the number of units processed will decline as the work proceeds through a series of work centers, as some units are rejected for various reasons. The production scheduler may be able to estimate the number of rejections, and so authorizes the initial production of a somewhat larger number of units than is actually needed, in the expectation that some units will not complete the entire process. A sample production order appears in the following exhibit.

Sample Production Order

Production Order							9082
Order: 4403	**Product:** PH-1000, Desk Phone					**Unit Quantity:** 1,000	
Released by: S. Bolero	**Release Date:** 06/14				**Deliver to:** Warehouse		
Work Station	Operation Number	Operation Description	Input Quantity	Scrapped/ Rejected	Start Date/ Time	End Date/ Time	
Base assembly	100	Keypad insertion	1,030	5	06/14 | 08:30	06/14 | 14:30	
Base assembly	200	Keypad solder	1,025	--	06/14 | 14:30	06/14 | 20:30	
Handset assembly	310	Microphone insertion	1,025	10	06/15 | 08:30	06/15 | 15:00	
Handset assembly	320	Shell closure	1,015	--	06/15 | 15:00	06/16 | 10:00	
Testing	400	Function test	1,015	15	06/16 | 10:00	06/17 | 18:00	
Packaging	450	Unit boxing	1,000	--	06/17 | 18:00	06/18 | 20:00	

In order to have the raw materials required for a production order, the system must release a material requisition to the warehouse staff. A *material requisition* lists the items to be picked from inventory and used in the production process. A sample requisition appears in the following exhibit. The requisition has three purposes, which are:

- To pick items from stock
- To relieve the inventory records in the amount of the items picked
- To charge the targeted job for the cost of the items requisitioned

Sample Material Requisition

Material Requisition				11033
Released to: Production			**Production order:** 9082	
Part Number	Description	Quantity	Unit Cost	Total Cost
PH-124A	Base	1,000	$2.40	$2,400
PH-400A	Keypad	1,000	1.90	1,900
PH-718C	Microphone	1,000	0.72	720
PH-032H	Cord	1,000	1.25	1,250
PH-320J	Shell	1,000	1.85	1,850
PH-900D	Speaker	1,000	0.65	650

Simpler products can be routed through the production process within quite a short period of time, resulting in a modest amount of documentation that can be relatively easily compiled into a product cost by the accounting staff. This is not the case for

166

more extensive projects that may last for months, such as custom machinery, airplanes, and satellites. In these situations, the assignment of labor, materials, and equipment to specific jobs needs to be carefully documented, so that an accurate product cost can be compiled.

Production Scheduling Controls

The most critical controls related to the production scheduling function are as follows:

- *Lock down production schedule.* When changes are made to the production schedule inside the point at which the company cannot order raw materials in time for the start of production, it will not be possible to initiate the impacted production jobs. This issue can be remediated by locking down changes to the production schedule in the short term.
- *Update demand forecast.* The demand forecast in the MPS should be adjusted on a regular basis to incorporate the latest customer demand estimates, to keep from under- or over-producing.
- *Update feasibility analysis.* The feasibility analysis for a preliminary MPS should be based on the most recent information about work center capacity levels, equipment downtime, staffing levels, and so forth, since this information is constantly changing.
- *Approvals.* An experienced production planner should review and approve the MPS, as well as all production orders, to minimize the risk that production orders are released with incorrect quantities, or when the constituent raw materials are not yet ready.
- *Material requisitions.* Material requisition forms should be used to authorize the movement of raw materials from the warehouse to the shop floor. Otherwise, the materials release process can be quite muddled, resulting in parts shortages or overages on the shop floor.

The key concept to focus on when designing production scheduling controls is that the MPS is constantly being altered – and therefore requires continual analysis via feasibility studies to ensure that the business can still produce to the plan.

Manufacturing Activities

Once a production order has been released to the shop floor, it enters the production process. It is nearly impossible to summarize the format of the manufacturing process, since it can vary substantially, depending on whether the business engages in lengthy production runs or one-off production, prefers to use automation versus manual labor, outsources significant parts of the manufacturing process, and so forth. A more advanced manufacturing environment may employ some mix of the following:

- *Lean work centers.* The shop floor is comprised of a cluster of work centers, each of which is configured to complete a specific task. These work centers are regularly adjusted to meet the needs of the MPS.
- *Computer-integrated manufacturing.* Most or all of the manufacturing process is controlled by computer, with feedback loops provided by real-time sensors. The labor component in this type of manufacturing can be quite minor.

Both of these approaches can allow a business to engage in the custom manufacturing of specialized products, and can also be highly scalable, so that a factory can easily reduce or increase its production volume.

Manufacturing Controls

The most critical controls related to the manufacturing function are as follows:

- *Material move receipts.* Whenever materials are moved, either from the warehouse to the shop floor or between work centers, someone should indicate receipt of the goods, thereby taking responsibility for them. This control may be minimized in a just-in-time environment where unit transfers are quite small.
- *Material returns.* Any materials returned to the warehouse are an indication that the bills of material call for more materials than are actually being used, so these returns should trigger a notification to the engineering staff to review the bills of material.
- *Additional material issuances.* Any requests from the shop floor for more materials can indicate multiple problems, such as incorrect bills of material, incorrect work instructions, theft, and low material quality. Thus, these requests should be targeted for significant management reviews.
- *Restricted access.* Passwords and encryption should be used to block unauthorized access to manufacturing process information and work instructions that could be used by competitors.

We have noted that there are many ways in which a manufacturing system can be configured, so it is difficult to specify controls that are applicable to all manufacturing processes. What we *can* do is monitor the materials input to the system to see if material shortages and overages are indicating the presence of underlying problems that require additional investigation.

Cost Accounting Activities

The cost accounting function supports the production cycle by providing information about the cost of products and manufacturing processes, which can also be used to value the cost of goods sold that appears in the income statement and the ending inventory balance that appears in the balance sheet. In order to provide this information, there needs to be a system for accumulating cost-related data. In most organizations, this is accomplished with either a job costing or process costing system, as described in the following sub-sections.

Job Costing

Job costing is used to accumulate costs at a small-unit level. For example, job costing is appropriate for deriving the cost of constructing a custom machine, designing a software program, or building a small batch of products. Job costing involves the following accounting activities:

- *Materials.* It accumulates the cost of components and then assigns these costs to a product or project once the components are used.
- *Labor.* Employees charge their time to specific jobs, which are then assigned to the jobs based on the labor cost of the employees.
- *Overhead.* It accumulates overhead costs into cost pools, and then allocates these costs to jobs.

Job costing is an excellent tool for tracing specific costs to individual jobs and examining them to see if the costs can be reduced later, on similar types of jobs.

EXAMPLE

Twill Machinery has just completed job number 1003, which is for a custom-designed milling machine ordered by a long-term customer. The costs assigned to the job include an allocation of $12,000 for 200 hours of rework on burrs discovered in numerous places on the metal edges of the machine. Further investigation reveals that the burrs were caused by improper metal stamping when the component parts were originally created.

Since the customer is likely to order additional versions of the same machine, management assigns a task group to investigate and correct the metal stamping process. Twill would probably not have found this problem if the job costing system had not highlighted it.

If a job is expected to run for a long period of time, the cost accountant can periodically compare the costs accumulated in the bucket for that job to its budget, and give management advance warning if costs appear to be running ahead of projections. This gives management time to either get costs under control over the remainder of the project, or possibly to approach the customer about a billing increase to cover some or all of the cost overrun.

Job costing demands a considerable amount of costing precision if costs are to be reimbursed by customers (as is the case in a cost-plus contract, where the customer pays all costs incurred, plus a profit). In such cases, the cost accountant must carefully review the costs assigned to each job before releasing it to the billing staff, which creates a customer invoice.

Process Costing

There are many situations where the volume of production is so high that there is no way to use job costing to track the cost of each individual product in a cost-effective manner. Also, it may be impossible to differentiate the costs associated with individual products. If either situation is the case, the usual solution is to use process costing, which calculates the average cost for all units produced. The classic example of a process costing situation is oil refining, where the cost of any individual gallon of fuel cannot be differentiated from another one.

In process costing, there are three methods available for generating a cost per unit. They are:

- *Weighted average costing.* Averages all costs from multiple periods and assigns them to units. This method is most applicable to simple costing environments, and where there are few cost changes from period to period. It is the simplest calculation method.
- *Standard costing.* Assign standard costs to production units and treat variances from actual costs separately. This method is used when a company has a standard costing system in operation.
- *First in, first out (FIFO) costing.* Assigns costs to production units based on the periods in which costs are incurred. This method produces the highest degree of accuracy, and is also the most complex to calculate. The FIFO method is most useful where costs vary substantially from period to period, so that management can see product cost trends.

The typical manner in which costs flow in process costing is that direct material costs are added at the beginning of the process, while all other costs (both direct labor and overhead) are gradually added over the course of the production process. For example, in a food processing operation, the direct material (such as a cow) is added at the beginning of the operation, and then various rendering operations gradually convert the direct material into finished products (such as steaks).

Cost Collection Issues

A cost accountant relies on a variety of data collection systems in order to compile costing reports. The type of data collection system used, as well as how that system is used, depends on the type of cost data being collected. To create a complete set of costs, the accountant needs access to labor costs, material costs, factory overhead costs, and machine usage data.

If labor cost data is being collected, the accountant can choose to collect it on timesheets, which are manually filled out by employees. This approach has the advantage of requiring no computer systems, but employees may not be diligent in identifying exactly which jobs they were working on, which reduces the utility of the resulting data. Another problem is that timesheets are typically only turned in once a week, so the data are not necessarily up-to-date. Conversely, an on-line system that mandates data entry by users will be filled out completely and be available to the accountant at once, but still suffers from the problem of potential data inaccuracy. Given the data inaccuracy consideration, it can be more cost-effective for the accountant to actively track labor hours only for those jobs in which tasks change frequently. When tasks do *not* change on a regular basis, the accountant can rely on an occasional survey of hours worked on those tasks; these surveys will probably reveal that labor cost assignments on standardized tasks vary little over time.

An additional consideration for the accountant is that direct labor costs are actually fixed in many situations, since the production manager needs to have a full staff on hand in order to run an assembly line, irrespective of the number of units actually produced. In this situation, direct labor can be considered a component of factory overhead, rather than a variable cost. This consideration can alter the content of the reports issued by the cost accountant.

If materials costs are being collected, the easiest approach for the accountant is to use the standard costs for each product, which are readily available by accessing the relevant bill of materials. However, much more detailed materials analysis is needed when standard costs do not approximate actual costs, or when costs are being reviewed for small-batch jobs or custom work. In these cases, there must be a system in place for tracking the cost of all materials going through the manufacturing area. This may be accomplished most easily with bar coded materials and a bar code identifying the job to be charged, so that workers only need to scan these codes to assign material costs to a specific job.

Factory overhead costs, such as utilities, supplies, and property taxes, are assigned to jobs, preferably using a basis of allocation that has a significant amount of resource usage. When production required a large amount of manual labor, overhead was routinely allocated to jobs based on the number of labor hours used. More recently, with many production tasks requiring large amounts of machine processing, a more appropriate basis of allocation is machine time used.

When allocating factory overhead costs, a concern for the accountant is that many of these costs will be incurred irrespective of the production of specific products. This being the case, the accountant needs to understand the uses to which allocated factory overhead costs will be put. If the intent is to record ending inventory, then generally accepted accounting principles mandate that the full amount of factory overhead costs be allocated to produced units. However, if the intent is to determine the lowest variable cost at which goods can be produced, then no overhead should be allocated at all. There are numerous other scenarios lying on the continuum between these two scenarios that will call for differing allocations.

It is possible to use *activity-based costing* (ABC) to more precisely allocate overhead to those items that actually use it. ABC does so by pooling overhead costs that are most closely related to certain activities, such as the storage of inventory or the painting of finished goods. There can be a number of cost pools. The costs in each of these cost pools are then assigned to *cost objects*[7] (usually products) based on the amount of usage by each cost object of the basis of allocation, which is called a *cost driver*. ABC works best in complex environments, where there are many machines and products, and tangled processes that are not easy to sort out. ABC information can be quite useful for learning about the cost of manufacturing activities, the cost of production facilities, whether to make or buy a product, how much distribution channels cost, customer profitability, and the minimum price point that can be charged to customers.

In short, the cost accountant needs to tailor the reports issued to the configuration of the manufacturing system and the uses to which the information will be put. This means that the contents of even standardized cost accounting reports that are issued on a repetitive basis will probably need to be adjusted from time to time.

Cost Accounting Controls

The most critical controls related to the cost accounting function are as follows:

- *Automated data collection.* There is a high risk of data inaccuracy when a manual data entry process is used, so use automated systems as much as possible. The use of bar codes is recommended, since they standardize a block of text for repetitive automated data entry. When manual data entry is mandated, do so through computer terminals, where the software can validate the data as it is entered.
- *Overhead allocation systems.* Activity-based costing can be used to more precisely allocate overhead to cost objects, so that management is using accurate costing data when making decisions.
- *Reconciliations.* The internal audit staff periodically traces raw material costs back to supporting supplier invoices, to ensure that the costs incorporated into product cost analyses are correct. Internal auditors can also examine whether the methodology used to allocate factory overhead to products is reasonable.
- *Reports.* There are several reports that can provide valuable feedback about problems in the production cycle, including the following:
  - Activity-based costing reports, where the emphasis shifts away from the cost of goods sold as a single number and toward the costs incurred for various activities, such as:
    - Materials handling
    - Picking
    - Quality inspections
    - Receiving
    - Shipping

---

[7] A cost object is any item for which a cost is compiled. Examples of cost objects are products, product lines, customers, and distribution channels.

- o Bottleneck reporting, where the focus is on operations that are running at their maximum capacity, and so cannot accept any additional work. Bottlenecks constrain a business from increasing its sales, so reporting on bottleneck operations will focus management attention on maximizing the efficiency of the bottleneck. This can include outsourcing work, increasing capacity, and adding staff.
- o Cost object reporting that shifts the emphasis away from a single cost of goods sold figure, instead focusing on revenues, expenses, and profit by product, product line, sales region, customer, and distribution channel.
- o Quality reporting that focuses on the following four types of costs:
  - *Prevention costs.* These are costs incurred to prevent quality problems from occurring, such as employee training, statistical process control, and supplier certifications.
  - *Appraisal costs.* These are inspection costs incurred to prevent quality problems from occurring, such as destructive product testing and the wages of inspection staff.
  - *Internal failure costs.* These are costs incurred when a defective product is produced, such as scrapped or reworked goods.
  - *External failure costs.* These are costs incurred when a product fails outside the company, such as product recalls, warranty claims, and field service.

  The outcome of quality reporting should be an emphasis on prevention activities, since these actions cost the least of the various costs of quality, and keep the other, more expensive costs from being incurred.
- o Throughput reporting, where throughput is the revenues generated by a production process, minus all completely variable expenses incurred in that process. Paying attention to increasing throughput will likely result in improved profitability over time, and focuses attention on only investing in resources that will increase throughput.
- o Warranty cost analysis, to identify specific part or design failures on products.

Summary

The production cycle incurs a large proportion of the total costs incurred by a business and is arguably its core operation, so it should be supported by especially robust systems. The product design function should use target costing to improve the probability that products are designed with the correct feature sets and costs to achieve targeted margins. The production scheduling function is managed by a master production schedule, which needs to be routinely tested to ensure that it is actually achievable, given known constraints. The efficiency of the manufacturing function can be enhanced with lean work centers, computer-integrated manufacturing, or some combination of the two. Finally, cost accounting is a key feedback loop that provides valuable information to management about the cost of every aspect of the production cycle, which can be used to fine-tune it.

The production cycle shares some data with the sales cycle, since the order entry staff needs to know when it can promise deliveries to customers. The production cycle also shares data with the expenditure cycle, to which it routes material requisitions for raw material purchases. A similar situation arises with the human resources cycle, to which it routes production staffing requirements. We deal with the human resources cycle in the next chapter.

Chapter 12
The Human Resources Cycle

Introduction

The human resources cycle includes all activities related to management of the personnel resources of a business. These activities include the following:

- Recruiting job candidates
- Interviewing job candidates
- Hiring employees
- Employee onboarding
- Training employees
- Compensating employees
- Coaching and mentoring employees
- Performance appraisals
- Terminating employment

All of the preceding activities are overseen by the human resources department, with the exception of the compensation activities, which are managed through the payroll function in the accounting department. An accounting information system (AIS) contains significant capabilities related to the processing of payroll, though it rarely supports the other activities. Though we will cover the entire human resources cycle in this chapter, our main focus will be on the processing of payroll.

Human Resources Cycle Overview

As a business grows and evolves, it needs to locate qualified personnel to operate its processes. These people need to have skills, experiences, and personalities that closely match the requirements of the business. Thus, a person who is ideally suited for a customer service position may be entirely different from someone who would be an excellent fit in the accounting department. In some organizations (especially in the tech industry), the skills of employees constitute the main competitive advantage of a company, which means that the human resources function is a central concern of the management team. The following activities are associated with these position fulfillment needs:

- *Recruitment.* The recruitment of new employees begins with a precise definition of the firm's needs, followed by the development of a recruitment pipeline that can provide a steady stream of candidates to the business. This activity involves heavy marketing of the capabilities of the business and the work environment that it offers its employees. One systems-related activity associated with recruitment is the provision of an on-line job application form to job candidates, as well as an internal application form for existing employees who want to apply for newly-opened positions. Another recruitment system is a resumes database, which contains the key skills and attributes of any qualified candidates who were not initially offered positions with the firm. When related positions become available, the database can be reviewed to see if any of the people listed in it might be a good match.

- *Interviewing*. The interviewing process involves an initial sorting through resumes to determine which candidates appear to be a good fit for the company. This task can be reduced by using resume analysis software, which looks for keywords in resumes that are indicative of possibly qualified candidates. Following this initial pass, telephone or video interviews may be conducted to further pare down the group, followed by in-person interviews. Once a final candidate is selected, there may be reference checks, background checks, and drug or polygraph testing before an offer is made.

- *Hiring*. Once a candidate has been selected, the human resources staff assembles a hiring packet that includes an offer letter. The letter will contain a compensation amount and benefits package, which should be based on the company's existing compensation rates and benefits for similar positions, as stored in its human resources database. There may also be an employment contract, including such terms as a noncompete clause, termination provisions, and scope of duties. There may be a contracts database in which these terms are entered, so that they are more readily accessible.

- *Onboarding*. An initial training period is needed to assist in integrating new hires into the organization. This includes learning about the organization and how it does business, its culture, policies and procedures, and the specific requirements of their jobs. These orientation activities can require a significant amount of staff time. A systems application that can apply to onboarding is an employee portal that gives them access to many types of information, such as summary information about the firm, online training modules, video presentations by management, social networking tools, a calendar of company events, and the answers to frequently asked questions.

- *Training*. Ongoing training is required to maintain employee skill levels that are closely aligned with the strategy of the business. This calls for training that may be custom designed for the specific needs of employees. As just noted for employee onboarding, a reasonable systems application related to training is to provide online access to self-paced online training programs. Significant support by management is needed to ensure that concepts learned are implemented in the workplace.

A systems-related activity associated with training is the use of a knowledge-management system, which stores the specific skills of all employees. Managers can peruse the database to see if anyone in-house already has needed skills, which can reduce the need to pursue talent outside the firm. This database reveals which skills are in short supply, which can be used to alter the job descriptions for positions to be filled. The database can also be used to store best practices information, which is especially valuable when knowledge needs to be shared across a multi-location company.

- *Compensation activities*. Payrolls are scheduled at fixed intervals for the collection of time worked information from employees and the calculation of their gross pay and deductions, resulting in their net pay. There is usually a well-defined process and supporting software package that are used to conduct error-free payrolls.
- *Coaching and mentoring*. An organization may provide coaching and mentoring to its employees in order to improve their overall productivity and creativity. Coaching enhances performance in the short term by helping a person close his knowledge or skill gaps, while mentoring focuses on the long-term personal growth of the individual. There are few systems available for enhancing the coaching and mentoring experience; the main application is a monitoring system for the frequency and outcome of coaching sessions.
- *Performance appraisals*. A performance appraisal is the process used to evaluate an employee's on-the-job performance, which tells her how well she is performing against expectations. The process leading up to the meeting involves collecting information about how the employee has performed against a set of predetermined goals and determining how to structure the meeting. During the meeting, the manager and employee discuss this prior performance against goals, and then address future plans. There are no significant systems that support performance appraisals.

The preceding activities are especially useful for reducing employee turnover. The prevention of employee departures can represent a massive cost savings for a business, since there are many costs associated with hiring a replacement, including job advertising, interviewing time by employees, onboarding activities, training costs, and the reduced productivity of new hires.

If there are failures in the systems that support the human resources cycle, a business could be subject to any of the following failures:

- Unqualified or larcenous employees are hired.
- Incorrect payments are made to employees.
- Payroll remittances to the government and other parties are not made or are made incorrectly.
- The business is liable to pay garnishments that it did not deduct from employee pay.
- Employees steal cash by creating payments to fake employees.
- Employment laws related to the hiring and firing of employees are violated.
- Employees are incorrectly classified as contractors, so that the company is liable for their payroll taxes.
- Confidential information, such as pay rates and performance evaluations, are used by an unauthorized party.
- Data are destroyed within the system, and there is no backup.

The preceding failures can result in significant monetary losses, as well as discord among employees if their confidential information is released.

Human Resources Controls

The most critical controls related to the human resources function are as follows:

- *Background checks*. Conduct a thorough background check on anyone being considered for employment, including verification of the applicant's education, employment history, and references. Also conduct a review for any criminal convictions. Doing so reduces the risk of hiring unqualified or larcenous applicants.
- *Employee documentation*. All decisions made in regard to the recruitment, hiring, and firing of employees are properly documented. This information may be needed in response to the legal actions of employees.
- *Employment law updates*. Conduct a periodic review of any applicable changes to the employment law, to see if they impact the company. Doing so reduces the risk of initiating illegal actions involving employees.
- *Segregation of duties*. Authorized human resources personnel are allowed to make changes to the employee master file, but only authorized payroll personnel can create paychecks. This will prevent payroll staff from being able to create new employees in the system.
- *Reports*. A number of reports can be used to gain feedback regarding the effectiveness of the various human resources activities. For example:
  - *New employee failure rate*. There may be significant differences in the turnover of new employees, depending on the sourcing mechanism used, such as advertisements, internal referrals, and recruiting firms. Management can use this report to target its resources at those recruiting sources that yield lower employee turnover rates and higher-quality employees.
  - *Recruitment costs*. This report itemizes the costs incurred to recruit, interview, hire, and train new employees. The results can be combined with analyses of the types of candidates hired to determine which recruiting approaches are the most cost-effective.
  - *Tardiness and absenteeism*. This report highlights cases of persistent tardiness and absenteeism, which can be an early indication of employee unhappiness that can eventually lead to heightened employee turnover.
  - *Change notices*. Any changes made to the employee master file can be summarized for the managers to whom employees report, so that they can verify that all changes made are valid.

Of the preceding controls, a robust system of background checks is the most important. These checks act as a gate that limits the hiring of underqualified or larcenous individuals, which could cause serious damage to the business if they were to be hired.

Payroll Activities

Nearly all activities within the human resources cycle occur continually, throughout the year. This is not the case for payroll, which operates as a well-defined batch process. Payroll is most commonly run either once a week, biweekly, semi-monthly, or monthly. Its outcome is payments made to employees, tax remittances to the government, and remittances to other parties for various deductions from employee pay.

A significant amount of coordination is required to successfully complete a payroll, because there are so many inputs to the system from outside the accounting department. These inputs are as follows:

- *All departments*. Every department in the company that employs hourly workers is responsible for collecting timesheets and forwarding these documents to the payroll staff.
- *Benefit providers*. The providers of benefits to employees, which are usually insurance companies, provide benefit cost information to the company for each person covered by their benefit plans.
- *Employees*. Depending on the nature of the system, employees may be able to update their own records in the system for the amounts and types of certain deductions taken from their pay, such as donations and pension plan contributions.
- *Governments*. Certain government agencies are responsible for setting tax or withholding rates, which are incorporated into payroll calculations. For example, state governments usually issue unemployment tax rates to employers near the end of each calendar year.
- *Human resources*. The human resources department is responsible for updating the employee master file in a timely manner with new hires, pay rate changes, and terminations.
- *Sales department*. The sales staff may be paid commissions, which are usually based on the sales generated by each salesperson. The sales department may need to verify the applicable sales information recorded by the accounting department before commissions can be calculated.

Multiple parties are impacted when a payroll has been completed. These parties include:

- *Employees*. Employees receive paychecks or electronic payments in the amount of the net pay owed to them.
- *Governments*. The company remits income tax withholdings to the government, along with social security, unemployment, and Medicare tax payments.

- *Benefit providers*. The company sends insurance premiums to insurance companies and pension payments to pension plan administrators.
- *Garnishing entities*. The company remits the amounts of any garnishments to the courts mandating these pay deductions.

Payroll processing begins with the employee master file, which is maintained by the human resources department. This file contains data pertaining to employment, such as employee names, birth dates, addresses, job titles, and pay rates. These data items are updated from documentation received by the human resources department, such as authorized pay rate change forms or termination notices issued by department managers.

The initiating payroll activity is the collection of time data for those employees who are paid wages. The data collected may also include job numbers and task codes, for those situations in which employees are charging their time to production jobs or billable work for customers. A timecard is usually printed on heavier-weight paper and is stored in a central timecard rack. Employees can fill it out by hand, or they can insert it into a punch clock, which stamps the time on it. There are separate columns for the beginning and ending times when regular hours and overtime hours are worked. There is also a small block next to each day of regular and overtime hours, in which the payroll staff enters the total time worked for that day. They then accumulate these daily totals into overtime and regular time totals at the bottom of the timecard. Both the employee and his or her supervisor should sign the card. A sample timecard appears in the next exhibit.

Sample Timecard

Employee Name		Timecard	
Overtime		Regular Time	
	1st Day IN		
	1st Day OUT		
	2nd Day IN		
	2nd Day OUT		
	3rd Day IN		
	3rd Day OUT		
	4th Day IN		
	4th Day OUT		
	5th Day IN		
	5th Day OUT		
	6th Day IN		
	6th Day OUT		
	7th Day IN		
	7th Day OUT		
Overtime Total		Regular Time Total	
Employee Signature Block			
Supervisor Signature Block			

A timesheet differs from the timecard in that there is no provision for a time stamp by a punch clock. Instead, employees are expected to fill out the timesheet by hand. This is a relatively simple document, as illustrated in the following exhibit. Employees state the time period worked and the number and types of hours worked. There is also space for supervisory approval of the document. The name of the supervisor is stated near the top of the form, in case the payroll staff wants to contact that person with a question about information on the timesheet.

Sample Weekly Timesheet

Weekly Timesheet

Employee Name
Supervisor Name
Week of ____ to ____

	Hours							
Day	Regular	Overtime	Vacation	Sick	Holiday	Leave	Other	Total
Monday								
Tuesday								
Wednesday								
Thursday								
Friday								
Saturday								
Sunday								
Total Hours								

Employee Signature
Supervisor Signature

In some organizations, time tracking is only intended for hours that can be billed to customers. In this situation, the timesheet is structured so that the employee can enter the name of the client, the project, and the task. This information is not used for the payment of employees (unless they are only paid for billed hours) but rather for creating customer invoices. A sample billing timesheet appears in the following exhibit.

Sample Billing Timesheet

Billing Information			Hours								
Client	Project	Task	Mon	Tue	Wed	Thu	Fri	Sat	Sun	Total	
		Total Hours									

Billing Timesheet

Employee Name

Supervisor Name

Week of ____ to ____

Employee Signature

Supervisor Signature

Rather than having employees fill out timesheets, there are several more advanced alternatives available, such as the following:

- *Computerized time clocks.* This is a time clock that accepts magnetic or bar coded employee badges to identify employee entrances and exits. A variation is to use RFID (radio frequency identification) badges, which can be waved in front of the time clock. The information is either stored in the time clock for later polling by the payroll system, or automatically transmitted as the information is recorded. This method is best for production environments where large numbers of employees are concentrated in one location.
- *Biometric time clocks.* This is a computerized time clock that requires a hand or fingerprint scan in order to positively identify an employee. These clocks scan rather slowly, but eliminate the risk of one employee punching in on behalf of an absent employee.
- *IP phone timekeeping.* If a business uses Voice Over Internet Protocol (VOIP), it is accepting and making phone calls through its computer network, rather than through the phone lines. If so, timekeeping information entered through VOIP phones can be stored in the payroll system.

- *Smart phone timekeeping.* A number of apps are available that allow the users of smart phones to record their time and activities via their cell phones, which can then be transmitted to the company. This approach is most useful for mobile employees, such as field service repair people and consultants.
- *Website timekeeping.* A business can develop its own timekeeping portal that is accessible to employees over the Internet, or rent the use of such a site from a third party provider (usually as part of an outsourcing payroll processing arrangement). This approach is useful for employees who are located outside the office.

The following table defines the circumstances under which a particular time tracking system will operate most effectively, as well as the levels of error and fraud risk associated with each system.

Time Tracking Usage Considerations

	Time Sheets	Time Cards	Computer Clocks	Biometric Clocks	Web Time Keeping	Smart Phones
Computer interface	None	None	Yes	Yes	Optional	Optional
Cost	Low	Low	High	High	Moderate	Moderate
Employee dispersion	Dispersed	Moderate	Concentrated	Concentrated	Dispersed	Dispersed
Error risk	High	Medium	Low	Low	Low	Low
Fraud risk	High	High	Moderate	Low	High	High
Number of employees	Few	Moderate	High	Moderate	High	High
Pay period	Short	Short	Any	Any	Any	Any
Production environment	Job cost	Standard	Any	Any	None	None
Summarization labor	High	High	Low	Low	Low	Low

Besides the basic recordation of hours worked in the payroll system, the payroll staff may also take input from a firm's incentive compensation software. This system is designed to track the most complex pay calculations, typically in regard to the calculation of commissions and bonuses paid to its salespeople. These systems should be able to handle the following commission and bonus arrangements:

- Bonuses for reaching various sales targets, such as quarterly and annual goals
- Caps on the commissions paid to departing salespeople
- Caps that limit the maximum possible commission that can be earned
- Commission rates that vary, depending on the volume of sales achieved
- Commission splits between several salespeople
- Guaranteed payments, as may be used for salespeople developing new sales regions
- Overrides to increase the amount of a commission, such as a commission boost when a salesperson generates sales in a new sales region

Incentive compensation software is useful for avoiding the calculation errors that would likely arise if the preceding compensation arrangements were to be handled manually.

The basic steps involved in the processing of payroll are as follows:

1. Review all submitted time data for accuracy, and to verify that there are manager approvals.
2. Verify that the payroll module is set to process the correct pay period.
3. Enter the amount of regular and overtime hours worked by each employee.
4. Verify that the hours submitted by all hourly employees have been entered.
5. Enter the amounts of any manual paychecks that have not yet been recorded in the system.
6. Enter any changes to the standard deductions from employee pay, including the following:

   - Cafeteria plan
   - Charitable contributions
   - Dental insurance
   - Disability insurance
   - Garnishments
   - Life insurance
   - Medical insurance
   - Pension plans

7. Have the system process all pay calculations for the period. For hourly employees, this calculation is the number of hours worked multiplied by the applicable wage rate, adjusted for other factors such as shift premiums and overtime. For salaried employees, this calculation is the applicable fraction of each person's annual salary. The amounts of any commissions, bonuses, and other incentive compensation are added to these pay totals.
8. Have the system process all pay deductions for the period. This involves subtracting all applicable deductions from the previously calculated gross pay figure for each employee to arrive at their net pay. Deductions fall into three general categories, which are:

   - *Payroll tax withholdings.* Includes withholdings for all types of income taxes, as well as charges for social security and Medicare taxes.
   - *Voluntary deductions.* Includes the premiums charged by insurers for various types of insurance, as well as pension plan contributions.
   - *Mandatory deductions.* Includes union dues and garnishments.

9. Print the following reports and review the underlying transactions for errors. Process payroll again until these issues have been corrected.

- Preliminary payroll register
- Sorted list of wages paid
- Trend line of payroll expense by department

10. Issue payments to employees. This also updates the cumulative earnings information for employees in the employee master file, which is used to produce annual earnings reports. The payment options are as follows:

- *Check payments.* The payment process is similar to the one used for accounts payable checks, as described earlier in the Expenditure Cycle chapter.
- *Direct deposit.* The payroll staff maintains a separate record for each employee to be paid by direct deposit, in which is stored the bank account number, employee name, and net pay amount. These records are transmitted to the firm's direct deposit processing firm, which in turn sends electronic messages to the paying banks with payment instructions.
- *Payroll cards.* When employees do not have a bank account, the company can pay them by loading funds into a debit card. To do so, it enters employee names, social security numbers, and net pay amounts into a file and transmits it to the payroll card processor, which loads the funds into employee payroll cards. The cards can then be used to make payments, or to withdraw cash from automated teller machines.

11. Issue payroll reports to management.
12. Lock down the payroll period in the payroll module for the period just completed.
13. Deposit payroll taxes and verify their transmission to the government.

Of the preceding reports produced by the payroll system, the most important one is the payroll register. This document itemizes the calculation of wages, taxes, and deductions for each employee for each payroll. There are multiple uses for the payroll register, including:

- *Investigation.* It is the starting point for the investigation of many issues involving employee pay.
- *Journal entries.* Journal entries to record a payroll are based on the information in the register.
- *Payments.* If manual check payments are being created, the source document for these payments is the register.
- *Reports.* The information on almost any government or management report related to payroll is drawn from the register.

The format of the payroll register is built into the payroll software, and so will vary somewhat by payroll system. If payroll processing is outsourced, the supplier will issue its own version of the payroll register as part of its basic service package. The following exhibit contains a typical payroll register format, with overtime and state and local taxes removed in order to compress the presentation.

Sample Payroll Register

Empl. Nbr.	Employee Name	Hours Worked	Rate/ Hour	Gross Wages	Taxes	Other Deductions	Check Nbr.	Net Pay
100	Johnson, Mark	40	18.12	724.80	55.45	28.00	5403	641.35
105	Olds, Gary	27	36.25	978.75	74.87	42.25	5404	861.63
107	Zeff, Morton	40	24.00	960.00	73.44	83.00	5405	803.56
111	Quill, Davis	40	15.00	600.00	45.90	10.10	5406	544.00
116	Pincus, Joseph	35	27.75	971.25	74.30	37.50	5407	859.45

If a company pays its employees with checks, it should issue not only the paycheck, but also a remittance advice that details the calculation of the payment. A sample paycheck and remittance advice is shown in the following exhibit. The presented format can be altered to include additional information, such as the remaining amount of earned vacation time.

Sample Paycheck and Remittance Advice

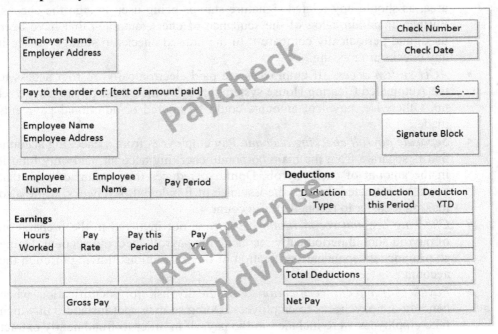

The paycheck and remittance advice shown here can also be adapted to direct deposit payments. The paycheck part of the document is stated as being non-negotiable, and that the payment was made by direct deposit. In all other respects, the document is the same.

Payroll Controls

The most critical controls related to the payroll function are as follows:

- *Restricted access.* Access to the employee master file should be restricted to authorized personnel. Otherwise, someone could access the system and alter pay rates, employee addresses, withholding percentages, and so forth.
- *Change log.* Activate the change log that tracks changes to the employee master file, and regularly review it to see if there were any unauthorized changes to employee data.
- *Verification of time entries.* Require supervisory approval of employee timesheets to verify that the hours they are claiming were actually worked. An alternative is to install biometric timeclocks that verify employees at the point of time recordation.
- *Payroll register review.* A manager should review and approve the preliminary payroll register before it is finalized. This step is needed to verify that all pay rates and hours worked that will be included in the payroll are reasonable.
- *Lock down check stock.* Unused payroll checks should be stored in a locked area, as should any related signature stamps being used to sign the checks. Further, maintain a log of the sequence of check numbers that have been used, and periodically compare it to the unused checks in storage, to see if any checks are missing.
- *ACH system access.* If employees are paid electronically, restrict access to the Automated Clearing House system through which these payments are set up. Otherwise, payment amounts could be altered or additional payments made.
- *Separate payroll checking account.* Pay employees from a checking account that is separate from the main corporate checking account, and only fund it in the amount of each payroll. Doing so reduces the amount of cash that could be extracted through the issuance of fraudulent paychecks, while also making it easier to reconcile the account.
- *Checking account reconciliation.* Someone not involved in the preparation of payroll should periodically reconcile the payroll checking account. Doing so provides independent verification of the transactions flowing through the account.
- *Paycheck recipient verification.* Periodically ask for identification when handing out paychecks to employees. Doing so may spot instances in which fake employees were included in the payroll in order to fraudulently extract cash from the company.

- *Unclaimed paycheck investigation.* Whenever paychecks are issued that are not claimed by employees, investigate why these checks were issued. The reason may be a control failure in the payroll system.
- *Earnings statement issuance.* Issue remittance advices to employees along with all payments to employees, as well as year-end earnings statements, and encourage them to review this information. They may spot incorrect earnings information.

Of the preceding controls, verifications are the most essential – this means the examination of submitted time reports by managers, as well as the verification of the preliminary payroll register. Errors and fraudulent entries are most easily detected at these two points, so these verifications should be mandatory.

Payroll Outsourcing

A typical in-house payroll department has many concerns. Besides the task of issuing paychecks, it may have to do so for many company locations where tax rates differ, employees are paid on different dates, and tax reporting to the various state governments must be made on a number of different forms. Worst of all is the tax remittance, which involves a heavy penalty if it is paid even one day late. All of these problems and costs can be avoided by handing over the payroll processing function to an outside supplier. More specifically, the following benefits are associated with the outsourcing of payroll:

- *Direct deposit.* Most payroll suppliers have the capability to issue payments to employees by direct deposit. Companies that process their payroll in-house can also do this, but only through the services of a third party that handles direct deposit.
- *Expert staff.* Suppliers have a core of highly-trained staff who not only know their systems and payroll regulations quite well, but who also provide training to clients, as well as advice over the phone.
- *Multi-location processing.* Larger payroll suppliers have locations in most major cities, and so can directly deliver paychecks to most urban locations. They send paychecks to more remote locations by overnight delivery service.
- *New hire reporting.* Each state government requires a company to report the hiring of new employees to them, so that they can determine if there are any garnishments outstanding against these individuals. Payroll suppliers usually offer this reporting service free of charge.
- *Pay cards.* Larger payroll suppliers offer payroll debit cards as a payment option. This is a good alternative to direct deposit for those employees who do not have bank accounts.
- *Reporting.* Suppliers have a standard set of "canned" payroll reports, and usually offer report writing software that allows a user to extract information and present it in formats that are specific to an employer's needs.

- *Software updates.* The employer no longer has to maintain any payroll software in-house, and so is no longer concerned with software updates. The supplier is responsible for all updates to its own software.
- *Tax remittances.* A supplier calculates all payroll taxes and remits them to the government without the company having to be involved. The savings from avoided tax remittance penalties may pay for the entire cost of the supplier.
- *Tax tables.* Suppliers maintain the most up-to-date records of tax rates charged by all government entities, and so can accurately calculate taxes payable to cities, counties, states, the federal government, and other special entities throughout the country.
- *W-2 forms.* All suppliers provide W-2 forms to employees after the end of each calendar year. Many also store this information on-line, so that employees can access their forms from previous years.

When payroll is outsourced, this rarely means that the entire payroll function is physically transferred away from the company. Instead, only the payroll calculation, tax remittance, and employee payment functions are shifted to a third party. The employer is still responsible for collecting information about hours worked, as well as inputting information about employees. The splitting of responsibilities between the employer and its payroll supplier are roughly as follows:

Employer responsibilities:

- Collect hours worked
- Collect employee allowance, deduction, and personal information
- Input the preceding information into the payroll system maintained by the supplier
- Distribute paychecks and remittance advices forwarded by the supplier
- Record payroll transactions based on reports issued by the supplier

Supplier responsibilities:

- Calculate wages based on hours worked
- Calculate tax deductions and withholdings
- Create paychecks, initiate direct deposit payments, and forward cash to payroll debit cards
- Remit taxes and withholdings to government entities
- Issue standard reports to clients
- Issue W-2 forms to employees following the end of the calendar year

The reason for this split is that payroll suppliers are focusing on the data processing aspects of payroll, where they use mainframe-based computers to handle the payroll processing for large numbers of clients. The fixed cost of these systems is high, but suppliers can achieve considerable profitability if they have many clients using their systems. What a payroll supplier wants to avoid is the low value-added and highly error-prone tasks of collecting information about employees and entering it into the payroll system. Thus, payroll suppliers are narrowly focused on the highest value-added portion of the tasks handled by the payroll department.

In short, there are many services available to a company that is willing to outsource its payroll function. The key factors are enhanced convenience and the elimination of any risk associated with not remitting payroll taxes on a timely basis.

Summary

The human resources cycle is typically supported by a cluster of systems that are targeted at very specific functions, such as automating the review of applicant resumes, calculating complex incentive pay, and providing on-line training to employees. The most overarching system in this area is payroll processing, which is a common feature in an accounting information system. Since a significant amount of funding flows through the payroll system and not the other human resources systems, controls tend to be clustered around payroll.

The human resources cycle is comprised of functions that mostly act in support of the other cycles described in the past three chapters, since it handles the employee hiring, training, and termination needs indicated by the other cycles. In addition, it produces costing data that can be incorporated into the cost accounting reports generated within the production cycle. The payroll expense data generated by the human resources cycle is carried forward into the general ledger, from which it is summarized into the financial statements, as described in the next chapter.

Chapter 13
Financial Reporting

Introduction

The financial reports issued by an accounting information system (AIS) reveal the financial position, financial results, and cash flows of a business, and constitute the primary report card for how well the organization is performing. In this chapter, we discuss the nature of these reports and how they are compiled, along with several related issues.

The Nature of Financial Reporting

External parties that want to understand a business will typically insist on receiving a complete set of financial statements, which are comprised of the following:

- *Income statement.* It shows the results of the firm's operations and financial activities for the reporting period. It reports on revenues, expenses, gains and losses, as well as the resulting profit or loss.
- *Balance sheet.* It shows the firm's assets, liabilities, and stockholders' equity as of the report date. It does not show information that covers a span of time.
- *Statement of cash flows.* It shows changes in the firm's cash flows during the reporting period.

The external parties receiving financial statements are usually creditors, lenders, and investors who are either lending to or investing in the business. Since they want to be assured that the financial statements fairly present the financial situation of a business, they will also want to receive an audit report along with the financial statements, in which an external audit firm states that it has no reservations about the financial statements.

If the business is subject to regulation, it may need to issue customized financial reports to the applicable government agencies. The format issued will be based on the requirements of the governing agencies, and so may be significantly different than the financial statements normally issued.

Internal reporting tends to be less detailed than the reports issued to outside parties. Managers are mostly interested in their specific areas of responsibility, so what they receive will be just those subsets of the financial statements that pertain to them (see the Responsibility Accounting section for more information).

The Income Statement

The income statement is an integral part of an entity's financial statements, and contains the results of its operations during an accounting period, showing revenues and expenses, and the resulting profit or loss.

There are two ways to present the income statement. One method is to present all items of revenue and expense for the reporting period in a statement of comprehensive income. Alternatively, this information can be split into an income statement and a statement of comprehensive income. Other comprehensive income contains all changes that are not permitted in the main part of the income statement. These items include unrealized gains and losses on available-for-sale securities, cash flow hedge gains and losses, foreign currency translation adjustments, and pension plan gains or losses. Smaller companies tend to ignore the distinction and simply aggregate the information into a document that they call the income statement; this is sufficient for internal reporting, but auditors will require the expanded version before they will certify a company's financial statements.

There are no specific requirements for the line items to include in the income statement, but the following line items are typically used, based on general practice:

- Revenue
- Tax expense
- Post-tax profit or loss for discontinued operations and their disposal
- Profit or loss
- Other comprehensive income, subdivided into each component thereof
- Total comprehensive income

A key additional item is to present an analysis of the expenses in profit or loss, using a classification based on their nature or functional area; the goal is to maximize the relevance and reliability of the presented information. If expenses are presented by their nature, the format looks similar to the following exhibit.

Sample Presentation by Nature of Items

Revenue		$xxx
Expenses		
Direct materials	$xxx	
Direct labor	xxx	
Salaries expense	xxx	
Payroll taxes	xxx	
Employee benefits	xxx	
Depreciation expense	xxx	
Telephone expense	xxx	
Other expenses	xxx	
Total expenses		$xxx
Profit before tax		$xxx

Alternatively, if expenses are presented by their functional area, the format looks similar to the following exhibit, where most expenses are aggregated at the department level.

Sample Presentation by Function of Items

Revenue	$xxx
Cost of goods sold	xxx
Gross profit	xxx
Administrative expenses	$xxx
Distribution expenses	xxx
Research and development expenses	xxx
Sales and marketing expenses	xxx
Other expenses	xxx
Total expenses	$xxx
Profit before tax	$xxx

Of the two methods, presenting expenses by their nature is easier, since it requires no allocation of expenses between functional areas. Conversely, the functional area presentation may be more relevant to users of the information, who can more easily see where resources are being consumed.

An example follows of an income statement that presents expenses by their nature, rather than by their function.

EXAMPLE

Lowry Locomotion presents its results in two separate statements by their nature, resulting in the following format, beginning with the income statement:

Lowry Locomotion
Income Statement
For the years ended December 31

(000s)	20x2	20x1
Revenue	$900,000	$850,000
Expenses		
Direct materials	$270,000	$255,000
Direct labor	90,000	85,000
Salaries	300,000	275,000
Payroll taxes	27,000	25,000
Depreciation expense	45,000	41,000
Telephone expense	30,000	20,000
Other expenses	23,000	22,000
Finance costs	29,000	23,000
Other income	-25,000	-20,000
Profit before tax	$111,000	$124,000
Income tax expense	38,000	43,000
Profit from continuing operations	$73,000	$81,000
Loss from discontinued operations	42,000	0
Profit	$31,000	$81,000

Lowry Locomotion then continues with the following statement of comprehensive income:

Lowry Locomotion
Statement of Comprehensive Income
For the years ended December 31

(000s)	20x2	20x1
Profit	$31,000	$81,000
Other comprehensive income		
Exchange differences on translating foreign operations	$5,000	$9,000
Available-for-sale financial assets	10,000	-2,000
Actuarial losses on defined benefit pension plan	-2,000	-12,000
Other comprehensive income, net of tax	$13,000	-$5,000
Total comprehensive income	$18,000	$76,000

The Balance Sheet

A balance sheet (also known as a statement of financial position) presents information about an entity's assets, liabilities, and shareholders' equity, where the compiled result must match this formula:

$$\text{Total assets} = \text{Total liabilities} + \text{Equity}$$

The balance sheet reports the aggregate effect of transactions as of a specific date. The balance sheet is used to assess an entity's liquidity and ability to pay its debts.

Here is an example of a balance sheet which presents information as of the end of two fiscal years:

Lowry Locomotion
Balance Sheet
As of December 31, 20X2 and 20X1

(000s)	12/31/20X2	12/31/20x1
ASSETS		
Current assets		
Cash and cash equivalents	$270,000	$215,000
Trade receivables	147,000	139,000
Inventories	139,000	128,000
Other current assets	15,000	27,000
Total current assets	$571,000	$509,000
Non-current assets		
Property, plant, and equipment	551,000	529,000
Goodwill	82,000	82,000
Other intangible assets	143,000	143,000
Total non-current assets	$776,000	$754,000
Total assets	$1,347,000	$1,263,000
LIABILITIES AND EQUITY		
Current liabilities		
Trade and other payables	$217,000	$198,000
Short-term borrowings	133,000	202,000
Current portion of long-term borrowings	5,000	5,000
Current tax payable	26,000	23,000
Accrued expenses	9,000	13,000
Total current liabilities	$390,000	$441,000
Non-current liabilities		
Long-term debt	85,000	65,000
Deferred taxes	19,000	17,000
Total non-current liabilities	$104,000	$82,000
Total liabilities	$494,000	$523,000

(000s)	12/31/20X2	12/31/20x1
Shareholders' equity		
Capital	100,000	100,000
Additional paid-in capital	15,000	15,000
Retained earnings	738,000	625,000
Total equity	$853,000	$740,000
Total liabilities and equity	$1,347,000	$1,263,000

The Statement of Cash Flows

The statement of cash flows contains information about the flows of cash into and out of a company; in particular, it shows the extent of those company activities that generate and use cash. It is particularly useful for assessing the differences between net income and the related cash receipts and payments.

In the statement of cash flows, cash flow information is to be reported within three separate classifications. The use of classifications is intended to improve the quality of the information presented. These classifications are:

- *Operating activities*. These are an entity's primary revenue-producing activities. Operating activities is the default classification, so if a cash flow does not belong in either of the following two classifications, it belongs in this classification. Operating cash flows are generally associated with revenues and expenses. Examples of cash inflows from operating activities are cash receipts from the sale of goods or services, accounts receivable, lawsuit settlements, normal insurance settlements, and supplier refunds. Examples of cash outflows for operating activities are for payments to employees and suppliers, fees and fines, lawsuit settlements, cash payments to lenders for interest, contributions to charity, cash refunds to customers, and the settlement of asset retirement obligations.

- *Investing activities*. These are investments in productive assets, as well as in the debt and equity securities issued by other entities. These cash flows are generally associated with the purchase or sale of assets. Examples are cash receipts from the sale or collection of loans, the sale of securities issued by other entities, the sale of long-term assets, and the proceeds from insurance settlements related to damaged property. Examples of cash outflows from investing activities are cash payments for loans made to other entities, the purchase of the debt or equity of other entities, and the purchase of fixed assets.

- *Financing activities*. These are the activities resulting in alterations to the amount of contributed equity and an entity's borrowings. These cash flows are generally associated with liabilities or equity, and involve transactions between the reporting entity and its providers of capital. Examples are cash receipts from the sale of an entity's own equity instruments or from issuing debt, and proceeds from derivative instruments. Examples of cash outflows from financing activities are cash outlays for dividends, share repurchases, payments for debt issuance costs, and the pay down of outstanding debt.

The *direct method* or the *indirect method* can be used to present the statement of cash flows. The direct method shows cash inflows and outflows in the operating section. The indirect method derives operating cash flows by modifying the net income figure. No matter which method is used, the total amount of cash provided or used by operations is the same. These methods are described in the following subsections.

The Direct Method

The direct method of presenting the statement of cash flows presents the specific cash flows associated with items that affect cash flow. Items that typically do so include:

- Cash collected from customers
- Interest and dividends received
- Cash paid to employees
- Cash paid to suppliers
- Interest paid
- Income taxes paid

Though additional disclosures can be made, entities tend to limit their reporting to the preceding line items. The format of the direct method appears in the following example. Also included in the example is a reconciliation of net income to cash from operating activities, which is required when the direct method is used.

EXAMPLE

Lowry Locomotion constructs the following statement of cash flows using the direct method:

Lowry Locomotion
Statement of Cash Flows
For the year ended 12/31/20X1

Cash flows from operating activities		
Cash receipts from customers	$45,800,000	
Cash paid to suppliers	-29,800,000	
Cash paid to employees	-11,200,000	
Cash generated from operations	4,800,000	
Interest paid	-310,000	
Income taxes paid	-1,700,000	
Net cash from operating activities		$2,790,000
Cash flows from investing activities		
Purchase of fixed assets	-580,000	
Proceeds from sale of equipment	110,000	
Net cash used in investing activities		-470,000
Cash flows from financing activities		
Proceeds from issuance of common stock	1,000,000	
Proceeds from issuance of long-term debt	500,000	
Principal payments under capital lease obligation	-10,000	
Dividends paid	-450,000	
Net cash used in financing activities		1,040,000
Net increase in cash and cash equivalents		3,360,000
Cash and cash equivalents at beginning of period		1,640,000
Cash and cash equivalents at end of period		$5,000,000

Reconciliation of net income to net cash provided by operating activities:

Net income		$2,665,000
Adjustments to reconcile net income to net cash provided by operating activities:		
Depreciation and amortization	$125,000	
Provision for losses on accounts receivable	15,000	
Gain on sale of equipment	-155,000	
Increase in interest and income taxes payable	32,000	
Increase in deferred taxes	90,000	
Increase in other liabilities	18,000	
Total adjustments		125,000
Net cash provided by operating activities		$2,790,000

The standard-setting bodies encourage the use of the direct method, but it is rarely used, for the excellent reason that the information in it is difficult to assemble; companies simply do not collect and store information in the manner required for this format. Instead, they use the indirect method, which is described in the following sub-section.

The Indirect Method

Under the indirect method of presenting the statement of cash flows, the presentation begins with net income or loss, with subsequent additions to or deductions from that amount for non-cash revenue and expense items, resulting in cash provided by operating activities. Adjustments to the net income figure that are needed to derive cash flows from operating activities include:

- Accrued revenue
- Accrued expenses, such as a provision for bad debt losses
- Noncash expenses, such as depreciation, amortization, and depletion
- Gains and losses from the sale of assets
- Change in accounts receivable
- Change in inventory
- Change in accounts payable

The format of the indirect method appears in the following example. Note that the indirect method does not include cash inflows and outflows in the cash flows from operating activities section, but rather a derivation of cash flows based on adjustments to net income.

EXAMPLE

Puller Corporation constructs the following statement of cash flows using the indirect method:

Puller Corporation
Statement of Cash Flows
For the year ended 12/31/20X3

Cash flows from operating activities		
Net income		$3,000,000
Adjustments for:		
Depreciation and amortization	$125,000	
Provision for losses on accounts receivable	20,000	
Gain on sale of facility	-65,000	
		80,000
Increase in trade receivables	-250,000	
Decrease in inventories	325,000	
Decrease in trade payables	-50,000	
		25,000
Cash generated from operations		3,105,000
Cash flows from investing activities		
Purchase of fixed assets	-500,000	
Proceeds from sale of equipment	35,000	
Net cash used in investing activities		-465,000
Cash flows from financing activities		
Proceeds from issuance of common stock	150,000	
Proceeds from issuance of long-term debt	175,000	
Dividends paid	-45,000	
Net cash used in financing activities		280,000
Net increase in cash and cash equivalents		2,920,000
Cash and cash equivalents at beginning of period		2,080,000
Cash and cash equivalents at end of period		$5,000,000

The key difference between the direct and indirect methods is the derivation of the cash flows from operating activities section, where the direct method requires the reporting of specific operating activity cash inflows and outflows, while the indirect method backs into this information.

The Preparation of Financial Statements

The preparation of financial statements is accomplished with a formal checklist that the accounting staff follows to ensure the production of accurate financial statements. This checklist will vary, depending on the nature of the business, its accounting policies and procedures, and the type of AIS used. Nonetheless, the following steps are commonly followed to prepare month-end financial statements:

1. Clear transactions from suspense accounts to the greatest extent possible. Transactions may be initially parked in a suspense account when there is uncertainty about how to record them, so clearing these items ensures that they are sent to the correct general ledger accounts. For example, a customer payment that does not identify the invoice being paid could be parked in a suspense account until the customer clarifies the nature of the payment.

2. Close all subledgers and roll forward their balances to the general ledger. Doing so ensures that there are no stray transactions in subledgers that have not been transferred to the general ledger.

3. Print a trial balance and verify that the grand total for the debits and credits match. The trial balance is described in the next section. If the debit and credit totals do not match, then do not issue financial statements until the cause of the imbalance can be found.

4. Post adjusting entries, which are intended to either accrue a revenue or expense that has not yet been recorded through a standard accounting trans-action, defer a revenue or expense that has been recorded but which has not yet been earned or used, or estimate the amount of a reserve, such as the allowance for doubtful accounts. Some of the more common adjusting en-tries are:

    -   To record depreciation and amortization for the period
    -   To record an allowance for doubtful accounts
    -   To record a reserve for obsolete inventory
    -   To record a reserve for sales returns
    -   To record the impairment of an asset
    -   To record an asset retirement obligation
    -   To record a warranty reserve
    -   To record any accrued revenue
    -   To record previously billed but unearned revenue as a liability
    -   To record any accrued expenses

- To record any previously paid but unused expenditures as prepaid expenses
- To adjust cash balances for any reconciling items noted in the bank reconciliation

5. Reconcile at least the major balance sheet accounts. Doing so is a good way to verify that the contents of each account are valid, and can be traced back to the supporting detail in the subledgers.
6. Print an adjusted trial balance and verify that the total of all debits still equals the total of all credits. Also, verify that ending account balances now match expectations following the posting of all adjusting entries.
7. Print preliminary financial statements and review them for errors. Also, accrue an income tax liability based on the preliminary profit or loss stated on the income statement.
8. Close the reporting period in the AIS and open the next reporting period. Doing so prevents any additional transactions from being inadvertently recorded in the preceding reporting period.

Technically, there is also a year-end closing journal entry in the last step of the process that zeroes out all revenue and expense accounts and transfers their net balance to the retained earnings account. However, this entry is automatically handled by the AIS, so there is no manual entry to be made to the general ledger.

If a business is publicly-held, it is required by the Securities and Exchange Commission (SEC) to take one additional step in the preparation of its quarterly and full-year financial statements, which is to convert them to the XBRL format. *XBRL* is a contraction of the term eXtensible Business Reporting Language. XBRL uses tags to specifically identify various types of information within a financial report, which are then used by software to convert the data into an electronic spreadsheet for further analysis. Thus, XBRL is a step in the process of converting plain-text financial information into a spreadsheet format for further analysis. Once the financial statements have been converted into the XBRL format, they are uploaded to the SEC's website.

See the author's *Closing the Books* course for a much more detailed discussion of the closing process.

The Trial Balance

The trial balance is a report run at the end of a reporting period. It is primarily used to ensure that the total of all debits equals the total of all credits, which means that there are no unbalanced entries in the accounting system that would make it impossible to generate accurate financial statements.

When the trial balance is first printed, it is called an *unadjusted trial balance*. Then, when the accounting team corrects any errors found or makes other adjustments, the report is called the *adjusted trial balance*. Finally, after the period has been closed, the report is called the *post-closing trial balance*.

The initial trial balance report contains the following columns:

1. Account number
2. Account name
3. Ending debit balance (if any)
4. Ending credit balance (if any)

Each line item only contains the ending balance in an account, which comes from the general ledger. All accounts having an ending balance are listed in the trial balance; usually, the accounting software automatically blocks all accounts having a zero balance from appearing in the report, which reduces its length. A sample trial balance appears in the following exhibit.

Sample Trial Balance

Account Number	Account Description	Unadjusted Trial Balance	
		Debit	Credit
1000	Cash	$60,000	
1500	Accounts receivable	180,000	
2000	Inventory	300,000	
3000	Fixed assets	210,000	
4000	Accounts payable		$90,000
4500	Accrued liabilities		50,000
4700	Notes payable		420,000
5000	Equity		350,000
6000	Revenue		400,000
7200	Cost of goods sold	290,000	
7300	Salaries expense	200,000	
7400	Payroll tax expense	20,000	
7500	Rent expense	35,000	
7600	Other expenses	15,000	
	Totals	$1,310,000	$1,310,000

The adjusted version of a trial balance may combine the debit and credit columns into a single combined column, and add columns to show adjusting entries and a revised ending balance. This format is useful for revealing the derivation of the line items in financial statements.

The following sample shows adjusting entries. It also combines the debit and credit totals into the second column, so that the summary balance for the total is (and should be) zero. Adjusting entries are added in the next column, yielding an adjusted trial balance in the far right column.

Sample Adjusted Trial Balance

Account Description	Unadjusted Trial Balance	Adjusting Entries	Adjusted Trial Balance
Cash	$60,000		$60,000
Accounts receivable	180,000	$50,000	230,000
Inventory	300,000		300,000
Fixed assets (net)	210,000		210,000
Accounts payable	-90,000		-90,000
Accrued liabilities	-50,000	-25,000	-75,000
Notes payable	-420,000		-420,000
Equity	-350,000		-350,000
Revenue	-400,000	-50,000	-450,000
Cost of goods sold	290,000		290,000
Salaries expense	200,000	25,000	225,000
Payroll tax expense	20,000		20,000
Rent expense	35,000		35,000
Other expenses	15,000		15,000
Totals	$0	$0	$0

Responsibility Accounting

Responsibility accounting is based on the assumption that all revenues generated and costs incurred must be the responsibility of one person. For example, the cost of rent can be assigned to the person who negotiates and signs the lease, while the cost of an employee's salary is the responsibility of that person's direct manager. This concept also applies to the cost of products, for each component part has a standard cost, which it is the responsibility of the purchasing manager to obtain at the correct price. Similarly, scrap costs incurred at a machine are the responsibility of the production manager.

By applying this concept to reporting, internal revenue and cost reports can be tailored for each recipient. For example, the manager of a work center on the production floor will receive a financial statement that only itemizes the costs incurred by that specific work center, while the production manager will receive a different report that itemizes the costs of the entire production department, and the chief executive officer receives one that summarizes the results of the entire organization.

Fewer responsibility reports are used for the more comprehensive types of reporting. For example, each person in a department may be placed in charge of a separate cost, so each one receives a report that itemizes their performance in controlling that cost. However, when the more complex *profit center* approach is used, these costs are typically clumped together into the group of costs that can be directly associated with revenues from a specific product or product line, which therefore results in fewer profit centers than cost centers. Then, at the highest level of responsibility center, which is the *investment center*, a manager makes investments that may cut across entire product lines, so that the investment center tends to be reported at a minimal level of an entire production facility. Thus, there is a natural consolidation in the number of responsibility reports generated by the accounting department as more complex forms of responsibility reporting are used.

Budget Reporting

A *budget* is a document that forecasts the financial results and financial position of a business for one or more future periods. At a minimum, a budget contains an estimated income statement that describes anticipated financial results. A more complex budget also contains an estimated balance sheet, which includes the entity's anticipated assets, liabilities, and equity positions at various points in time in the future. A prime use of the budget is to serve as a performance baseline for the measurement of actual results.

A completed budget is loaded into the AIS in order to present a budget versus actual reporting format for the income statement and balance sheet. This report reveals any variances between the budgeted and actual amounts. The format of such a report is similar to the one in the following exhibit.

Sample Budget versus Actual Income Statement

	Actual Results	Budget Results	Variance ($)	Variance (%)
Revenue	$1,000,000	$1,100,000	-$100,000	-9%
Cost of goods sold:				
Direct materials	300,000	330,000	30,000	9%
Direct labor	100,000	90,000	-10,000	-11%
Manufacturing overhead	150,000	155,000	5,000	3%
Total cost of goods sold	550,000	575,000	25,000	4%
Gross margin	$450,000	$525,000	-$75,000	-14%
Administration expenses	175,000	160,000	-15,000	-9%
Sales and marketing expenses	225,000	205,000	-20,000	-10%
Net profit or loss	$50,000	$160,000	-$110,000	-69%

This report format does not reveal a great deal of information by itself, since it only notifies management of the presence *of* a variance, not the reason *for* the variance. Further, the budget upon which the variance is calculated may be so far out of line with actual results that the variance is essentially meaningless.

A subtle variation on this report format is to position the largest-dollar items at the top of the report, so that the areas in which variances are likely to be largest are where management can more easily see them. The following exhibit illustrates the concept.

Sample Sales and Marketing Department Monthly Report

Expense Item	Actual	Budget	$ Variance	% Variance
Wages	$85,000	$82,000	-$3,000	-4%
Commissions	18,000	19,500	1,500	8%
Payroll taxes	8,000	7,500	-500	-7%
Trade shows	25,000	28,000	3,000	11%
Travel and entertainment	11,000	7,000	-4,000	-57%
Office expenses	6,500	3,500	-3,000	-86%
Promotional materials	5,000	5,000	0	0%
Other	1,200	500	-700	-58%
Totals	$159,700	$153,000	-$6,700	-4%

Note how the preceding report is structured to place wages and related expenses at the top of the report; this is because compensation costs are the largest expenditure for many departments, and so should be the center of attention.

An alternative format is one that presents a historical trend line of revenues and expenses for each line item in the income statement. Doing so eliminates the risk of comparing a completely inaccurate budget to actual results. A sample report format follows, where unusual blips in the trend line are highlighted.

Sample Trend Line Report Format

	Jan.	Feb	Mar.	Apr.	May
Accounting fees	$1,000	$1,100	$1,050	$1,900	$1,150
Legal	0	0	5,000	0	250
Maintenance	550	575	400	600	3,250
Office expenses	925	2,800	890	790	850
Travel and entertainment	6,500	1,200	1,350	1,400	995
Utilities	500	310	420	1,600	375
Totals	$9,475	$5,985	$9,110	$6,290	$6,870

The key assumption behind a trend line report is that most expenses do not vary much from period to period. If that assumption is true, then the report is excellent for highlighting anomalies over time.

No matter which of the preceding report formats are used, it is rarely sufficient to simply issue financial information to managers without at least some explanation of the larger variances. Instead, the accounting staff investigates the larger variances and issues a separate report that delves into the reasons for them. The following sample report states the amount of each expense or revenue item that requires explanation, and then spends a fair amount of time describing the situation.

Sample Variance Discussion Report

Line Item	Discussion
Product Alpha revenue	Revenues were $100,000 lower than expected, due to a product recall and free replacement. The problem was a design flaw that is being investigated by Engineering. Recommend stopping sales until an engineering change order is released.
Direct materials expense	Freight expense was $40,000 higher than expected, due to air freight of late delivery from overseas supplier. Recommend sourcing the part locally.
Rent expense	Expense was $20,000 lower than expected, due to renegotiation of building lease. Note that the lease now runs an additional three years.
Travel and entertainment expense	Expense was $25,000 higher than expected, due to damage to rental party room during company Christmas party.
Utilities expense	Electricity cost was $15,000 higher than expected, due to unusually cold December temperatures. Recommend additional building insulation.

Note that the best reports of this type clearly quantify the issue and state the exact cause of the problem, possibly with an accompanying recommendation. The report needs to be sufficiently detailed that management can use it to resolve the underlying problem.

Flexible Budgeting

Many income statements are issued in a budget versus actual format, along with a calculated variance from the budget. This format allows managers to view how well the business is performing in comparison to expectations. The problem with this form of presentation is that the traditional budget model is a static one – that is, it does not change even if the underlying activity level of the business differs during the budget period from the level assumed when the budget was constructed. This can be a major problem when the actual activity level *does* change, because the reported variances may be not only quite large, but also irrelevant. Instead, a budget model needs to be used that changes based on the level of actual activity.

A possible solution is the *flexible budget*, which calculates different expenditure levels for variable costs, depending upon changes in the amount of actual revenue or other activity measures. The usual way to update a flexible budget model is to input actual revenues or other activity measures into it once a reporting period has been completed, resulting in a revised budget model that is specific to the inputs. This revised budget is then compared to actual results in the budget versus actual report. The steps needed to construct a flexible budget are:

1. Identify all fixed costs and segregate them in the budget model.
2. Determine the extent to which all variable costs change as activity measures change.
3. Create the budget model, where fixed costs are "hard coded" into the model, and variable costs are stated as a percentage of the relevant activity measures or as a cost per unit of activity measure.
4. Enter actual activity measures into the model after a reporting period has been completed. This updates the variable costs in the flexible budget.
5. Enter the resulting flexible budget for the completed period into the AIS for comparison to actual expenses.

This approach varies from the more common *static budget*, which contains nothing but fixed amounts that do not vary with actual revenue levels. Budget versus actual reports under a flexible budget tend to yield variances that are much more relevant than those generated under a static budget, since both the budgeted and actual expenses are based on the same activity measure. This means that the variances will likely be smaller than under a static budget, and will also be highly actionable. The following two examples show a flexible budget in action.

EXAMPLE

Quest Adventure Gear has a budget of $10 million in revenues and a $4 million cost of goods sold. Of the $4 million in budgeted cost of goods sold, $1 million is fixed, and $3 million varies directly with revenue. Thus, the variable portion of the cost of goods sold is 30% of revenues. Once the budget period has been completed, Quest finds that sales were actually $9 million. If it used a flexible budget, the fixed portion of the cost of goods sold would still be $1 million, but the variable portion would drop to $2.7 million, since it is always 30% of revenues. The result is that a flexible budget yields a budgeted cost of goods sold of $3.7 million at a $9 million revenue level, rather than the $4 million that would be listed in a static budget.

EXAMPLE

Quest Adventure Gear has always budgeted for sales of its polycarbonate climbing helmets using a static budget, but sales have differed markedly from expectations, resulting in large variances in its production budget. For the new budget year, Quest is experimenting with a flexible budget. This budget is divided into variable cost and fixed cost components, with the variable costs being tied to the number of unit sales of the helmet. The resulting budget is shown in the following table, which notes both budgeted and actual results for the first month of the budget period.

Helmet Production Department	Budgeted Unit Costs	Budget January	Actual January	Variances
Revenue (at $90/unit)		$135,000	$135,000	$0
Units sold		1,500	1,500	
Variable costs:				
Helmet components	$21.50	32,250	33,100	-850
Fixed costs:				
Direct labor crewing		18,000	19,500	-1,500
Manufacturing overhead		41,500	40,750	750
Gross margin		$43,250	$41,650	-$1,600

The budget model multiplies the $21.50 budgeted unit cost of the helmet components by the 1,500 actual units sold to arrive at budgeted variable costs for the month of $32,250. All other costs shown in the budget are fixed.

Financial Reporting Controls

Businesses go to great lengths to ensure that their financial reports are as accurate as possible, for several reasons. First, they will soon lose the faith of their creditors and investors if they repeatedly issue financial statements that prove to be incorrect. Second, management may take action based on incorrect financial statements, resulting in changes that are not beneficial to the company. And third, regulators may penalize a business that issues incorrect financial statements. Consequently, there are strong incentives to issue accurate reports.

Financial statement accuracy can be enhanced by installing a suite of robust controls around the general ledger and the processes used to generate financial statements. These controls include the following:

- *Closing checklist*. The use of a closing checklist should be enforced. This is a good way to verify that all steps required to close the books have been taken.
- *Access restrictions*. The source of the data that is summarized into the financial statements is the general ledger, so access to the general ledger should be strictly controlled. Ideally, only the general ledger accountant should be allowed to make journal entries, so that all changes to the general ledger can be traced to one person. Further, read-only access to the general ledger and the ability to view or print financial statements should also be restricted, especially in publicly-held companies where early access to financial information can be used to illegally manipulate stock prices.
- *Change log*. A change log should be used to track all changes to the general ledger. This log is regularly reviewed to ensure that all changes made are appropriate.

- *Audit trail.* Ensure that the system supplies reviewers with a clear audit trail that documents the flow of transactions. It is used to investigate how a source document was translated into an account entry, and from there was inserted into the financial statements. It can also be used in reverse, to track backwards from a financial statement line item to the originating source document.
- *Standardized adjusting entries.* Standardized templates should be used for the adjusting entries that modify the general ledger for month-end reporting. The use of templates reduces the risk that adjusting entries will be prepared incorrectly, leading to incorrect financial statements.
- *Account reconciliations.* Balance sheet accounts should be reconciled at the end of each reporting period, to ensure that their balances are comprised of valid transactions. Reconciliations will sometimes detect items that should be recognized in the current period, thereby shifting them from the balance sheet to the income statement.
- *Analytical review.* Compare the preliminary financial statements to the results of the past few periods to see if there are any anomalies in the various line items, and investigate as necessary. This could be a simple search for blips in the trend line of results, or a more quantitatively-precise approach where changes of a specific dollar amount or percentage are investigated.
- *Spreadsheet review.* There may be calculation errors in the spreadsheets used to create journal entries, so periodically review the calculations to verify that they are correct.
- *Cutoff analysis.* Review significant transactions occurring near the end of the reporting period to see if they are being recorded in the correct period. It is possible that some of them relate to the following reporting period.
- *Customized report analysis.* When a special version of the financial statements is created within the AIS, there is a good chance that some accounts will not be included in the custom report, or that they will be repeated. These issues can be found by comparing the original default financial statements to the modified versions.
- *Reversing entry review.* Some adjusting entries are set to automatically reverse at the beginning of the next reporting period. A manual review of these entries in the next period can detect whether any reversals did *not* take place, usually because the general ledger accountant did not set a flag in the journal entry to reverse itself.
- *Budget file protection.* It is quite easy for someone to access the completed budget file and inadvertently make changes to it. To avoid this issue, impose password protection on the file. In addition, archive the file, preferably in an off-site location. Further, consider printing and binding a copy of the budget, and storing it in the corporate archives.
- *Loaded budget matches approved budget.* Once the budget has been approved, load it into the AIS in order to generate financial statements in an

actual versus budget format. Given the volume of budget information to be entered, it is quite likely that some of the budget information will be entered into the AIS incorrectly. Consequently, match the loaded version of the budget to the approved version, and adjust the loaded version for any errors found.

Of the preceding controls, the one that will avoid the most problems is the closing checklist. Without a formal listing of activities to be completed, it is quite likely that a closing process will be flawed, resulting in the release of incorrect financial statements.

Summary

Financial reporting is derived from the general ledger, so it is critical to tightly control the transactions flowing into it. This means limiting access to the general ledger, as well as to the subledgers posting to it. In addition, the AIS should have a strong audit trail, so that the flow of transactions through the system can be easily monitored, both from source documents into the financial statements and from the financial statements back to the source documents.

The accuracy of the information that appears in the financial statements is driven by many issues, such as how well the accounting staff follows the closing checklist, ensures that subledgers have posted to the general ledger, reconciles accounts, and investigates anomalies. Thus, a significant amount of effort is needed to ensure that financial reports are issued that fairly represent the actual financial situation of a business.

Chapter 14
Systems Development and Analysis

Introduction

Organizations are routinely outgrowing their old systems as they expand in size or shift into new market niches. When this happens, the old systems no longer meet their requirements, resulting in slow response times, missing capabilities, or ongoing patches to the system to add new features. The tipping point when management sees the need for a replacement system is when one or more of the following conditions are present:

- *Acquisitions.* A business that is acquiring others may experience a drastic increase in transaction volume coming from its acquired businesses. If the intent is to operate the acquirees on a common platform, then a much more robust system will be needed.
- *Age.* Existing systems may be so old that it is difficult to find qualified people to maintain them, let alone provide updates to their features.
- *Competition.* A business may find that it needs to acquire a new system just to keep up with the competition. This is a particular concern when new systems at competitors are allowing them to provide new services to customers that the company cannot match.
- *Costs.* When the cost of the old system is significantly higher than that of other systems in the marketplace with comparable capabilities, it may be time to switch systems, if only to strip costs out of the business. This is also the case when the acquisition of a new system will enhance processes or improve productivity to such an extent that costs can be significantly reduced.
- *Features.* Management may find that it is in need of an essential feature in its systems that it cannot obtain or build into those systems. When a missing feature is a cornerstone of the business strategy, there may be no choice – a new system must be acquired.
- *Incompatible systems.* An older business may have acquired separate systems for each of its functional areas, and those systems are not compatible with each other. When this is the case, the acquisition of an integrated solution can be used to sweep away these old systems.
- *Regulatory changes.* If a business is operating in a highly regulated environment, the regulator may impose requirements that can only be met by a limited number of systems.

Given the multitude of reasons for replacing a system, it should be no surprise that most organizations have some sort of systems development project going on at all times. In this chapter, we address the planning process that goes into the design of an information system, as well as implementation, project oversight, and numerous other related issues.

Systems Development Concerns

Engaging in an in-house systems development project is not for the faint of heart. These projects routinely take longer than expected, are more expensive than expected, and deliver results that are less than expected (usually all three). Some projects fail so miserably on all three counts that they are cancelled. The situation is exacerbated by the presence of *scope creep*, where the requirements of a proposed system are gradually expanded over the course of a project, greatly increasing its cost and delaying its completion date.

When viewed from a longer-term perspective, the situation is even more dire. If management does not follow a long-term plan for how it intends to roll out new systems or enhance existing ones, it is quite likely that the result will be a patchwork of systems that do not interact, and for which there is no clear upgrade path.

In the following sections, we cover many planning topics related to the development of systems that can be used to minimize these concerns.

Systems Planning

Ideally, a business should create an overarching plan for its systems that is closely aligned with the overall corporate strategy. The plan outlines which systems will be installed, how they will be acquired or developed in-house, and the resources required. It will also prioritize projects, which can be useful when full funding for all proposed systems is not available. This information will be laid out on a timetable that typically covers multiple years, since many systems require several years of effort to complete. Doing so has the following advantages:

- *Management support.* Since there is a clear linkage between the systems plan and corporate strategy, management is much more likely to support the systems plan, providing it with adequate resources.
- *Software coordination.* Because the systems plan outlines which systems will be installed, as well as where and how they will interact, there is a high likelihood that these systems will be designed to share data as soon as they are installed.
- *System selection process.* An ancillary document that may be developed along with the systems plan is a standardized system selection process. Using the same criteria to select *all* systems improves the odds of acquiring systems that will perform beyond minimum standards.
- *Waste reduction.* By adopting a coordinated approach to the development of systems, the organization is more likely to save money by avoiding duplicated efforts.
- *Awareness of change.* With a plan in place, management has adequate warning to find sufficient funding to pay for systems acquisitions. Also,

since some systems will impact the company's hiring and training needs, the human resources department can use the plan to develop its own recruiting, training, and layoff plans.

A corporate systems plan is by no means frozen for an extended period of time. Instead, the information technology staff should stay abreast of the latest improvements in the industry, and advise management regarding the need to incorporate these changes into the plan. Further, it is advisable to reissue the plan once a quarter, so that the most recent project status information can be incorporated into the plan.

Systems Development Life Cycle

The systems development life cycle describes the process of planning, creating, testing, and deploying an information system. This life cycle can be used to describe software installations, hardware installations or a mix of the two. The stages in this life cycle are as follows:

1. *Analysis*. Involves a review of user requirements and how well they are met by the existing system. A survey of the current system may be triggered, which includes gaining an understanding of existing operations, procedures, and software capabilities by reviewing system documentation, observing operations, and interviewing employees. If there is a need for a replacement system, a cost-benefit analysis is completed, along with a feasibility study to determine how difficult the proposed project will be. Several alternative solutions may be considered. If the proposed system appears to be both cost-beneficial and feasible, then a proposal document is prepared for the review and approval of management.
2. *Design*. This includes the development of specifications for the system, including necessary inputs, processing capabilities, business rules, and outputs. The design includes descriptions of the controls and procedures that must accompany or be built into the system. This information is used to decide whether to construct the system in-house or buy it from a supplier.
3. *Development*. Write the code for the proposed system, along with input and output forms, files, controls, and procedures.
4. *Implementation*. Write an implementation plan that includes hardware and software installations, user training, and the switchover to the new system, followed by actual implementation.
5. *Testing*. The system is tested in a variety of ways to see if it conforms to the requirements specified in the design stage, that its various modules work together as anticipated, and that it operates at reasonable speed under maximum user load conditions.

6. *Documentation*. Develop user documentation that describes the actions needed to complete various tasks within the system.
7. *Evaluation*. Entails an analysis of the effectiveness of the completed system. The evaluation may also include a review of any additional enhancements that may be made to it.

Given the high probability that a systems development project will fail, there is a strong need for the systems development life cycle. By following the progression of steps described in the cycle, one can evaluate projects at many points during the development process to decide whether there is a need for additional resources, scope changes, or changes to the implementation schedule. By constantly reviewing a project, one can decide as early as possible whether to make changes to advance the project, or to withdraw funding and kill it.

There are several ways to improve the odds of having a successful systems development process. First, involve users throughout the design process, since they are in the best position to understand what is needed. Second, the management team needs to visibly provide significant support throughout the process, as well as monetary support, so that users understand that this system *will* be completed. And finally, management must continue supporting the system for a long time after it has been installed, in order to overcome any residual resistance to it.

Feasibility Study

One of the tasks noted in the last section for the analysis phase of the systems development life cycle is the completion of a feasibility study. A *feasibility study* is the evaluation of a proposed activity to see if it meets the following criteria:

- *Cost-benefit*. Will the project generate a benefit that equals or exceeds its costs? This determination is usually made using a capital budgeting technique, typically involving one or more of the following:
  - o *Discounted cash flows*. Estimate the amount of all cash inflows and outflows associated with a project through its estimated useful life, and then apply a discount rate to these cash flows to determine their present value. If the present value is positive, accept the proposed project, subject to funding availability.
  - o *Internal rate of return*. Determine the discount rate at which the cash flows from a project net to zero. The project with the highest internal rate of return is selected.
  - o *Constraint analysis*. Examine the impact of a proposed project on the bottleneck operation of the business. If the proposal either increases the capacity of the bottleneck or routes work around it, thereby increasing throughput, then fund the project.
  - o *Breakeven analysis*. Determine the required sales level at which a project will result in positive cash flow. If the sales level is low enough to be reasonably attainable, then accept the project.

217

- o *Discounted payback*. Determine the amount of time it will take for the discounted cash flows from a project to earn back the initial investment. If the period is sufficiently short, then accept the project.
- o *Real options*. Focus on the range of profits and losses that may be encountered over the course of the investment period. The analysis begins with a review of the risks to which a project will be subjected, and then models for each of these risks or combinations of risks. The result may be greater care in placing large bets on a single likelihood of probability.

When analyzing a possible investment, it is useful to also analyze the system into which the proposed project will be inserted. If the system is unusually complex, it is likely to take longer for the outcome of the new project to function as expected. The reason for the delay is that there may be unintended consequences that ripple through the system, requiring multiple adjustments before any gains from the initial investment can be achieved.

- *Technical challenges*. Can the stated goals of the project be achieved with existing technology? More specifically, can the goals be achieved with the current technological capabilities of employees, or must new skills be acquired?
- *Legal requirements*. Will the proposed system meet all regulatory and legal requirements? This is a particular concern when a business operates in a regulated industry.
- *Schedule attainment*. Is it likely that the system can be rolled out within the time period allotted for it? This is a particular concern when a delayed completion date will significantly increase the costs incurred.
- *Operational capability*. Will employees use the proposed system? Conversely, what level of employee pushback can be expected from the implementation of this system?

Feasibility studies are quite common for larger systems projects, where the high degree of complexity and uncertainty presents a significant risk of failure. These larger projects can last for months or years, so it is reasonable to revisit the initial feasibility study at intervals over the life of a project, to see if the original conclusions still apply. It is quite possible that a serious problem encountered somewhere along the project timeline will lead to a conclusion that a project is no longer feasible, resulting in its termination.

Conceptual and Physical Systems Design

The design step noted earlier in the systems development life cycle can be broken down further, into conceptual and physical systems design. A significant amount of time should be spent on these activities, since a clear delineation of a proposed system makes it much easier to generate code that does not require correction at a later date.

In the conceptual design phase, the focus is on assessing the feasibility of meeting the designated objectives, as well as on developing a broad overview of the system. The following activities are typically included in the conceptual design phase:

1. *Define the problem.* Clearly define the problem to be solved. This may involve consideration of the organization's mission, objectives, and plans.
2. *Set objectives.* Quantify the objectives to be met.
3. *Identify constraints.* Identify all bottlenecks, both within and outside the company that can impact the project. This typically involves non-cooperation by employees, lack of management support, and/or lack of resources.
4. *Determine information needs.* Specify what users want from the system, as well as those information items needed to achieve the firm's objectives.
5. *Determine information sources.* Specify all information sources, including internal records and key personnel.
6. *Develop design alternatives.* Create several possible designs, from which the optimum design can be selected that meets the requirements of the business in a cost-effective manner. For example, should the delivery of goods to a customer via a company-operated truck involve the use of paper transfer documents, or a screen on a tablet computer? Or, should the process of picking goods from stock involve a paper pick list or a headset that conveys audio instructions? The following exhibit presents examples of other design alternatives.
7. *Document the design.* Document the overall flow of the system, including all inputs to and outputs from it. The design document should specify the data elements needed to produce required output, and include the content of any reports and screen output generated, as well as how they are formatted.

Sample System Design Alternatives

Design Topic	Possible Alternatives Available
Data input method	Input alternatives include manual keying, bar coding, RFID, and point of sale
Data storage	Storage alternatives include hard drive and solid state
Data transmission	Transmission alternatives include wireless, Internet, and satellite
Form of processing	In batch mode if update speed is not critical, or in real time if it is critical
Operational responsibility	Responsibilities for operating the system can be in-house or a supplier
Output medium	Alternatives include screen output, paper report output, and audio output
Print format	Alternatives are the use of preprinted forms or system-formatted output
Software usage	Alternatives are on-line, commercial, customized commercial, or in-house

Physical systems design involves translating the conceptual design into detailed requirements that are used as the basis for writing software. The physical design incorporates the following activities:

1. *Design the output.* This is an iterative process of designing preliminary reports and then working with users to refine the initial concepts. This process is most critical for scheduled reports, such as a monthly sales report by region, since they will be used many times. The report design effort tends to be somewhat reduced for special-purpose reports that will be used less frequently.
2. *Design the file structure.* This step requires designers to pay attention to the underlying file structure and data formats, so that records can be more easily shared with other applications. Other considerations include the type of processing to be used, the number of records expected, and the proportion of these records that will be added, changed, or deleted each year.
3. *Design the input.* This step includes the design of the forms used to manually collect data, as well as the design of the screens used to input data into the computer. There are many considerations, such as the incorporation of a logical flow, the grouping of similar data, and the avoidance of clutter. These decisions are driven by where the data comes from, the volume to be entered, the frequency of data entry, and the skill level of the people being asked to engage in data entry tasks.
4. *Design the program.* This extensive step can be broken down into several activities, which are:

    a. *Write the software.* The previous design steps are used as the basis for writing the software, for which the coding is typically broken down into a series of smaller modules. Dividing the programming work into modules makes it easier to modify and debug the software.
    b. *Test the software.* Several types of testing regimens are used to see if the code contains logic errors, handles invalid data correctly, interacts properly with other modules, operates properly under heavy user volumes, can recover from system crashes, can block attempted access by unauthorized parties, and meets the requirements of users. Copies of real transactions may be used on a copy of the software, to see how the system handles "live" data.
    c. *Document the software.* Once the software has been tested and so is unlikely to change further, it can be documented. This involves a full explanation of what each block of code is intended to do, as well as the nature of the data being stored and manipulated. Flowcharts, record layouts, and data flow diagrams may be added to enhance user understanding of the software.
    d. *Prepare the site.* The hardware needed to support the software may need to be housed in a special room with air conditioning, fire suppression systems, an emergency power system, raised floors, and humidity controls. The site should be completed, the hardware installed, and software run on it before users can begin their training sessions.

    e. *Train the users.* Training materials are prepared that are intended to show employees how to use the system's functionality, along with any related policies and procedures. These materials may define key terms used, explain the purposes of various forms and input screens, and walk users through a series of test transactions. The training given to users must be sufficient to give them a working knowledge of the system; if training is inadequate, user acceptance will likely decline, and it may take months for them to figure out the functionality of the software on their own. The system should be scheduled to go live as soon as user training has been completed; otherwise, users will rapidly forget how the system works.

5. *Design related controls.* Any system will likely need to be matched with a few controls to ensure that inputs to the system are accurate, thereby increasing the quality of the data being processed. These controls may be incorporated into the procedures associated with a system, or they may be built into the software itself.

6. *Design related procedures.* Most software is embedded in a set of procedures that control who can access the system, how they are supposed to use it, and what they should do with the output from the software. These procedures are developed immediately after the software has been finalized, and may be incorporated into online help screens or printed user manuals.

Systems Implementation

An essential part of the process of going live is switching over from the old system to the new one. Depending on the complexity of the system, this conversion can be quite complex, since it also involves shifting records from the old system to the new one as seamlessly as possible. There several ways to conduct this conversion, each one with varying risks and costs. The available options are:

- *Cold turkey.* As the name implies, this conversion involves shutting down the old system and turning on the new one. This approach can be the least expensive (if it works), since there is no parallel processing of the two systems. However, it places the business at significant risk of a shutdown if the new system does not function properly. This approach works best when the system is relatively minor and has no impact on other systems.

- *Parallel processing.* Both the old and the new system are run concurrently for a period of time. Doing so allows testers to compare the results of the two systems to make sure that the new system is producing the same results as the old one. This is a safer approach than a cold turkey changeover, since the company is still running the old system if the new one fails. However, it also requires employees to enter transactions twice – once in the old system and once in the new one.

- *Phased conversion.* This approach involves changing over to the new system one software module at a time. Doing so minimizes the dislocation involved with a changeover. However, it can result in a significant expenditure to build temporary interfaces between the newly-installed modules and the modules in the old system with which they share data. Also, this approach can result in quite a lengthy implementation process – quite possibly stretching through several years for a larger installation.

- *Pilot installation.* Instead of attempting to install the entire system across the organization, it is piloted at a single location, such as a subsidiary or a single retail store. The system can be thoroughly tested in this location over an extended period of time to ensure that all possible issues have been detected and dealt with. Once the installation team is satisfied with the performance of the system, they can roll it out on a company-wide basis with a much lower risk of failure. Though a relatively safe approach, the use of pilot installations can greatly prolong the time period needed to complete a full rollout of a system.

A particular concern with systems implementation is the difficulty associated with converting data from the old system into the record format needed by the new system. This can be a major problem when fields in the old system have been deleted in the record structure employed by the new system, since there is no way to exactly match the old fields to the new fields. Given these concerns, the data conversion process should be scheduled with plenty of extra time to deal with errors in the conversion routine, as well as for extensive validation testing to ensure that the data have been converted to the new system correctly.

Once the preceding steps have been completed, users are given access to the system. This includes the use of interfaces with other systems that can port data into and out of other applications. Even if a significant amount of training has been provided to users, one can expect a substantial amount of user uncertainty in the first few days. To deal with this issue, a large part of the implementation team should be made available for user support, either in the field or through a centralized user helpline. The types of questions fielded by this group may indicate the need for additional tweaks to the system, the training, or the user documentation.

Once the implementation is complete, users can be expected to initiate requests for changes to the system, which may include suggested enhancements to its inputs, processing, and outputs. These changes may prove to be considerable, especially if changes to the company's operating or regulatory environment require it to alter its systems to match the environmental changes.

Change Management

One of the line items noted earlier for a feasibility study was an analysis of operational capability, one component of which was whether employees will push back on the proposed system implementation. Since systems underlie much of the work performed by employees, it would be reasonable to assume that any proposed changes to their activities would be a concern for them. Consequently, when evaluating whether a prospective change can be applied to an organization, it is useful to evaluate the environment on which it will be imposed. If the environment is especially toxic, it may be necessary to focus on fewer projects, and assume longer completion timelines and larger budgets in order to have any chance of success. Here are several environments that can cause trouble for a project:

- *Prospect of change.* Any initiative that is likely to result in a layoff is sure to trigger either passive or active resistance by employees. Even if there are assurances from management that there will be no layoffs, projects still represent changes to established work patterns, which may be viewed with trepidation.
- *Jaded employees.* Employees have experienced so many failed initiatives in the past that they believe nothing will work for the company. Their response is to shrug off new projects and wait for the supporting managers to give up and go away.
- *Off-site plotting.* There is a culture of having little discussion during meetings, after which there is intensive discussion in private meetings, usually to derail proposed initiatives. In this environment, those most able to plot and play politics control the corporate agenda.
- *Reactive culture.* Managers avoid taking risks by heaping criticism on new initiatives, thereby squashing them before they get started. This environment is especially likely when the managers of functions or subsidiaries have substantial power, and so can easily fend off senior management's initiatives with a few well-chosen critiques.

All of the preceding environments can be deeply ingrained within the culture of a business, and so are especially difficult to eradicate.

To overcome these problems, one can follow a specific series of steps that have been proven to work. Each step in this process must be thoroughly addressed before a change can be considered to have been successfully completed. To greatly improve the odds that a change initiative will be accepted within an organization, follow these steps:

1. *Create a sense of urgency.* This involves the discussion of existing or looming crises facing the business, as well as major opportunities. If there is no sense of urgency, it is nearly impossible to budge people from their zones of complacency. This is a particular problem in businesses that have had a history of success, where employees have no experience with problems that could obliterate sales and profits.
2. *Assemble a guiding coalition.* Locate those key people within the business who are willing to lead a change effort, and assemble them into a functioning team. This group must have sufficiently powerful titles, budgets, expertise, and networks within the business to drive through change.
3. *Develop a vision.* Devise a vision for the change effort, as well as an overarching strategy for how that vision will be achieved. This should be an easily understandable and compelling vision, not a complicated laundry list of improvement efforts. An organization can rally around a clear vision, but

will be put off by an excessively detailed or unfocused one. Be sure to develop a *reasonable* vision, to avoid unrealistic expectations by employees for what will be achieved.

4. *Communicate constantly.* Use multiple communication channels and a high degree of repetition to communicate the vision and supporting strategy throughout the business. These communication channels may include not just the usual e-mails and newsletters, but every possible form of communication, such as during performance reviews, training classes, and quarterly financial reports. Further, the coalition leading the change effort should present an example of the best possible behavior needed to support the change. Only comprehensive messaging will shape the opinions of employees.

5. *Eliminate obstacles.* Any obstacle interfering with the change effort must be eliminated. This may include the replacement of existing processes, structures, and personnel. In essence, any bottleneck interfering with a project should be anticipated and dealt with as expeditiously as possible. When a serious obstacle remains in place for any period of time, the probability of success declines precipitously.

6. *Create wins.* Plan for a series of short-term and highly-visible wins, and reward employees for achieving them. These wins should be measurable and therefore unambiguous, so that naysayers cannot claim that the wins are really just a matter of opinion. Examples of short-term wins to be celebrated are:

   - Increase in inventory record accuracy
   - Increase in on-time shipping percentage
   - Increase in market share
   - New products are rolled out

7. *Roll forward.* With the initial wins just noted, the project earns an increased amount of respectability, allowing the guiding coalition to establish more goals, implement more changes, and eliminate more barriers to success.

8. *Lock in changes.* Once change initiatives have succeeded, integrate them into the fabric of the business, so that there will be no backsliding. This can involve integration into policies and procedures, employee training, and compensation plans.

All of the preceding steps must be followed, or else a project will experience a high risk of failure. However, if just one of the preceding steps must be targeted as being absolutely essential, it is the creation of a guiding coalition. More specifically, the group responsible for pushing change must not simply be a slight variation on the existing corporate hierarchy. If the existing hierarchy were managing the business effectively, there would be no crisis that requires change. Consequently, the coalition needs to operate outside of the normal operating structure of the business, working as an independent entity.

Project Monitoring

It is essential to monitor the progress of systems development projects, since many of them are highly complex and difficult to keep track of. Two of the more common monitoring tools are the Gantt chart and the program evaluation and review technique, which are described in the following sub-sections.

Gantt Charts

A *Gantt chart* is a visual portrayal of the task assignments and task durations within a project. This information is displayed in the form of a horizontal bar chart. The chart can be enhanced with shading to show the level of completion of each task, or a vertical line through the chart that shows today's date. The chart can also show dependencies between the different activities, where one task must be completed before the next task can begin; this means it is relatively easy to identify critical tasks or bottlenecks that might prevent a project from being completed by its planned due date. A simplified Gantt chart that outlines the tasks associated with installing a warehouse bar code scanning system appears in the following exhibit.

Sample Gantt Chart

	Day								
	1	2	3	4	5	6	7	8	9
Take delivery of hardware									
Install location labels									
Test scanner operability									
Test in production environment									
Conduct training									
Go live with scanners									

In the sample chart, note that certain tasks are dependent upon the completion of prior tasks. For example, the testing of scanner operability cannot begin until the bar coded location labels have been installed. Similarly, employees cannot be trained until production testing has been completed. These dependencies are critical to project completion, since a delay earlier in the process has a ripple effect that pushes dependent tasks further out into the future. However, other tasks can be worked on concurrently, since there is no dependency between them. There is more likely to be an overlap in the timelines for these tasks. For example, the installation of location labels could take place prior to the receipt of the bar code scanning hardware.

The Gantt chart is one of the simplest project monitoring tools, and yet can be quite effective, especially when dealing with a relatively uncomplicated project. The complexity of a larger project might instead call for the PERT technique, which is described next.

Program Evaluation and Review Technique (PERT)

The *program evaluation and review technique* identifies every task involved in a project, the time required to complete each one, and the dependencies between tasks. The result is a network diagram that clarifies where the critical path is located in a project. The critical path is that sequence of tasks that requires the longest total time period to complete. There may be several paths within a PERT chart, each comprised of a different set of interrelated tasks that must be completed. Whichever path has the longest duration is the critical path, since shrinking this path will compress the duration of the entire project.

The critical path must be closely monitored to ensure that a project is completed in a timely manner. If a task on the critical path is delayed, this also delays the entire project. A remedial action is to overload tasks on the critical path with additional resources.

PERT allows for the inclusion of variable amounts of time for each task. Thus, each task has a most likely, pessimistic, and optimistic duration attached to it. These three estimates are then combined to arrive at a single estimated duration for each task. This probability feature means that PERT is especially useful when dealing with projects for which there is some uncertainty about completion dates.

The main problem with PERT is the large amount of data that must be incorporated into the planning process. This makes it expensive to maintain, which usually limits its usefulness to larger and more complex systems projects.

Purchased Software

Once the specifications for a new system have been developed, management has the choice of writing custom software or of buying commercial off-the-shelf software. Since writing custom software can be fraught with problems, many businesses opt in favor of purchasing software. If they elect to do so, they can select from the following alternatives, which are presented in increasing order of the amount of expertise required by the company:

- *Application service provider.* This is a supplier that maintains its software from a central location. The advantage is that the company does not have to maintain the software in any way. Instead, its users simply access the software over the Internet.
- *Turnkey solution.* This is when the supplier installs everything – software and hardware – and tests the system before turning it over to the company. Though the cost of a turnkey solution is higher, it is quite attractive to companies that have limited in-house information technology resources.
- *Software-only solution.* This is when the company buys the software and manages the rest of the installation itself. This approach is only possible

when there is sufficient in-house expertise to install and maintain the software.

- *Software-only with modifications.* This involves the acquisition of prepackaged software that is then modified to more precisely meet the company's needs. Since the software now diverges from the supplier's standard software offering, it is difficult (if not impossible) to install any subsequent software updates provided by the supplier.

When considering which of these alternatives to take, management should consider the following additional factors:

- *Requirements addressed.* No commercial off-the-shelf software will exactly match a company's requirements for a system, and it is possible that the software provider will never make the adjustments needed to bring its software perfectly into alignment with those needs. Consequently, the analysis of prospective software packages must include detailed consideration of the features that are *not* provided, as well as discussions about how to work around these shortcomings.
- *Scalability.* Some software solutions are only configured to handle the needs of a relatively small number of users, and will become slow or entirely unworkable if there are too many users. This issue can be overcome by acquiring more robust software, but the highest-end systems can be quite expensive. Consequently, a company may elect to start with an inexpensive, modest software package that can only accommodate a few users, and then have to replace the system later, when its needs expand. This problem can be avoided by using an application service provider, which maintains robust software for all users.
- *Upgrades.* Software providers typically issue updates on a regular basis. When this happens, the updates may erase any customized changes that the company has made to its software, including any interfaces written to link the software to other systems. Consequently, the customization decision effectively eliminates the option of updating the software.
- *Supplier support.* A company with relatively modest in-house information technology expertise may need significant support from its software supplier. If so, the presence of a local supplier office or 24×7 customer support may be significant deciding factors in selecting a supplier.
- *Supplier finances.* A supplier may go out of business, leaving the company with software for which there is no support. Accordingly, part of the supplier selection process should include a discussion of the firm's finances, as well as the size of its user base.

In order to engage in a thorough evaluation of the preceding alternatives, it is useful to aggregate the company's needs into a *request for proposal* (RFP) document, which states the company's exact system needs, differentiating between mandatory functionality and other features that are considered desirable but not necessary.

Suppliers are requested to respond by indicating whether their software meets each of the stated requirements. A review team can then compile the responses into a summary-level analysis of the suitability of each software package. If a supplier exceeds the minimum threshold score on this analysis, it is invited to demonstrate its software before a group of users. Following these demonstrations, the reviewers select a winner based on an array of criteria, which may include the points noted in the following exhibit.

Sample Supplier Evaluation Criteria

Supplier Criteria	Software Criteria	Hardware Criteria
Financial stability	Ability to meet specifications	Compatibility with existing systems
Financing availability	Compatibility with existing systems	Expandability
Installation support	Controls environment	Maintenance cost
Local support staff	Frequency of updates	Purchase cost
Number of customers	Modifications needed	Response times
Quality of references	Query capabilities	Stability of the system
Reputation	Response times	Storage capacity
Support plan	Training and documentation	Underlying technology used
Years in business	Warranties provided	Warranties provided

To introduce some quantitative rigor into the supplier selection process, the review team should devise a listing of which criteria are most important and assign higher weightings to them. It then assigns a score to each supplier for each criterion, which is multiplied by the weighting system to arrive at a weighted final score. The supplier with the highest weighted score is awarded the contract. A sample point scoring system appears in the following exhibit.

Sample Evaluation Matrix for Software Purchase

Criterion	Score	Weight	Weighted Score
Availability on mobile devices	2	20	40
Compatibility with existing software	4	50	200
Comprehensiveness of controls	10	80	800
Frequency of software updates	8	60	480
Interface availability for other software	2	40	80
Portability to other platforms	4	10	40
Query capabilities	8	20	160
Supplier support	8	60	480
Usability of documentation	6	40	240
Usability of mandatory functionality	7	90	630
User group influence on software updates	5	70	350
			3,500

A problem with the point scoring system is that the weightings can be adjusted to alter the outcome, so that a sale is awarded to the most favored supplier, even if that supplier does not actually have software that is the best fit for the company's needs. For example, in the previous exhibit, the supplier described in the exhibit could be awarded a higher weighted score simply by increasing the weighting for any criterion for which it has been awarded a high score. In the exhibit, the supplier was given a high score of 8 for its query capabilities, but the current weighting system tends to discount that category; merely increasing the weighting from 20 to 40 would double the supplier's weighted score for that criterion.

To make the costs of competing software bids more comparable, one should also create estimates for what it would cost to develop any mandatory functionality that is not included in a supplier's current software offering (if this is even possible). An additional consideration is whether a supplier's existing software would be usable while such development is underway. If not, then the selection committee also has to consider the effect of a potentially prolonged delay in the rollout of purchased software.

Once a supplier has been provisionally selected, the selection committee should conduct on-site interviews with the supplier's references, which includes observing the system being used and querying its users about usability, issues found, and supplier responsiveness in dealing with problems. This last step is critical, since it allows the committee to see the system in a live production environment, rather than in a demonstration that is controlled by a salesperson.

Custom Software

There may be instances in which it makes more sense to develop software in-house. This may be necessary under the following circumstances:

- *Competitive advantage.* A business could use the software to develop a competitive advantage over its rivals. For example, an insurer could provide mobile access to its insurance adjustment software, so that its insurance adjustors can complete reimbursement payments in the field.
- *No software.* There may be no commercially available software that meets the firm's specific needs. This is most common for niche applications, where there are so few potential customers that a supplier cannot justify developing the software.
- *Interfaces.* When a business owns several software packages that are not designed to share data, it may be necessary to construct interfaces that do so. These interfaces may need to be revised at regular intervals, if updates to the software packages crash earlier versions of the interfaces.

In most cases, there will be many possible commercially-available software packages on the market, which are more stable and less expensive than any software that could be developed in-house. Consequently, many businesses assume that they will acquire software for most applications, and reserve custom software for a small number of select situations where commercial software is not the best answer to their needs.

When considering whether to develop software in-house, one should first decide whether any of the following problems could impact the development effort:

- *Duration.* It can take a substantial amount of time to complete a software development project, with major projects sometimes requiring years of effort.
- *Scope creep.* Users periodically demand more functionality as the project progresses, resulting in continual expansion of the project scope. This increases the cost and duration of the project.
- *Management support.* Management may initially be behind a project and will fully fund it, but as the project continues, management's attention (and money) may shift elsewhere.
- *Staffing.* It can be quite difficult to obtain the top-notch programming talent needed to design software. The use of less-competent staff can significantly delay the completion of a project, if it can be completed at all.

Management may decide to have a third party develop software instead of doing so in-house. This approach has the advantage of giving the company access to (hopefully) a first-rate development team. However, there will still be significant potential issues to consider. First, the developer may not have any experience in the company's industry, and so is not familiar with the unique aspects of transaction processing in this environment. Second, if the company does not continually provide guidance to the developer, it may spend inordinate resources pursuing development work that will not fit the needs of the company. And third, the developer has an incentive to expand the scope of the project, so that it can bill more to the company. Given these concerns, one must be careful to hire a software development firm with the right kinds of expertise and experience, and to then closely monitor its development activities on behalf of the company.

The Outsourcing Option

A business may decide that it is being bogged down by problems in its information technology function, to the point where these issues are detracting from the management of its core competencies. In this situation, it can make sense to outsource some or all of the information technology area to a third party. For example, a business could shift its AIS to an application service provider, thereby eliminating the related software and hardware from the premises. Or, it could shift the management of its personal computers to a supplier, or its help desk operations. The decision to outsource can have the following positive outcomes:

- *Renewed focus*. Management can refocus its attention on those parts of the business from which it derives a competitive advantage.
- *Sale of assets*. The company can sell its information technology assets to the supplier, thereby providing an immediate influx of cash. In addition, it no longer has to pay for the ongoing maintenance or replacement of its systems.
- *Cost reduction*. Suppliers can offer lower prices than a business would incur if it were to retain its in-house IT functions, because they can purchase hardware and software in massive quantities, and can reduce data storage costs by shifting data storage into consolidated server farms.
- *Technology focus*. Suppliers can offer more cutting-edge technology, which a business might not otherwise have been able to support with its in-house staff.

Though these benefits may appear substantial, there are also several negative issues to consider, which are:

- *Duration*. Outsourcing contracts can run for years. If so, and the relationship sours, it may be difficult for the company to break out of the arrangement.
- *Loss of expertise*. Once employees in the information technology area are laid off or hired by the supplier, the company loses *all* of its in-house information technology expertise. This can be a concern if the company ever wants to take back its information technology function, since it will have to rebuild this expertise from scratch.
- *Cost to take back*. If the company wants to terminate the outsourcing arrangement, it may have to incur significant costs. First, the supplier may have shifted the software and data off-site, so taking back the information technology function may require a significant investment to purchase replacement hardware and software. And second, terminating the arrangement

early may call for the payment of a significant termination fee to the supplier.

- *Loss of competitive advantage*. A company may not realize that some aspects of its information technology functions *do* provide a competitive advantage, so that outsourcing prevents it from having control over that advantage.
- *Service*. The service level provided by the supplier may be lower than expected, so that help desk queries are not resolved promptly. A further concern is that the supplier may not be willing to provide frequent software updates or to migrate the company to new technologies.
- *Supplier failure*. There is a risk that the supplier will go bankrupt, which could lead to all outsourced functions failing.

There is no clear decision arising from these pluses and minuses. Outsourcing has proven to be a major benefit for some companies and an outright failure for others. These outcomes have been driven by many factors, such as the level of communication between the parties, the level of specificity in the outsourcing contracts, the level of oversight by both parties, and expectations for service levels and cost savings.

Electronic Spreadsheets

A common ancillary function to an information system is the electronic spreadsheet. Accountants routinely compile and analyze data on a spreadsheet, rather than attempting to configure the system to provide this functionality. Spreadsheets allow one to construct an application in a few hours, rather than submitting a request to the programming staff and waiting months for it to be developed. A significant benefit of spreadsheets is that they have offloaded the need for custom applications from the system, which can be maintained in a pristine state, without modifications.

As examples of spreadsheet usage, one might employ a spreadsheet to compile a monthly depreciation journal entry for a group of fixed assets, or to maintain the detail for balance sheet accounts, or to analyze why the cost of goods sold has been increasing for the past few months. While spreadsheets are highly useful and can massively enhance the productivity of the accounting department, one should be aware of the following concerns:

- *Complexity*. As a spreadsheet increases in complexity, the probability of having one or more formula errors increases, along with the possibility of incorrect ranges, faulty logic, or incorrect inputs.
- *Minimal testing*. Users tend not to be overly rigorous in testing whether their spreadsheets are correct, which increases the probability of generating incorrect results.
- *Documentation*. The documentation for a spreadsheet is usually nonexistent, making it more difficult for someone other than the spreadsheet creator to understand how it functions.

232

- *Quantity limitations.* When the number of transactions included in a spreadsheet is quite large, it makes more sense to track the transactions in a database that is designed to do so. Thus, a small business could track its inventory quantities on a spreadsheet as long as there are only a hundred or so items in stock, but should switch to a formal inventory management system once the inventory expands beyond that point.

Summary

Accounting software is available through dozens of suppliers, as individual software modules for specific applications, or in the form of comprehensive, seamless systems that cover all possible applications of an accounting information system. Consequently, accounting information systems are nearly always purchased. The use of custom software tends to be limited to very specific niche applications around the edges of an AIS.

A business may operate in an industry whose requirements are so unique that it might appear to require an entirely custom-built AIS. This is rarely advisable, since the bulk of an AIS' functionality does not vary by industry. And even in those cases where an industry has very specific accounting requirements (such as casinos, mining, or construction), commercially-available applications have been developed for those industries. In short, it rarely makes sense to custom-develop an AIS.

Glossary

A

Accounting information system. A formal structure used to collect, store, manage, and report an organization's financial information.

Activity-based costing. A methodology for precisely allocating costs to those items that actually use it.

Adjusted trial balance. A trial balance that includes all adjusting journal entries used to produce period-end financial statements.

Advance shipping notice. A notification send from a seller to a buyer, detailing the estimated delivery date and time of a shipment.

Audit. The examination of an entity's financial records and physical assets.

Audit plan. A document that states the detailed steps to be followed in the conduct of an audit.

Audit risk. The risk that an auditor will not detect errors or fraud while examining a target area.

Audit strategy. A document that sets the direction, timing, and scope of an audit.

Audit trail. The documented flow of a transaction from its point of origin to its final point of use.

Authorization. The restriction of user access to specific parts of a system, as well as defining the actions they are allowed to take within those areas.

Automated control. A control that is operated automatically by a computer system.

B

Balance sheet. A financial report that summarizes the assets, liabilities, and equity of the reporting entity.

Batch processing. When record updates are made at extended intervals, such as once a day or month.

Bill of lading. A document that states the type and quality of goods being sent to a customer, as well as the method of shipment and how it will be routed.

Bill of materials. A listing of the contents of a product.

Budget. A document that forecasts the financial results and financial position of a business for one or more future periods.

Business process. A set of connected tasks that result in the completion of a goal.

Business process diagram. A diagram that graphically depicts the flow of business processes.

C

Chart of accounts. A listing of all accounts used in the general ledger.

Cold site. A separate business location that is rented as a backup to the normal data center, but not necessarily with the required computer equipment.

Concurrent audit techniques. The ongoing automated examination of processes.

Context diagram. A diagram that portrays a data processing system, not the detail of its component parts.

Continuous controls monitoring. The use of automated tools to examine business transactions as they occur.

Control account. A summary-level account in the general ledger that contains aggregated totals for transactions that are individually stored in subledgers.

Control environment. The comprehensive set of actions taken by management that sets the tone for how employees engage in their day-to-day activities.

Cost driver. Something that triggers a change in the cost of an activity.

Cost object. Any item for which a cost is compiled.

Credit memo. A document issued to a customer, reducing the amount that the customer owes to the seller.

Cycle billing. The process of issuing invoices to customers on a rotating basis.

Cycle counting. The process of counting small amounts of inventory each day, with the intent of cycling through the entire inventory on an ongoing basis.

D

Data. Facts that are collected, stored, and used by an organization.

Data dictionary. A central repository of information about data.

Data flow diagram. A diagram that portrays the flow of information for a process, including data sources and uses.

Data processing cycle. The set of operations used to transform data into useful information.

Data warehouse. A large store of data that has been accumulated from a number of sources, and which is used to assist in the formulation of management decisions.

Database. An organized collection of data that is designed to make data more easily accessed, manipulated, and updated.

Database management system. A software program that defines, manipulates, retrieves, and manages the data stored in a database.

Detective control. A control that detects a control breach after it has occurred.

Digital signature. A mathematical approach to verifying whether a digital document is authentic.

Direct method. A format for the statement of cash flows that shows cash inflows and cash outflows in the operating section of the report.

E

Electronic data interchange. A system for sending electronic transactions in a standard format to other business partners.

Embezzlement. The theft or misappropriation of funds.

Encryption. A method by which data are converted from a readable form to an encoded version that can only be read by someone having access to a decryption key.

Endpoint device. Any computer hardware device connected to a network, such as a computer or printer.

Enterprise risk management. A set of activities that are designed to mitigate or otherwise work with the portfolio of risk to which an organization is subjected.

Evaluated receipts settlement. A situation in which payments to suppliers are based on the quantities received, rather than a supplier invoice.

Expenditure cycle. All activities related to the purchase of inventory in exchange for current or future payments.

Exposure. The potential monetary loss from a threat.

F

Feasibility study. The evaluation of a proposed activity to see if it meets several predetermined criteria, such as cost thresholds, legal issues, proposed duration, and technical challenges.

Financing cycle. All activities related to obtaining debt or equity funding, as well as the payment of dividends, principal, and/or interest.

Firewall. Part of a network that is designed to block unauthorized access to the system, while permitting outbound communications.

Flexible budget. A budget model that calculates different expenditure levels for variable costs, depending on changes in actual revenue.

Flowchart. A diagram that graphically describes a system.

Foreign key. A field in one table that uniquely identifies a primary key in another table.

Fraud. The false representation of facts, resulting in the object of the fraud receiving an injury by acting upon the misrepresented facts.

Fraud triangle. Three conditions that increase the likelihood of fraud being committed, which are perceived pressure, opportunity to commit fraud, and rationalization of the need to do so.

G

Gantt chart. A visual portrayal of the task assignments and task durations within a project.

General ledger. The master set of accounts that summarize all transactions occurring within a business.

Give-get exchange. The swapping of one item for another, such as selling goods for cash.

H

Hot site. An off-site location that is maintained with all necessary equipment to support company computing operations.

Human resources cycle. All activities related to interactions with job candidates, through their hiring, training, evaluation, and eventual discharge.

I

Income statement. A financial report that summarizes the revenues generated, expenses incurred, and any resulting profit or loss for a reporting period.

Indirect method. A format for the statement of cash flows that derives operating cash flows by modifying the reporting entity's net income figure.

Information. Data that have been organized and processed within a context that gives it meaning and relevance.

Internal controls. The interlocking set of activities that are layered onto the normal operating procedures of an organization, with the intent of safeguarding assets, minimizing errors, and ensuring that operations are conducted in an approved manner.

Intrusion detection system. Software that monitors a network for malicious activity or policy abuses.

Investment center. A business unit that is responsible for its revenues, profits, and assets.

Invoice. A document submitted to a customer, identifying a transaction for which the customer owes payment to the issuer.

J

Job costing. A system for accumulating costs for a specific job.

K

Kanban. An authorization to produce goods or withdraw goods from a supply bin.

Kaizen costing. The process of continual cost reduction after a product design has been completed and is in production.

L

Lead time. The sum of the time required to place a replenishment order and for the supplier to then deliver the ordered goods.

Ledger. A book or database in which accounting transactions are stored or summarized.

M

Manual control. A control that requires a person to perform it.

Master production schedule. A production plan that states which products will be manufactured, as well as their amounts and start dates.

Material requisition. A document that states the items to be picked from inventory and used in the production process.

Multi-factor authentication. When two or more forms of evidence must be presented in order to gain access to a system.

N

Negative approval. A situation in which supplier invoices will be paid unless the responsible manager notifies the payables staff not to do so.

O

Online analytical processing. A tool for analyzing database information.

P

Packing slip. A document that describes the contents of a delivery of goods to a customer.

Payroll register. A report that summarizes the payments made to employees as part of a payroll.

Perpetual inventory. A system for continually updating inventory records so that they reflect current physical inventory balances.

Petty cash. A small amount of bills and coins that are kept on the premises to pay for minor expenditures.

Picking ticket. A list used to gather items to be shipped from a warehouse.

Positive pay. When a payer sends a file to its bank, containing information about the checks it has issued. The bank then compares this information to the checks being submitted for payment, to detect any fraudulent checks.

Post-closing trial balance. A trial balance as of the end of a reporting period, when the books have been closed.

Posting. When the balance in a subledger is shifted into the general ledger.

Preventive control. A control that keeps a control breach from occurring.

Primary key. A unique address for a row within a table.

Process costing. A process for accumulating costs for a period of time and then allocating them to the units produced during that time on a consistent basis.

Production cycle. All activities related to the conversion of raw materials into finished goods.

Production order. A document that states the number of units to be manufactured, the date when the order is released for production, and where the units should be delivered once they have been completed.

Profit center. A business unit that generates revenues and profits or losses.

Program evaluation and review technique. A project management technique that identifies the time taken by each step in a project, as well as the total time required for its completion.

Public-key algorithm. When an encryption algorithm uses a public key, which is available to anyone, and a private key.

Purchase order. A document used to order goods and services from a supplier.

Purchase requisition. A formal request made to the purchasing department to buy goods or services.

R

RAID system. Acronym for redundant arrays of independent drives.

Real-time mirroring. When identical copies of a database are maintained at two different data centers, and those databases are continually updated in real time.

Real-time processing. When records are updated as soon as a transaction occurs.

Receiving report. A report that is used to document the contents of ongoing deliveries to a business.

Reconciliation. The process of matching two sets of records to see if there are any differences.

Recovery time objective. The targeted time period within which a business process must be restored in order to avoid any unacceptable consequences related to a break in the continuity of business operations.

Relational database. A set of tables from which data can be accessed or reassembled in many ways without having to reorganize the underlying tables.

Remittance advice. A statement that accompanies a payment to a supplier, detailing what was paid.

Remote deposit capture. When a check scanner is used to create an electronic image of a check, which is then transmitted to a bank instead of making a physical deposit.

Request for proposal. A document sent to suppliers, detailing a buyer's needs and requesting a pricing response.

Reverse auction. An online bidding process in which suppliers can repeatedly bid their prices lower in order to win a purchase contract.

Risk. The probability that events will vary from expectations.

S

Safety stock. Excess inventory that acts as a buffer between forecasted and actual demand levels.

Sales cycle. All activities related to the sale of goods or services in exchange for current or future payments.

Sales order. A document generated by a seller for its internal use in processing an order.

Schema. A diagram that describes the tables and corresponding fields contained within a database.

Social engineering. The act of representing oneself as a valid user who has lost access information, in order to extract this information from a business.

Source document. The physical basis upon which business transactions are recorded.

Spend management. The process of collecting and analyzing purchasing data in order to decrease procurement costs.

Statement of account. A summary of all open invoices owed by a customer.

Statement of cash flows. A financial report that shows the changes in a firm's cash flows during a reporting period.

Static budget. A budget model that is fixed for the entire period covered by the model.

Subsidiary ledger. A ledger designed for the storage of specific types of accounting transactions.

Symmetric-key algorithm. When an encryption algorithm uses the same cryptographic keys for both encryption and decryption.

Systems development lifecycle. The process of planning, creating, testing and deploying an information system.

T

Target costing. A process for integrating a target selling price and margin into the design of a product.

Transaction. A business event that has a monetary impact on an organization's financial statements, and which is recorded in its accounting records.

Trial balance. A report that lists the ending balance in each general ledger account.

Turnaround document. A document sent to a third party, who is supposed to fill in the document and return it to the company.

U

Unadjusted trial balance. A trial balance before any adjusting journal entries have been made in preparation for the issuance of financial statements.

V

Virtual private network. The use of an encrypted connection over a less secure network, where users must employ authentication methods to gain access to the VPN server.

X

XBRL. An acronym for eXtensible Business Language Reporting. This reporting format is required for submissions made to the Securities and Exchange Commission.

Z

Zone picking. The process of combining customer orders into a master batch, so that multiple orders are picked at the same time.

Index

CPSIA information can be obtained
at www.ICGtesting.com
Printed in the USA
FFHW011322251119
56472076-62266FF

9 781642 210194